JOURNAL FOR THE STUDY OF THE NEW TESTAMENT
SUPPLEMENT SERIES

35

JSOT Press
Sheffield

The Proverbs of Jesus

Issues of History and Rhetoric

Alan P. Winton

Journal for the Study of the New Testament
Supplement Series 35

To my mother
and the memory of my father

Published by JSOT Press
JSOT Press is an imprint of
Sheffield Academic Press Ltd
The University of Sheffield
343 Fulwood Road
Sheffield S10 3BP
England

Printed in Great Britain
by Billing & Sons Ltd
Worcester

British Library Cataloguing in Publication Data

Winton, A.P.
The proverbs of Jesus
1. Jesus Christ. Teaching
I. Title II. Series
232.9'54

ISSN 0143-5108
ISBN 1-85075-219-2

CONTENTS

PREFACE

This study represents research for the degree of Doctor of Philosophy, undertaken in the department of Biblical Studies at the University of Sheffield. In the course of my research there were many people who gave help and support. The work was begun under the supervision of Rev. Dr Bruce Chilton, and completed with Rev. Dr David Hill: I am grateful to both for their guidance and encouragement. I am also particularly indebted to three fellow students, David Orton, Steve Fowl, and Mark Brett for their friendship and support. Mark was kind enough to read through the whole of this work, and I am most grateful for his stimulating and constructive comments.

The thesis was completed in the summer of 1987, and has undergone some revisions in the intervening months.

For financial assistance my thanks are also given to the awarding committee of the Petrie Watson studentship of the University of Sheffield, to the Rt. Rev. David Lunn, Bishop of Sheffield, and to my mother. However, in defiance of Ben Sira's sentiments (25.22) I am happy to acknowledge that the main financial burden for the luxury of several years of research has been borne by my wife, Pippa. She knows how grateful I am for her help, her love and friendship.

Alan P. Winton
Strasbourg
Summer 1988

ABBREVIATIONS

ATR	*Anglican Theological Review*
Bib	*Biblica*
BR	*Biblical Research*
CBQ	*Catholic Biblical Quarterly*
ET	English translation
ET	*Expository Times*
FFC	*Folklore Fellows Communications* (Helsinki)
HBT	*Horizons in Biblical Theology*
Int	*Interpretation*
JAAR	*Journal of the American Academy of Religion*
JAF	*Journal of American Folklore*
JBL	*Journal of Biblical Literature*
JR	*Journal of Religion*
JSNT	*Journal for the Study of the New Testament*
JTC	*Journal for Theology and the Church*
JTS	*Journal of Theological Studies*
MJLF	*Midwestern Journal of Language and Folklore*
NT	*Novum Testamentum*
NTS	*New Testament Studies*
RB	*Revue Biblique*
RR	*Radical Religion*
RSR	*Religious Studies Review*
SJT	*Scottish Journal of Theology*
TDNT	*Theological Dictionary of the New Testament*
ThLZ	*Theologische Literaturzeitung*
VT	*Vetus Testamentum*
VT Supp	*Vetus Testamentum Supplement*
WF	*Western Folklore*
ZAW	*Zeitschrift für die alttestamentliche Wissenschaft*
ZNW	*Zeitschrift für die neutestamentliche Wissenschaft*

SYMBOLS

>	leads to
≯	does not lead to
=	equals
≠	does not equal
→	causes
∞	cannot cause

Note: biblical quotations, where they are not my own translation, are from the NASB, the Old Testament apocryphal quotations are from the RSV Apocrypha, Qumran citations are from G. Vermes: *The Dead Sea Scrolls in English* (Harmondsworth: Penguin, 1970), and for Jewish pseudepigrapha J.H. Charlesworth (ed.), *The Old Testament Pseudepigrapha* I & II (London: Darton, Longman and Todd, 1983, 1985).

INTRODUCTION

The argument pursued here concerns the place of proverbial wisdom in the Synoptic presentations of Jesus. A great deal of work has been done on the parables of Jesus as a characteristic form of speech, but the shorter proverbial sayings have been largely overlooked. This is perhaps due to the difficulty of assigning them a significant place in the message of Jesus, as it is traditionally understood. How, therefore, might one best proceed in treating this material? To begin with a straightforward exegetical or historical-critical study soon proved inadequate: all the most important issues had already been decided without serious reference to the material under consideration. I have therefore found it necessary, in the course of this study, to address much broader issues of interpretation and method in Gospel studies. Of these aspects of the work, two deserve particular mention.

First, there is a danger that the position argued in this work regarding the historical reconstruction of Jesus' speech may be misunderstood. In essence, the conclusion of the fourth chapter is that there exists no reliable method for the task of reconstructing Jesus' speech. The evidence is difficult to assess, and traditional critical (and conservative) approaches are unpersuasive. Although I am unable to suggest an alternative to current practice, it does seem worthwhile to attempt a more holistic assessment of the Synoptic presentation of Jesus. Thus, what is offered in the final chapter may be merely the preliminary to a more comprehensive attempt to understand Jesus' message in its literary form. Alternatively, it may be viewed as an attempt to approach the historical question in a different and much more tentative way.

Second, the question of eschatology deserves special mention. Any writer concerned to look critically at the consensus on the eschatological nature of Jesus' message and mission runs the risk of being considered weak-hearted—unable to face up to the strangeness of Jesus to twentieth-century eyes. Alternatively, such a critic may simply have his or her work assigned to one of the tolerably acceptable categories of scholarship, such as 'realized eschatology'. I can only hope that this attempt, in the interests of historical accuracy, to offer a balanced assessment of the significance of eschatology in the Synoptic presentations of Jesus, and hence to give some significance to the role of proverbial wisdom, will be considered on its own terms.

The preliminary chapters look at ways in which 'wisdom' as a 'tradition' is thought to bear on our understanding of the Gospels, and then at how to describe and classify the relevant proverbial material. Chapter 3 is a review of some of the most important modern works on the interpretation of proverbial wisdom, drawing out the main issues for consideration in terms of history and rhetoric. The fourth chapter examines some of the relevant problems in the historical reconstruction of Jesus' speech, and the fifth offers a fresh approach to the rhetoric of proverb performance. Finally, there is an attempt to draw together conclusions on the significance of proverbial wisdom through a reconsideration of the nature of Jesus' Kingdom proclamation in the Synoptic Gospels.

Chapter 1

ASPECTS OF WISDOM IN THE SYNOPTIC GOSPELS

1. *Introduction*

Our concern in this work is with the function and significance of the proverbial sayings attributed to Jesus within the Synoptic tradition. In the literature of New Testament scholarship the designation of this material as proverbial inevitably leads to the question of the significance of 'wisdom' features in the Gospels, since in the study of Old Testament and Jewish literature the proverb is considered a part of the 'wisdom tradition'. In this chapter we wish to look critically at the way in which 'wisdom' as a 'tradition' is thought to bear upon our understanding of the gospels, and to look at some of the main areas in which 'wisdom influence' has been posited.

2. *Wisdom Tradition and Wisdom Influence*

In recent years, the question has been raised concerning the scope of the wisdom tradition and its influence throughout the Old Testament, so that G.T. Sheppard can speak of 'a fascination with the presence and significance of "wisdom elements" in non-wisdom literature'.[1] Classic studies of this kind would include J. Fichtner's work on Isaiah[2], and G. von Rad's reading of the Joseph Narrative;[3] indeed, there are few examples of Old Testament literature in which wisdom influence has not been suggested.[4]

The course of earlier research in this area was not often marked by much self-conscious reflection on the method employed. This led to a rethinking of the situation, such that some have sought to define wisdom more precisely and to offer explicit criteria by which the influence of wisdom can be judged.[5]

In general, the wisdom tradition is defined in terms of the 'wisdom' literature of the Old Testament and intertestamental period (this would include, at least; Proverbs, Ecclesiastes, Job, Ben Sira, and the Wisdom of Solomon).[6] The question of influence is usually posed through the comparison of vocabulary, forms of speech, and content. There is a seemingly inevitable circularity in this approach. One has to be able to say what wisdom is before looking for its impact in so-called non-wisdom contexts. In his attempt at a rigorous treatment of wisdom influence based on tangible linguistic evidence, R.N. Whybray states the problem as follows:

> In order to determine which words, occurring both in the acknowledged 'wisdom books' and in some passages in other books, are characteristic of the intellectual tradition, it has been necessary to some extent to pre-judge the question whether those passages belong to that tradition or not.[7]

The same problem arises if one bases the approach on forms of speech or content. In seeking a more precise study of the influence of wisdom on other literature, one is forced into a narrow definition of what constitutes the tradition. Precision in method seems to require the delimitation of the 'tradition' in what may subsequently prove to be an arbitrary way.

It seems as though the way in which the question is posed leads inevitably to reasoning which is at times circular or based on arbitrary formulations. Perhaps the categories in which the discussion has proceeded are in need of some review.

a. *Problems with the language of 'influence'*

To a large extent the discussion of influence is, of necessity, carried on only with respect to literary influence. When we study one body of literature such as the Gospels, and posit the influence of another tradition, we are making a literary claim. The 'wisdom tradition' is known chiefly through a number of representative texts.[8] When we speak of the influence of wisdom we are, in effect, positing the 'influence' of one text on another.[9] The problem is that talking of 'influence' introduces an unhelpful notion of causation, about which it is difficult to comment with any degree of certainty.

We speak of influence when we notice similarities between the text we are studying and another type of literature, and we believe that by positing some connection between the two we might be better able to understand the original. However, the question arises whether it is really necessary to talk of influence at this stage. Could we not simply talk of an affinity between texts, without describing the relationship in causal terms, while still realizing that our understanding of the one text may be enhanced by reading it alongside the other?

The recognition of affinity between texts need not only lead to an argument for some causal link, but also the possible observation of shared traditions across material previously thought unrelated. This could be explicable in terms of a common stock of language and ideas, or could lead to a re-appraisal of the boundaries of the original tradition.

In an interesting article on 'The Limits of Historical Explanation', Quentin Skinner offers a critique of the notion of influence as it is employed in the History of Ideas. His main point is that proving influence requires a great deal of evidence, and that the suggestion of the influence of one text or tradition upon another may simply be a confession of ignorance. To posit influence, for Skinner, is merely to claim that one item reminds the critic of another. It might be, however, that if the critic knew the ideas contained in a series of other texts or traditions, some of them would have brought to mind the original item even more strongly.

> It is .... clear that on this formulation it will be impossible to assign any unambiguous meaning to the concepts of influence and inner connectedness as explanatory hypotheses, short of a complete knowledge about all of the relevant items in the aggregate of historical information.[10]

Interestingly, Skinner speaks of a 'conventional canon' of figures whose influence is posited. In the case of biblical studies this is a most appropriate phrase, since discussions about influence often seem to reflect our ignorance in the face of such a limited canon of relevant and available literature (even including canonical and non-canonical literature in the theological sense).

b. *This leads us on to a questioning of the concept of 'tradition' which is prevalent in much biblical research.*

In an interesting collection of essays published in 1971, J.M. Robinson and H. Koester write about *Trajectories through Early Christianity*, reflecting on the crisis which they observe in the categories of New Testament research. Robinson focuses particularly on the notion of 'background' which he sees as a static category, and wishes to replace it with the more dynamic, process-oriented category of 'trajectory'. He comments:

> The religious world through which early Christianity moved has been conceptualized as strangely immobile. Rabbinic Judaism, Gnosticism, an oriental cult, a given mystery religion—each was presented as a single position.[11]

Robinson favours what he terms a 'reconceptualization', whereby we think more in terms of developing movements through the Hellenistic world.

In a similar way, the category 'tradition' is perhaps too static. It is becoming increasingly apparent that the idea of separate, well-defined traditions, such as 'wisdom', 'prophecy' and 'apocalyptic', are impossible to maintain.[12] It is also difficult to support the view that different traditions relate to specific social groupings.

The notion of the 'wisdom tradition' is, in effect, an abstraction based on the content of those books which are designated as wisdom literature, largely on the grounds of shared terminology. This is then set in opposition to the 'prophetic tradition', for example, which again is developed from a similar body of literature. These traditions are then often related to sociological settings or groupings such as 'the wise', 'the clan', 'the court', 'the cult'. Thus, when we speak of 'traditions' we are dealing both with literary and sociological phenomena.

One may make observations about 'affinities' between 'traditions' based on literary comparisons, as an aid to understanding; however caution, and other evidence, are required in moving from here to the sociological implications. The language of 'influence' between 'traditions' and texts takes us into the much more complex world of sociological phenomena. This is not to say that interest in the sociological implications of observed literary traditions is unimportant; rather we are insisting that, in this case, further evidence is necessary before moving from literary phenomena to sociological claims.[13]

It is important to realize that what we term 'traditions' are simply the result of the kind of literature which has come down to us. We should therefore be cautious in our use of this notion of 'tradition'; thus, for example, we should hesitate in using 'traditions' as the basis for certain historical judgments. In studying a text which we assign to a particular tradition, the presence of 'unexpected' material could either lead to a reassessment of the nature of that tradition, or to a historical judgment about secondary material intruding, or a chronological claim.

These are questions to which we will return in the course of our thesis, but our observations make it necessary to proceed with caution when we encounter claims about the 'influence' of 'the wisdom tradition'.[14]

The important role of the 'wisdom tradition' in the New Testament has been posited in a number of ways.

> Jesus of Nazareth may be the culmination of other traditions but he is no less the culmination of the Wisdom tradition.[15]

> All I wish to point out is the survival of the form and content of the wisdom tradition in the books of the primitive Christian community.[16]

We wish to consider briefly the main aspects of wisdom that have been recognized in the study of the Gospels, and also to mention other places in the literature of early Christianity where wisdom seems to be an important category.

3. *Christology*

In the realm of New Testament Christology, wisdom has become an important category. The influence of speculative reflection on the figure of Wisdom in the Old Testament and intertestamental literature has been posited in connection with various christological passages in the Pauline epistles, Hebrews, John's Gospel, and the Synoptics.[17]

a. *The question of the figure of Wisdom in pre-Christian Judaism*

The figure of Wisdom, or Wisdom personified, can be seen in a number of key passages: Proverbs 1 and 8, Job 28, Ben Sira 1 and 24, Baruch 3–4, Wisdom of Solomon 6–11, *1 Enoch* 42.[18] There is a vast literature on this subject both in Old Testament and New Testament research, which raises a number of important and disputed issues.[19] However, for present purposes, we wish to focus on the issue of the way in which this material is handled as 'background' to christological affirmations in the New Testament.

There appear to be two main ways of formulating the evidence for the figure of Wisdom.

First, the various passages cited above can be read as a coherent and developing picture of Wisdom. Thus, J. Dunn:

> if we set out the passages in the most likely chronological order, it becomes evident that there is. . . . a development in the talk about Wisdom.[20]

H. Gese argues even more strongly for a consistent development from the Old to the New Testament. This is in the context of supporting the idea of a biblical theology, and rejecting ideas about 'pagan' influence and background to the figure of Wisdom.[21]

This approach suggests a consistent and well-developed picture of Wisdom which is appropriated by the New Testament writers. Thus, Dunn can ask:

> What or who was this Wisdom whose descriptions and functions are attributed to Christ in such a broad sweep of New Testament writings?[22]

Dunn seems to be suggesting that mention of the idea 'Wisdom of God' would evoke a whole set of expectations in the reader's mind, i.e. particular functions and characteristics based on the development of Wisdom throughout Jewish literature.

It is questionable whether this is a suitable way of describing the evidence for the figure of Wisdom, or for describing how this tradition should be conceived as background for the New Testament writers.

In an attempt to map out the development from Jesus of Nazareth to Paul and the Christology of the Early Church Fathers, M. Hengel focuses on the figure of Wisdom personified.[23] He addresses the question of the reticence of the New Testament writers in identifying Jesus with the Wisdom of God,[24] and in the process he argues against the development of a consistent Wisdom myth, favouring recognition of the diversity of the picture presented, both in the pre-Christian sources and in the individual Wisdom texts in the New Testament.[25]

A more thorough critique of the use of Wisdom as a background to New Testament Christology is offered by E. Schüssler Fiorenza in an article which focuses particularly on the hymnic material.[26]

Fiorenza argues against any kind of basic myth of Wisdom, or consistent developing myth as background to the New Testament christological hymns. She speaks of 'reflective mythology'[27] in an attempt to do justice to the variety of mythical language about Wisdom in the Jewish Tradition, and to the various foreign mythical goddesses which have been posited as the source of this conception. For Fiorenza,

> reflective mythology uses mythical materials as thought categories for its own theological reflection and conception.[28]

This is an argument against reductionism whereby diverse texts are reduced to one basic myth, rather than seeing them in their different functions within distinct theological contexts.

Thus, when we consider Proverbs 1–9, or Ben Sira 24 we conceive the relationship between the texts and the original living myth or myths, not as 'background' or 'influence', but as a more dynamic theological reflection which uses the language and features of myth for its own ends.

In a very important conclusion, Fiorenza states:

> Neither the background nor the parallels define the theological content and aims of the New Testament Christological hymns, but rather the theological interest of these hymns determines the mythological language and material which is appropriated and accentuated.[29]

This is an important corrective to much New Testament research in which the influence of earlier traditions is posited in such a way that the New Testament writer appears to be taking on a whole set of ideas which determine his thinking, rather than using theologically the traditions of the past to express his own understanding of present events. In Fiorenza's view, the determinative role is given to the New Testament writer, rather than to the strength or effect of the tradition. Thus, attention is directed to a careful exegesis of the text in which there is posited the influence of (or affinity with) an older tradition; rather than an effort to discover all the features and characteristics of the tradition in order to explicate the present text.

The thesis put forward by Fiorenza has as its weakest point the emphasis upon the mythological nature of the figure of Wisdom, and the rejection of the notion of Wisdom as a poetic personification of a divine function.

> Since most of the characterizations and descriptions of Wisdom use the language of myth, Wisdom cannot be explained as a metaphorical personification of certain attributes of Yahweh.[30]

It is questionable whether Fiorenza's distinction between myth and poetic personification can be maintained, or is indeed helpful. Her argument against the latter is based on the recognition that the figure of Wisdom 'appears less...of an abstract concept than a real personal being'.[31] This judgment seems to reflect a rather strange view of the poet's capabilities to create a believable image. However, for our purposes, the discussion of the exact nature of the language about Wisdom is not so important as the issue of the way that we conceive the New Testament writer's use of this 'traditional' material. Fiorenza reminds us that the focus of meaning resides with the present text rather than allowing the past tradition to determine meaning.[32]

b. *Jesus and the Wisdom of God*

In the Synoptics, the evidence for a connection between Jesus and the Wisdom of God is limited to a few main texts.[33] The discussion of these texts most frequently focuses on the questions of if, and when, the identification of Jesus and Wisdom took place. The tendency seems to be to place the identification of Jesus (and John) as the envoy of Wisdom at the 'Q' stage of the tradition:

> Nowhere in Q can we say with any confidence that Jesus himself was identified as Wisdom .... Throughout the earliest stages of the Synoptic tradition prior to Matthew, but including Luke, Jesus is presented not as Wisdom, but as the messenger of Wisdom, as the eschatological envoy of (God in his) Wisdom.[34]

Some go on to see an explicit Wisdom Christology, i.e. an identification of Jesus and Wisdom, in Matthew's Gospel. This position has been most notably affirmed by M.J. Suggs in *Wisdom, Christology and Law in Matthew's Gospel*.[35] The question of Jesus' own identification of himself with Wisdom is usually answered in the negative.[36]

Lk. 7.31-35 and Mt. 11.16-19 are often seen as evidence for the distinction between Q's identification of Jesus as Wisdom's envoy, and Matthew's Wisdom Christology (cf. Dunn, p. 198). Matthew is thought to have introduced the term 'works' in v. 19 to connect with the reference to the 'works of Christ' in v. 2: thus, there is an identification between Wisdom and Jesus. On the other hand, Luke retains the more original 'children' such that John and Jesus (and perhaps also their disciples) are thought to be Wisdom's children, i.e. her envoys. It is surely questionable whether the metaphor in Lk. 7.35 and Mt. 11.19b is a clear enough allusion to invoke the thought of Wisdom personified, and hence either christological speculation or talk of 'envoys': indeed, the force of the saying in both cases is not dependent on such an allusion.[37]

The evidence of the comparison between Lk. 11.49-51 and Mt. 23.34-36 is also ambiguous. Where Lk. 11.49 has 'the Wisdom of God' speaking, Matthew has Jesus speaking. While some would see this as evidence of Matthew's identification of Jesus with 'Wisdom'

(Dunn, p. 202), Matthew's text could equally suggest a desire to distinguish Jesus and Wisdom.

To speak of a 'Wisdom Christology' in the Synoptic Gospels does seem to be overstating the case. We would not dispute the idea that there is some affinity between Gospel texts and passages which describe the functions and significance of the figure of Wisdom. Indeed, it may be that the soteriological and revelatory functions of Wisdom were used to make explicit the significance of Jesus in this respect;[38] however, these traditions are not used uncritically, and are not really essential to our understanding of the Gospel texts. With regard to Mt. 11.28-30, G. Stanton comments:

> The use of some Wisdom themes in 11.28-30 is not being disputed, but they do not seem to be the key to the passage as it now stands in Matthew's Gospel.[39]

Stanton raises the question of who is issuing the invitation here? Traditionally this has been answered with reference to Ben Sira 51 (and also 24.19, 20),[40] but Stanton points out that Matthew's text describes the speaker as 'gentle and humble in spirit', a description which, appropriately, coheres better with the picture of Jesus in the Synoptics, than with the figure of Wisdom in the Jewish literature to which reference is usually made.[41] It seems that affinity with Wisdom may not in this case be as significant as is sometimes claimed.

We find the evidence too sparse and ambiguous to speak of an actual 'Wisdom Christology', i.e. an explicit, reflective affirmation that Jesus of Nazareth can be identified with the figure(s) of Wisdom, active in creation and throughout Israel's history. The desire to see Jesus as Wisdom's envoy may also be reading too much back into the texts.

However, the possible linking of Jesus with Wisdom 'traditions' and ideas from the speculative stream of thought is interesting in view of the presence of further affinities with Wisdom throughout the Synoptics. Thus Johnson raises the question of the relation between Jesus as 'the incarnation of Wisdom' and as a teacher of wisdom. R.H. Fuller argues for an explicit wisdom Christology in the Synoptics as the formation of the post-Easter community 'on the basis of the traditions about Jesus as a teacher of wisdom'.[42] In Mt. 12.42/Lk. 11.31 either Jesus or his message is described as 'something greater than Solomon'. This could be construed as further evidence of a Wisdom Christology, but alternatively suggests a connection between Jesus and wisdom of a less speculative kind. There are a few other points at which attention is drawn to Jesus' possession of wisdom (Mt. 13.54; Mk 6.2; Lk. 2.40, 52), and it may well be that the Synoptic tradition is more interested in Jesus' wise utterance and action than in the speculative stream of wisdom thought.

Before we go on to consider these other aspects of wisdom in the Synoptics, we should briefly mention the question of 'Wisdom Christology' elsewhere in the New Testament.

The influence of Wisdom is posited in the Johannine presentation of Jesus. In speaking of the important revelatory function of Jesus in the Fourth Gospel, R.E. Brown comments:

> We suggest that in drawing this portrait of Jesus, the evangelist has capitalised on an identification of Jesus with personified Wisdom as described in the Old Testament.[43]

Obviously, many have seen in the figure of Wisdom the background to the 'logos' concept in the Prologue,[44] but Brown wishes to see John's narrative presentation of Jesus also as related to Wisdom.[45] However, he distinguishes the Johannine from the Synoptic picture:

> In the Synoptics, Jesus' teaching shows a certain continuity with the ethical and moral teaching of the sages of the Wisdom Literature; in John, Jesus is personified Wisdom.[46]

In the epistolary literature, the idea of 'Wisdom Christology' is applied to the Pauline material, 1 Peter and Hebrews.[47] Wisdom influence is invoked on account of the cosmic significance assigned to Christ in many of these passages, and particularly with regard to the idea of his pre-existence. Later developments saw the figure of Wisdom incorporated in a decisive way in the presentation of Jesus in the *Gospel of Thomas* and on into Gnostic texts.[48]

With regard to the Synoptics we cannot speak of an explicit Wisdom Christology, but neither can we rule out the possibility that 'traditions' concerning the figure(s) of Wisdom may have been alluded to in order to give further content to the significance of Jesus' mission.

4. *Social Identity: Jesus as a Wise Man*

In *The History of the Synoptic Tradition* Bultmann includes a section on the Logia or Proverbial sayings under the title 'Jesus as a Teacher of Wisdom'.[49] This tantalizing, but passing reference has been echoed in the work of others. Thus McKenzie writes:

> The scribes were the heirs of the wise men, and Jesus who can be designated by no other word typical of any class within the Jewish community, was a teacher—that is to say, a wise man.[50]

This quotation introduces, albeit unintentionally, something of the difficulty which surrounds any comment on the role/social identity of Jesus. The terms 'scribe', 'wise man', and 'teacher' are difficult to distinguish; indeed, assertions about the different sociological groups and roles identifiable within Palestine at the time of Jesus often rest on little evidence. What evidence there is, is to a large extent tendentious[51] or temporally distant.[52]

The issue of Jesus' social identity is raised by the continuity between much of the material attributed to Jesus in the Synoptics and the literature of wisdom. The question arises whether there was an established social role of 'wise man', or 'wisdom teacher', by means of which his contemporaries would have begun to understand Jesus. This is to aim at a more precise description of Jesus' social identity than the designation 'teacher'. It may be, on the other hand, that the use of proverbs attributed to Jesus in the Synoptics should not lead us to the assertion that Jesus fulfilled a specific 'wisdom' role.[53]

In the field of Old Testament study the question of the sociological groupings and roles which lie behind the wisdom 'tradition' is a complex and disputed one.[54] We have already urged caution in moving from literary phenomena, i.e. an apparently coherent wisdom 'tradition', to making sociological claims, i.e. the existence of a class of 'the wise' or of 'schools'.[55]

In the intertestamental literature we have the example in Ben Sira, especially 38.24–39.11, of someone commenting reflectively on 'the wisdom of the scribe'. Here the 'scribe' appears to be a wisdom figure who is concerned with the Law (39.1) and proverbs and parables (39.3). There is an interesting apocalyptic or charismatic element to his role (39.2-8), but the emphasis on the high social and economic status of the scribe makes it unhelpful as a model for Jesus' social identity.[56]

H. Koester has noted the significance of an interesting reference in Josephus which might bear on our understanding of the role of Jesus. He wishes to emphasize the similarities to Jesus' ministry of Josephus' messianic or 'sign prophets'.[57] Koester argues that what is peculiar to Jesus' ministry must be argued in relation to these figures, rather than in comparison with the expectation of messianic figures in Jewish apocalyptic literature. In this connection he focuses on the wisdom teaching of Jesus, and notes the important comment by Josephus in *Ant*. 18.63.

> About this time there lived a wise man, if indeed one ought to call him a man.

Koester sees the use of the term σοφὸς ἀνήρ as a probable remnant of Josephus' original characterization of Jesus; it is of interest that he does not use the term σοφός for any of the other messianic prophets of that period. However, the passage from Josephus which refers to Jesus is notoriously problematic, with many critics seeing a Christian interpolation at this point. Various attempts are made to reconstruct the original form of the passage, but it seems impossible to achieve any degree of certainty. The most problematic phrase is the claim 'He was the Messiah'; however, some would suggest that the term σοφός is an alteration of the more derogatory term σοφιστής. Although Josephus' comment may be an interesting designation of Jesus as a wise man, a study of the use of that designation elsewhere in his work reveals that it can have the meaning of cunning or shrewd person (*Bell*. 3.376; *Ant*. 2.54), one who interprets oracles (*Bell*. 6.313), one who interprets dreams and mysteries (*Ant*. 10.197, 198, 237), the term may be connected with the role of the seer (*Ap*. 1.236,256), it is also used of Solomon's wisdom (*Ant*. 8.53), and can be used to describe those who perform magical deeds (*Ant*. 2.285). Such a designation as σοφός, even if it could be shown to be original, would not necessarily show that Josephus was describing Jesus in terms of his wisdom; and the concept is too vague to serve as evidence for Jesus' social identity.[58]

M. Hengel offers a thorough analysis of possible explanations of Jesus' social identity in *The Charismatic Leader and his Followers*.[59] He discusses the roles of rabbi, scribe, wisdom teacher, and prophet. He seems to dismiss the designations rabbi and scribe as inadequate on the grounds that the Old Testament was no longer the central focus for Jesus' message. In support of this he quotes Käsemann with approval:

> The portrayal of the teacher of wisdom accords but ill with that of the rabbi, because the former lives by immediacy of contemplation, such as is familiar to us from the parables of Jesus, while the latter's existence is determined by meditation and by the bond which keeps him tied to Scripture.[60]

Hengel is keen to show links between wisdom and prophecy, thus he points to the example of Ben Sira as a teacher of wisdom who used prophetic forms and compared himself to a prophet. Also in 'David's Composition' from Qumran[61] David is seen as a wise man who speaks through prophetic inspiration. Thus for Hengel,

> Jesus as a 'teacher' using so-called 'wisdom' forms, and Jesus as an 'eschatological charismatic' or 'messianic' prophet, are in no sense contraries; the reverse is true: each conditions the other, the unheard-of, revolutionary content of Jesus' message sought the stamp and polish of an established form.[62]

Jesus is to be distinguished from the rabbi or scribe, but his designation as wise man must also be seen in the light of the prophetic element in his vocation. In the end, Hengel settles for the designation 'eschatological charismatic'[63]; the wisdom aspect apparently becoming simply a formal element in his message.

Perhaps what Hengel's analysis, and the rest of our comments, show most clearly is the fact that any attempt to reduce the social identity of Jesus to one title will not do justice to the diverse themes and concerns of his ministry. There are elements of wisdom, charismatic aspects, prophetic/eschatological concerns, miracle working and healing stories.[64] It is also true that our knowledge of the social roles and types in first-century Palestine is extremely limited. There is a good deal of confusion and overlapping in the very terms we wish to distinguish.

It has also become clear that the designation of Jesus as a wise man or teacher of wisdom is often simply a statement about the form and content of his message, which in places is seen to have affinities with the wisdom tradition. However, since there is so little clear evidence about the actual social role(s) through which his contemporaries would have understood him it would be wise not to place too much emphasis on this kind of designation. The question of Jesus' social identity remains, at the moment, an interesting and elusive one.[65]

5. *Forms of Speech and Literary Forms*

In this final section we wish to consider some formal aspects of wisdom in the Synoptics and instances of wisdom terminology. We are here concerned to identify forms which have an affinity with wisdom, while being aware of the fact that their present position and context may have brought about significant transformations.

The example of the parable is an important instance of a form of speech sometimes associated with wisdom[66] which is generally thought to undergo a transformation when placed in the context of Jesus' eschatological proclamation.[67] The beatitude and woe are also forms of speech which may be associated with wisdom[68], but also are to be found in prophetic contexts. Parable, beatitude and woe are associated with both wisdom and prophecy in the Old Testament and Jewish literature, and also, we shall find, in the Synoptic presentation of Jesus' message.

Wisdom terminology is associated with the parables,[69] and occurs in descriptions of Jesus,[70] and in certain of his comments to the disciples.[71] There are some other passages in which wisdom terminology may be observed, or which seem best understood in the context of wisdom. Mt. 7.24-27 compares the wise (φρόνιμος) and foolish (μωρός) men in terms of their ability to take action in response to Jesus' words. Whether this parable can be fitted into an eschatological scheme as easily as some suggest[72] may be open to question. It certainly does cohere well with the Christian 'wisdom' which can be found in the epistle of James.[73]

Various commentators seek to understand other Synoptic passages in terms of wisdom. Thus, for example, J.L. McKenzie:

> I can explain the exchange between Jesus and the mysterious Syro-Phoenician or Canaanite woman, for instance (Mt. 15.21-28; Mk 7.24-30) only as a typical wisdom duel of wits.[74]

While McKenzie leaves us no evidence for similar 'typical' duels of wits from the wisdom literature (or from elsewhere), it is clear that the exchange between Jesus and the woman is concluded by competing proverbial sayings, and it is the wisdom of the woman which is superior.

An interesting thesis concerning 'sayings of the sages' or *logoi sophōn*, has been put forward by J.M. Robinson, with respect to the hypothetical source 'Q'.[75] Rather than pursuing the connection between sayings of Jesus and wisdom literature in terms of Christology, Robinson take up the fact that in the 'Q' logia Jesus appears as a teacher of wisdom. Robinson is interested in the Gattung of 'Q' as a wisdom form, and so moves from an interest in forms of speech to literary forms.

Robinson notes the interesting formula 'and it came to pass when Jesus completed these logoi' (Mt. 7.28; 19.1; 26.1, compare also Lk. 9.28; 9.26/Mk 8.38). Here we can trace the beginning of a designation of the collections of sayings as logia.[76] Next we must look for examples of the Gattung prior to and subsequent to 'Q'. Thus Robinson notes in Prov. 22.17f. there is the superscription 'sayings of the sages', which the LXX renders *logoi sophōn* (compare also Eccl. 12.11 and the Ahikar collection). He sees the *Pirke Aboth* as a collection of sayings which corresponds formally to the Gattung *logoi sophōn*, and notes overlap between the 'testament' and the 'sayings of the sages'.[77]

The development subsequent to 'Q' leads most interestingly to the *Gospel of Thomas*. Aside from the obvious formal similarities, the incipit of the *Gospel* refers to logoi, and Robinson argues that it is only for obvious polemical purposes that the text ends with the title: 'the Gospel according to Thomas'. He raises the question of whether the 'sayings' Gattung had an inherent tendency that could lead to the Gnostic variant 'secret sayings'?[78] When seen in the light of the Sophia speech in Mt. 23.34-39 and Bultmann's myth of divine Wisdom, Robinson can conclude:

> Bultmann's suggestions of an early Christian association of Jewish Wisdom literature's personified Sophia with Jesus, and of the absorption of part of a collection of wisdom sayings into a collection of Jesus' sayings, may in their way point to the prehistory of a gattung that, though apparently not gnostic in origin, was open to a development in that direction, once a general shift toward Gnosticism had set in.[79]

Robinson's claims are made concisely in a subsequent essay on 'Jesus as Sophos and Sophia: Wisdom Tradition and the Gospels',[80] in which he maintains that the editor/author of 'Q' seems to be part of the wisdom tradition, since he cast his material into a wisdom genre, i.e. 'sayings of the sages'. Whether Robinson's thesis concerning the literary form of 'Q' is convincing or capable of being tested, is not necessary to discuss here.[81] It does, however, draw attention to the presence of a large number of wisdom sayings in the Synoptic tradition, and it is to that material that we must now turn.

Wisdom Sayings

A good deal of the speech attributed to Jesus is cast in a form which has obvious affinities with proverbial forms of speech found principally in the wisdom literature.[82] At this point, we wish only to introduce the variety of what can generally be termed 'wisdom sayings' in the Synoptics; in our next chapter we will focus the treatment of this material more precisely.

There are four main kinds of 'wisdom saying' apparent in the Synoptics:

1. The Imperative saying or Admonition has been studied in some detail by D. Zeller.[83] This refers, for the most part, to those sayings in the imperative mood, which explicitly call for some kind of response from the hearer or reader. An example would be Mt. 7.1: 'Do not judge lest you be judged'.
2. There is a smaller group of interrogative sayings or questions, such as Mt. 6.26, 27, 28.
3. There are some longer sections of wisdom discourse, where a number of wisdom sayings are joined together (such as Mt. 6.25-34, or 7.16-20), or where a theme is developed in a lengthier saying (such as in Mk 2.21, 22).
4. The Descriptive saying, in contrast to the Admonition, is in some non-imperative mood, usually the indicative. It describes a state of affairs or offers a principle, rather than explicitly calling for a response from the hearer or reader. Examples would include Mk 2.17b, and Lk. 16.15b. It is true, however, that some apparently descriptive sayings do appear to have imperative force.[84] In the following discussions we will use the term 'proverbial sayings' to refer principally to this kind of material.

6. *What is Wisdom?*

In conclusion, we wish to stress the diverse nature of 'wisdom' both in the Old Testament and Early Jewish literature, and in the way that we have reviewed aspects of wisdom in the Synoptics. The 'wisdom tradition' is not a homogeneous entity, and any discussion of wisdom and the Gospels needs to be clear about the aspect(s) of wisdom under consideration. Briefly, we would identify four ways of construing wisdom.

(i) *Speculation about the figure of Wisdom/personified Wisdom*

We have already commented on this at some length, and remain unconvinced about the significance given to 'Wisdom Christology' in some work on the Synoptics. However, we would agree that this is an important theme in Old Testament and Jewish wisdom literature.

(ii) *Wisdom as a human attribute*
The designation of someone as 'wise' is a common feature of Hellenistic and Early Jewish literature, but the range of meanings for such a comment is fairly broad,[85] and may not always be very closely related to the use of proverbial sayings.

(iii) *Wisdom as insight (mantic wisdom)*[86]
In this case, wisdom is associated with the interpretation of dreams, knowledge of the future, and special understanding. For example, Daniel's wisdom concerns the understanding of secret things (especially chapter 2), and in 2.27 the wise man is linked with 'conjurers, magicians, and diviners' in the task of explaining the meaning of a mystery. As we noted earlier, Ben Sira's vision of the ideal scribe includes elements of such wisdom (39.1-3, 6-8).

(iv) *Proverbial (experiential) wisdom*
Wise utterance and instruction overlaps in some respects with the preceding two categories. One feature of proverbial wisdom is to encapsulate different aspects of wise behaviour: to describe the way things are, or to give advice about the wise choice. It is this form of wisdom with which we are most concerned in our study of the Synoptics, for Jesus' language is similar in form to Jewish proverbial wisdom, and shares many common themes. However, the other three forms of wisdom are probably all reflected in the Synoptic presentation of Jesus, and will be of some importance in the following chapters.

We therefore conclude our survey of the various aspects of wisdom relating to the Synoptics; a number of the issues raised in this section will be discussed further, and we hope to move on from the somewhat tentative comments that this general introduction has generated. However, it will have been worthwhile if it encourages a more cautious and reflective use of the categories 'wisdom', 'tradition', and 'influence'.

Chapter 2

CLASSIFYING AND ANALYZING PROVERBIAL SAYINGS

1. *Questions of Definition*

Our work in this section will focus specifically on what we have termed the 'proverbial saying': that is the Descriptive wisdom saying, as opposed to the Wisdom Admonition, Question or longer sections of discourse. We have chosen to narrow our attention at this stage, partly on account of the bulk of material involved in a study of all the wisdom sayings, but more importantly, because of the way in which the proverbial sayings sharpen the question of the place of 'wisdom' in Jesus' message.[1]

It is not appropriate here to enter into discussion with the vast amount of form-critical work on the Proverb in Old Testament and Jewish literature.[2] The main interest of a good deal of this work is to demonstrate the origins of proverbial material in certain groups, and to give relative datings to the more and less sophisticated sayings. These issues are of little value at this stage of our work on the tradition of proverbial speech attributed to Jesus. The few works which touch on the form of proverbial sayings in the Gospels are not particularly helpful for our goal of classifying and analyzing the material.[3] We will have more to say in this regard later in the chapter.

For the present, however, we need to address two important questions. The first concerns the issue of definition and vocabulary with regard to the designation 'proverb', while the second concerns the justification for the selection of a specific body of material from within the Synoptics, to be grouped together as 'proverbial'. It is obvious that these are related questions.

Anyone who is acquainted with the literature on the proverb, either in biblical, literary or folklore studies, will be well aware that questions of terminology and definition recur frequently. We have, thus far, used the expressions 'wisdom saying' and 'proverbial saying': the list of related speech forms is long, and the problems in differentiating the individual items often appear insurmountable. Indeed, in the scholarly literature, a number of terms seem interchangeable: proverb, aphorism, maxim, gnome, epigram, sententious saying, motto, slogan, apophthegm, witticism, idiom, Wellerism, and proverbial phrase are all closely related. Some would attempt to distinguish, for example, a proverb from an aphorism on the grounds of the latter's association and origin with an individual, whereas the proverb is a saying popular among 'the folk', with a folk origin. However, Jolles argues against the view of a folk origin: every proverb must have been at one stage an individual utterance, i.e. an aphorism.

> Jede Schöpfung, Erfindung, Entdeckung rührt immer von einer Einzelpersönlichkeit her. Irgendwo und irgendwann muss jedes Sprichwort einmal zuerst ausgesprochen worden sein.[4]

On the other hand, to claim that a particular saying is an aphorism on the lips of an individual must always be an argument from silence. When we speak of the tradition of Jesus' sayings the question of their origin, either in popular currency or as examples of Jesus' originality, is a difficult one. It seems inappropriate at this stage to speak of Jesus' aphorisms;[5] we will use the expression proverbial sayings in a more neutral sense without making a judgment about origin.[6] However, it is possible, in theory, to describe at least three different kinds of sayings in the Synoptic record of Jesus, although it will, in practice, be difficult to decide to which group any particular saying belongs.

1. There will be some sayings, for which we can often locate precedents, which have sufficiently similar form and content to warrant the designation proverb.

2. Other sayings may have a proverbial form, but have some feature which prevents them being termed proverbs, i.e., some kind of specific referent.

3. There might be some sayings which have their origin at the stage of literary fixation, and could be termed literary proverbs/ aphorisms.

With regard to the Gospels, it is obvious that the first and second types of saying could be derived, like other material, from Jesus or have entered the tradition of his sayings at some later stage. We will give examples of these types of saying in our classification of material.

A fourth category would be proverbial phrases; that is, proverbial expressions which do not form complete sayings, but nonetheless appear to have popular currency. In most cases these would be metaphorical phrases, e.g. Mt. 24.27 'strain out a gnat and swallow a camel'.

Having introduced a little of the complexity in discussions of the proverb and related speech forms, we need to address the question of definition. A. Taylor is sceptical about this enterprise.

> The definition of a proverb is too difficult to repay the undertaking. . . . no definition will enable us to identify positively a sentence as proverbial.[7]

We cannot accept this position, since our concern requires us to give some explanation for our choice of material from within the Synoptics, for which we are claiming relatedness, and an affinity with the proverbial sayings found elsewhere in Israel's wisdom literature.

D. Zeller in *Die weisheitlichen Mahnsprüche bei den Synoptikern*[8] offers some guidelines for a general definition of proverbial material along functional and linguistic lines, and this proves helpful in delimiting our material.

1. Perhaps the most important point is one which unites both form and content in the proverbial saying. In terms of function, Zeller claims,

> es formuliert eine gemachte Erfahrung so bündig, dass dadurch immer wieder neue Situationen erhellt werden können.[9]

In both form and content the saying exhibits a generalizing character which allows it to be applied in similar situations. Thus, an important feature is that the referents are non-specific, or they refer to roles which might be filled by a number of different people: 'he who'—Lk. 7.47c, 'whoever'—Mt. 10.38, 'everyone'—Lk. 12.48b; 'those who'—Mt. 11.8c; 'all who'—Mt. 26.52b.

There may be generalizing groups within the saying: 'the good'—Mt. 12.35; 'the evil'—Mt. 5.45b; 'the first'—Mk 10.31; 'the least'—Lk. 9.48.

There may be non-personal general referents: 'all things'—Mt. 19.26c. 'the day'—Mt. 6.34b.

These may function metaphorically: 'the tree'—Mt. 12.33c.

The situation described is not unrepeatable; the referent is within the reach of a later hearer or reader, either through metaphor or the subject/object's generic form: 'das Sprichwort steht nicht in einem einmaligen Situationskontext'.[10] A proverbial saying is not bound to one situation only, or applicable to a particular group of people in one situation only.

In the Synoptic tradition there are many examples of sayings attributed to Jesus which exhibit a proverbial form in some ways, but include a specific referent that ties them to a particular situation, or fixes them in a particular literary context. One such is Mt. 5.19, 'Whoever annuls one of the least of these commandments, and so teaches others, shall be called least in the Kingdom of Heaven; but whoever keeps and teaches them, he shall be called great in the Kingdom of Heaven'. Here, the reference to 'these commandments' ties the saying to the preceding verses. Again, the series of sayings at Mt. 18.4-6 are proverbial in form, but are tied to the narrative context by reference to 'this child', 'one such child', and 'one of these little ones'.

2. The function described above leads on to further characteristic linguistic features.

Of primary importance is the fact that *the proverbial saying is seen to be independent of context; there is a sense in which it can 'stand on its own'*. Thus Zeller, 'es ist unabhängig von weiterer Rede oder literarischem Kontext'.[11] Crossan speaks of the 'external isolation from continuing discourse'.[12] There is a certain ambiguity here in that we do not want to play down the importance of context in the understanding of the proverbial saying. We are aware of the increasing stress on contextual studies in paroemiology; however, our point is merely a formal marker for designating material as proverbial. As such it is tied to the linguistic observation of the necessity for syntactic completeness in the proverb: 'syntaktisch ist das Sprichwort ... ein geschlossenes Gebilde'.[13] Of course this characteristic is not determinative of the proverb, but it is a necessary condition.

3. Zeller considers *binary form as a common feature of proverbial sayings*, 'Oft realisiert das Sprichwort sein Ordnungsgefüge in binärer Form'.[14] This observation is also made by Dundes in his work towards a structural definition of the proverb, to which we will soon turn. The binary form is observed most clearly in contrasting semantic word pairs: 'good–evil', 'righteous–unrighteous', 'first–last'.

4. *Certain stylistic features are common in proverbial sayings which help to distinguish them from ordinary speech.* The proverb exhibits a certain succinctness and employs elevated language or poetic style. There are, of course, prosaic sayings, and some cases in which the length of the saying makes the designation proverbial seem of dubious value. Mt. 5.15 'Men do not light a lamp and put it under the peck-measure, but on a lampstand; and it gives light to all who are in the house'. This demonstrates the flexibility of wisdom forms from the proverb to the parable, and suggests a connection between the proverb and longer narrative forms.

With regard to stylistic features, Zeller raises the question of whether *parallelismus membrorum* is the fundamental form of the proverbial saying. Against Bultmann, he wishes to stress the essential importance of parallelism, and thus, supports Hermisson's idea that we should see 'die Form des synonymen Parallelismus als ein geeignetes Instrument zur sprachlichen Fixierung einer Ordnung'.[15] It is true that parallelism appears to be an important feature of Hebrew and Aramaic poetry, and as such, it is not strange that it should be one of the devices present in Jesus' proverbial wisdom.[16] However, there are also many single-limbed sayings attributed to Jesus, which indicates that parallelism is not an essential feature of the form.

The question of metaphorical language as a further stylistic feature is raised by Zeller; but, again, as with a majority of Old Testament proverbs, it is not always a feature of Jesus' usage.

5. *The proverb may be distinguished from the riddle on account of the lack of clarity in the sense of the riddle*, whereas 'das Sprichwort sagt sofort, was es meint, und bedarf nicht noch späterer Auflösung'.[17] However, it may be disputed whether the distinction between riddle and proverb can be made so easily; or alternatively the question may be raised as to whether some of Jesus' sayings would be better described as riddles. In some cases in the Gospels, the context in which the saying is placed makes for difficulties in interpretation. Indeed, often the effect of a proverbial saying seems to be to cause the reader to come to a sharp halt, demanding reflection, and a question as to the object(s) of reference.

A list of such linguistic and functional features does not provide us with a 'pure' or 'original' form against which we should measure 'corruptions'; such a use of form-criticism would represent the worst aspects of the method. It does, however, help us to describe a group of sayings with enough in common to warrant their study separately from other groups, and it gives us some means to justify the inclusion or exclusion of material on more than merely intuitive grounds.

2. *Classifying Proverbs*

Having covered some initial questions concerning the definition and selection of material, we must turn to the problem of method in our analysis and classification of proverbial sayings. Our interest is to find a descriptive method of study which will enable a manageable classification.

A good deal of biblical (cf. n. 2) and older folklore studies are historical in their interest, or in the case of some biblical studies, they focus on the poetic features of the sayings.[18] More recent work in paroemiology has involved structural and contextual studies.[19] In arguing that the proverb should be defined and studied in structural terms,[20] Alan Dundes rejects functional approaches, maintaining that other genres may share the same function as proverbs: in New Testament studies, the influential work of W.A. Beardslee betrays an overriding interest in function.[21] For Dundes, the initial question is not what a proverb does, but what it is: he wishes to describe the essential structural features of the proverb. In describing structure, one's focus is confined to the text of the sayings as they now stand, and no attempt is made to place different structures in a line of development from 'original' to 'most sophisticated'.

Dundes is also dissatisfied with the work of M. Kimmerle who attempted a classification closely tied to linguistic and syntactic formulas.[22] As we examine his work in more detail we shall see why concern for syntax and linguistic features is not adequate.

For Dundes, a central question is whether there are underlying patterns of 'folkloristic structure' which can be identified and classified.[23] At this point, two questions arise.

First, what does Dundes mean by underlying patterns of 'folkloristic structure'? He does not deal with this explicitly in his essay, but we will see more clearly what he intends by this term as we consider the detail of his analysis. Meanwhile, we would suggest that 'folkloristic structure' seeks to describe the conventional ways in which we conceptualize, both consciously and unconsciously; it refers to the patterns in which our thought is structured. We will see that one of the basic patterns common among proverbs is 'opposition', and this 'structural' pattern is seen to be expressed in a number of 'linguistic' features. The most common of these is the contrastive semantic pair; another example would be the contrast of active and passive voices.

The second question is raised and answered by Dundes himself, and concerns the nature of what precisely it is that we are analyzing in our structural study of the proverb.

There are three aspects of the proverb capable of being analyzed:

1. Proverb 'image': this is based on the literal or textual level of the saying, and may or may not involve metaphor,
2. Proverb 'message': this is the fundamental meaning of the saying as illustrated by the image.
3. 'Architectural formula': it is upon this that the image is constructed and the message conveyed.

Dundes considers it appropriate to analyze the architectural (or compositional) formula, since unlike image and message, differences in content do not necessarily mean there are correlative differences in underlying (architectural) structure. He considers his analysis to be concerned with deep structure, whereas the kind of classification, mentioned before, which is closely tied to linguistic and syntactic features, operates more at the level of surface structure. However, this sort of characterization of the analysis of architectural formula and linguistic formula as sharply differentiated may be a little misleading, for there are many points at which Dundes' analysis of architecture seems quite akin to linguistic description. This may be due to the simple nature of the proverb: thus the saying 'The harvest is plenty, but the labourers are few' displays an oppositional structure, which can be seen in the opposition between the linguistic terms 'harvest' and 'labourers', which can be construed as labourer = actor, harvest = acted upon. The structural opposition is reflected in an opposition easily observable at the level of content.

Obviously, Dundes' approach includes studying the linguistic features and syntax structurally (as deep structure), rather than in conventional linguistic or syntactic terms (as surface structure). Thus, although there is a concern with syntax and linguistics, the analysis is not ultimately tied at that level, for similar structure (i.e. architectural formula) can be seen in differing syntactic frameworks. To approach the proverb through the study of the structure of the architectural formula involves syntactic and linguistic analysis, but recognizes that there are more fundamental patterns which lie behind such 'surface' features. We therefore see that although the approach is concerned with 'deep' structure (in Dundes' terms), it remains descriptive, and is connected with recognizable linguistic and syntactic features. These distinctions should become clearer as we consider the method in detail, and in practice; and it is on the basis of the descriptive competence and subtlety of the approach that we will employ it in our task for the purpose of a descriptive classification of the material in the Synoptics. M. Kuusi makes clear the descriptive value of the approach:

> Structural analysis is not a skeleton key to all the locked doors of paroemiology, but it is a key that opens the way from seeming equivalences and differences to an ordered perception of essential similarities and contrasts.[24]

It is to Dundes' analysis of the structure of the proverb that we now turn.[25] His comments on the proverb depend to a large extent on an earlier essay dealing with the riddle;[26] indeed, Dundes assumes a close relationship between the structure of the proverb and riddle structure.

He begins by stating that the proverb consists of one or more descriptive elements; that is, one topic and one comment.

> The topic is the apparent referent; that is, it is the object or item which is allegedly described. The comment is an assertion about the topic.[27]

Proverbs with only one descriptive element are always non-oppositional, they are identificational:

'Money talks'.	'Time flies'.
Topic—Comment	Topic—Comment

However, such single descriptive element proverbs are rare. Proverbs with multi-descriptive elements are more common, and they can be either oppositional or non-oppositional:

'He who receives a prophet in the name of a prophet shall receive a prophet's reward'.

The topic here is the pronoun 'he', and there are several comments. Again the structure is non-oppositional; there is a transformation of the simple identification A = B, such that A leads to B, which can be written A > B. This structure often occurs in the form 'He who is A, shall be B'.

'Those who are healthy do not need a physician, but those who are sick'.

There are two descriptive elements here: 'those who are healthy', and 'those who are sick'. The structure here is oppositional, and is a transformation of the simple form A does not equal B ($A \neq B$), which may be written, 'Not A, but B'. The opposition is reinforced by the contrast healthy–sick.

We see that there are two basic categories of proverbs: the non-oppositional/identificational proverbs which equate; and the oppositional proverbs which contrast. Indeed, Dundes summarizes by saying that all proverbs are fundamentally propositions which compare and/or contrast.

1. *Non-oppositional proverbs*

The basic equational proverb is $A = B$, 'Business is business', 'Boys will be boys'.

There are then transformations of this simple formula, which are expressed in set linguistic patterns: 'He who is A, is B', and 'Where there's an A, there's a B'.

> Where your treasure is, there will your heart be also.

Another transformation would be the causal saying, 'A leads to B', $A > B$.

Further transformations of the basic equational structure consist of a series of two or more descriptive elements, in which the descriptive elements are often linked by a repetition of either the topic or the comment.

> Many men, many minds. First come, first served.

Occasionally, there are series which are more coordinate, or conjunctional than equational.

> Live and learn. Live and let live.

2. *Oppositional proverbs*

There are a number of different forms of opposition found in proverbs.

One of the simplest is the negation, where $A \neq B$ is the basic formula:

> Two wrongs don't make a right.

Here the opposition is reinforced by the contrasts—Two $\neq$ One, Wrong $\neq$ Right.

A slightly more complex form of basic opposition would be:

> Not even when one has an abundance does his life consist of his possessions.

The structure of this proverb could be written—$A \neq B$, or A does not lead to B ($A > B$).

Among oppositional proverbs, Dundes distinguishes three kinds of contradictive sayings:

- the antithetical contradictive
- the privational contradictive
- the causal contradictive

Each of these can be produced by affirmation or negation.

(a) Antithetical contradictive

In describing this form of opposition, Dundes draws an analogy with the notion of 'complementary distribution', which is used in linguistic theory. It simply means that the two ideas presented cannot occur together.

> If you have A, you cannot have B;
> if you have B, you cannot have A.

Dundes draws an example from a Sumerian text:

> Who builds like a lord, lives like a slave;
> who builds like a slave, lives like a lord.

The two ideas are said to be in complementary distribution, since building like a lord and living like a lord cannot occur together: the opposition is therefore antithetically contradictive.

It is not always the case that the contradiction is worked out so fully, through reversal in a second line.

> You can't have your cake and eat it too.

This is an example of antithetical contradiction, since 'having your cake' is mutually exclusive with 'eating it'; yet the full extent of the contradiction is not worked out explicitly in the proverb.

An example in the Synoptics would be Mt. 5.14b.

> A city set on a hill cannot be hidden.

In this case, being 'set on a hill' and being 'hidden' are mutually exclusive; the opposition is therefore of antithetical contradiction.

(b) Privational contradictive

This class of opposition refers to the proverb where a logical part or attribute of an object is denied. Dundes gives the example:

> The mob has many heads, but no brains.

Here we see the second of a pair of descriptive elements denying a natural attribute of the first. There are also privational contradictive oppositions in which an associative part or function is denied.

There do not appear to be any examples of privational contradiction in the Synoptics.

(c) Causal contradictive

This refers to the kind of opposition where normal effects or consequences are denied. There are many non-oppositional, causal proverbs in which 'A simply causes B', $A \rightarrow B$:

> Familiarity breeds contempt.

In oppositional, causal proverbs the cause is denied or deemed impossible, 'A cannot produce or yield B', $A \infty B$. Dundes gives the example:

> You can lead a horse to water, but you can't make him drink.

The opposition results from what 'can' be done, and what 'can't' be done; since one might expect the latter to be possible, it is considered causally contradictive.

In some causal contradictive oppositions, the second of the pair of descriptive elements explicitly denies the expected or natural consequence of the action contained in the first descriptive element.

In others, the second descriptive element simply contains an assertion which is contrary to the expected or natural consequence. Dundes continues:

> The causal contradictive opposition is unlike the antithetical contradictive opposition in that there is no complete negation of one descriptive element by another. Nor is there a part or function of an object lacking as there is in the privational contradictive opposition. One of the distinguishing characteristics of the causal contradictive opposition is its time dimension. The two descriptive elements in opposition are separated by time. Specifically, one is necessarily prior to the other. In contrast, antithetical and privational contradictive oppositions are synchronic; that is, the descriptive elements in opposition are not separated by time.[28]

A Synoptic example of causal contradiction would be Mt. 23.11,

> But the greatest among you will be your servant.

Here the opposition is emphasized by contrasting 'greatest' and 'servant', and this opposition may be termed causally contradictive, since greatness does not usually lead to servanthood: the normal causation is contradicted.

Finally, Dundes notes another form of causal contradiction which plays upon the possibility of having the normal effect being illogically placed before the cause: thus, the proverb reverses the usual chronological priority of actions A and B.

In addition to these three categories of contradiction, Dundes notes the importance of contrast, in various forms, as a feature of oppositional proverbs.

The most simple form of contrast would be in the formula 'A, but B'.

> The spirit is willing, but the flesh is weak.

There are various other common contrastive formulas: 'A is less than B', 'A is greater than B', 'Better A than B'. However, perhaps the most common way of creating opposition in proverbs is through the use of contrastive word pairs. Thus in our previous example, 'the spirit is willing, but the flesh is weak', we see the contrastive formula 'A, but B'. This is reinforced by the use of two sets of contrastive word pairs: willing—weak, spirit—flesh.

The latter pair is an example of traditional semantic opposites, whereas the former are merely used contrastively in this instance.

Other semantic pairs would include: few—many, good—evil, light—darkness, first—last, least—greatest.

Contrastive word pairs are a very common feature of proverbial sayings, but this should not lead us to see such sayings only in terms of oppositional features. It is important to notice that many proverbs contain both oppositional and non-oppositional features.

3. *Mixed features*

> The longest way round is the shortest way found.

There is an equation here which suggests identification; however, it involves the contrast 'longest'—'shortest', which is clearly oppositional.

Luke 9.48 provides an interesting example of this sort:

> for he who is least among you, this is the one who is great.

The structure of this saying includes an identificational frame, A = B, 'he who is A, is B'. However, this identification involves the traditional semantic pair 'least'—'great'.

The contrast may be more subtle than that:

> He who has been forgiven little, loves little.

The structure of the frame is identificational, being a transformation of 'he who is A, is B'. The identification is reinforced by the repetition of the comment 'little'. However, a contrastive feature is also created through the voice and the consequent change from object to subject:

A is passive, B is active.

A is object, B is subject.

Another example of mixed features:

> Where your treasure is, there will your heart be also.

Again the frame is identificational, 'where A, there B', but although 'treasure'—'heart' could not be called a contrasting semantic pair, there is a fundamental contrast implied between what is external to a person and what is internal. To miss this contrast would be to miss an essential aspect of the structure (and content) of what would otherwise be considered a simple transformed equational proverb.

In some cases, it is possible to state which structural features are dominant, but this will not always be the case.

We have seen how Dundes' approach to proverb analysis can describe the structural features of the underlying architectural formula.

Such features may be oppositional, non-oppositional, or a combination of both. They will include the various transformations of identificational features, ranging from the simple equational proverb A = B, to the causal proverb A > B. Oppositional features can be seen in terms of the various kinds of contradictives and contrasts, often employing contrasting semantic pairs, or certain basic oppositions. There are then a whole range of proverbs with combinations of features, such as the identificational frame employing contrastive pairs.

Such analysis will not give us completely watertight categories into which we can fit all Synoptic proverbial sayings, but will at least provide us with sufficient descriptive tools to make comparisons and differentiations within the material, so that we may begin to discern any characteristic patterns or features in the sayings attributed to Jesus.

There are obviously other levels of analysis which are important: we have mentioned message and image, but might also include context, function, and actual linguistic features. We need mention these at this stage only as they assist our descriptive analysis.

3. *The Structure of Synoptic Proverbial Sayings*

a. *Sayings with primarily non-oppositional features*

1. Transformations of simple identificational features
There are many examples of these sayings in the Synoptics.

(a) Mt. 11.8c

> Those who wear soft clothing are in King's palaces.

Luke 7.25b

> Those who are splendidly clothed and live in luxury are in royal palaces.

The structure is a transformation of A = B, 'Those who are A, are in B'. Note the use of relatively prosaic language here.

(b) Mt. 24.28

> Wherever the corpse, there the vultures will gather.
>
> Wherever the body, there also the vultures will gather.

This is a simple transformation of an identificational saying; 'Where A, there B'.

(c) Mt. 10.41

> He who receives a prophet in the name of a prophet shall receive a prophet's reward; and he who receives a righteous man in the name of a righteous man shall receive a righteous man's reward.

Here we have an example of compound doubling[29] which is identificational throughout.

In each line the structure may be written A > B; the causation is natural, and is reinforced through repetition. Between the lines there is identification; 'as A, so B'. The relationship between the terms 'prophet' and 'righteous man' is non-oppositional, and thus reinforces the overall identification.

Other examples include: Mt. 6.34b; Mt. 10.10c, Lk. 10.7b; Mt.

19.26c, Mk 10.27, 9.23[30]; Mt. 15.14; Mt. 12.25; Lk. 11.17; Mk 3.24-25; Mt. 16.2b, 3a[31]; Mk 7.20; Mk 10.15, Lk. 18.17; Mt. 18.3; Mt. 7.8, Lk. 11.10; Mt. 21.22; Mk 3.35, cf. Mt. 12.50.[32]

2. Identification, but with various contrastive features

(a) Mt. 6.22a

The lamp of the body is the eye.

Lk. 11.34a

The lamp of the body is your eye.

The structure is primarily identificational, A = B. However, there is a contrast present between the whole and the part, expressed in the pair 'body' and 'eye'.

(b) Mt. 12.34b

For the mouth speaks out of the fulness of the heart.

Lk. 6.45c

For his mouth speaks out of the fulness of his heart.

The structure is primarily identificational; the relationship is causal, A > B, 'A speaks out of B'. Again there is a contrast: in this case it is between that which is external and the internal, mouth—heart. The Lukan form is tied to its literary context by 'his', which refers to 'the good man'.

(c) Mt. 6.21; Lk. 12.34

For where your treasure is, there will your heart be also.[33]

The structure is primarily a simple identification; 'where A, there B'. Again, however, there is a basic external—internal opposition expressed in the contrast, treasure—heart.

(d) Mt. 7.2b; Mk 4.24b

In what measure you measure, it will be measured to you.

Lk. 6.38

With what measure you measure, it will be measured to you.

The structure is primarily identificational, 'as in A, so B', or A > B. However, there is the contrast of 'you' as subject, compared with 'you' as object; and also the active—passive contrast.

(e) Lk. 12.48b

> And from everyone who has been given much, much shall be required; and to whom they entrusted much, all the more they will ask of him.

In this example of compound doubling, the structure is identificational both within and between the lines.

Within the lines the relationship is causal, transforming A > B, 'from A, B'. There is, however, important contrast as well:

given—required   entrust—ask of

The relationship between the lines is 'as A, so B', and this is reinforced by the repetition 'much'—'much', 'much'—'all the more'.

Other examples include: Mt. 11.19c; Lk. 7.35; Mt. 12.33c; Lk. 6.44a; Mt. 7.2a; Lk. 7.47c; Mt. 5.45b; Lk. 9.48; Lk. 6.44b; Lk. 15.10; Mt. 10.25.

3. Primarily identificational: with identification within the lines, but some contrast between the lines

(a) Mt. 6.22b, 23a

> If therefore your eye is clear, your whole body will be full of light;
> but if your eye is bad, your whole body will be full of darkness.

Within the lines the structure is primarily identificational, 'if A, then B', or A > B. This is reinforced by 'clear'—'light', 'bad'—'darkness'. However, there may be contrast in the pair 'eye'—'body'.

Between the lines the relationship is contrastive, 'A, but B'. This is reinforced by the contrasting pairs:

clear—bad   light—darkness

(b) Mt. 12.35

> The good man, out of his good treasure, brings forth what is good;
> and the evil man, out of his evil treasure, brings forth what is evil.

Lk. 6.45

> The good man, out of the good treasure of his heart, brings forth what is good;
> and the evil man, out of the evil treasure, brings forth what is evil.

Within the lines the structure is identificational, A > B. This is reinforced by the repetition of 'good' and of 'evil'.

Between the lines there is contrast, 'A, but B', reinforced by: good man—evil man; good treasure—evil treasure; good—evil.

In the sayings in this class the contrast between lines is not emphatic, but has a certain identificational force as well, in that the causation is natural. This is reinforced by similar syntax in both limbs. Other examples include: Lk. 16.10; Mt. 7.17; Mk 16.16.

b. *Sayings with primarily oppositional structure*

4. Simple oppositional and contrastive sayings and transformations
(a) Mt. 9.12; Mk 2.17; Lk. 5.31

Those who are healthy do not need a doctor, but those who are sick.[34]

The structure is contrastive, 'not A, but B'. This is reinforced by the word pair 'healthy'—'sick'.

(b) Mt. 26.41b; Mk 14.38b

The spirit is willing, but the flesh is weak.

The structure is contrastive, 'A, but B', and is reinforced by the contrastive semantic pair 'spirit'—'flesh', and also the contrastive pair 'willing'—'weak'.

The structure and linguistic construction in this saying is identical with the following saying: note μὲν. . . . .δέ

(c) Mt. 9.37; Lk. 10.2.

The harvest is great, but the workers are few.

The structure is contrastive, 'A, but B', and is reinforced by the contrasts 'harvest'—'workers', 'great'—'few'.

(d) Mt. 15.26 (with slight variants in Mk 7.27b)

It is not good to take the children's bread and throw it to the dogs.

The structure is oppositional, and can be written in a number of ways: 'A is not B', or 'if A, not B'.

The style of the saying is somewhat prosaic, but still warrants the description proverbial saying. The reply by the woman, 'even the dogs feed on the crumbs which fall from their master's table', is identificational. It plays on the contrast between 'the dogs'—'their master', as this saying involves the contrast 'children'—'dogs'.

(e) Mt. 8.20; Lk. 9.58

> The foxes have holes, and the birds of the air have nests, but the Son of Man has nowhere to lay his head.

It is doubtful whether this should be classified as a proverbial saying, since the referent is specific (Son of Man), and means that the generalizing nature of the saying is lost. It may be best to speak of this as a saying which is merely proverbial in form. Its structure is contrastive, 'A, but B'. The first line builds up identification, and there is comparison between 'foxes'—'birds', and 'holes'—'nests'. However, the second line creates contrast: 'foxes and birds'—'Son of Man', 'holes and nests'—'nowhere'.

Other examples include: Mt. 19.24; Mk 10.25; Lk. 18.25; Mt. 22.14; Lk. 15.7; Mk 9.40; Lk. 9.50; Lk. 6.40;[35] Mk 2.27; Lk. 18.27; Lk. 16.15b; Lk. 12.15b; Lk. 16.8.

5. Contrast within the lines, but identification between lines

(a) Mt. 12.30; Lk. 11.23

> He who is not with me is against me;
> and he who does not gather with me scatters.

The structure of the lines is contrastive, 'not A = B', or A ≠ B. This is reinforced by the contrastive semantic pairs, 'with'—'against' 'gather'—'scatter'. There is identification between the lines, 'as A, so B'.

(b) Mt. 7.18.

> A good tree cannot produce bad fruit,
> nor can a rotten tree produce fine fruit.

Lk. 6.43 is similar.

> For there is no good tree which produces bad fruit,
> nor, on the other hand, a bad tree which produces good fruit.

The structure is contrastive within the lines, A * B, and reinforced by the contrasts 'good'—'bad', and in Matthew's case 'rotten'—'fine'. There is also the contrast of 'tree'—'fruit'.

The relationship between the lines is identificational, 'as A, so B' and this is reinforced by matching syntax.

Other examples include: Lk. 12.23; Mt. 10.24.

6. Causal Contradictive

(1) Simple examples:

(a) Mk 9.35

> If anyone wishes to be first,
> he will be last of all and servant of all.

The structure is causally contradictive; this is brought about through the affirmation of an abnormal causation. The contradiction is reinforced through the opposition of 'first'—'last/servant'.

There is some question with this, and indeed all the other simple causal contradictives, whether they are truly descriptive, or whether ἔσται, the future indicative, actually has imperative force. A judgment on this question appears to be essentially a problem of interpretation; most commentators seem to favour a reading with imperative force.

This 'family' of sayings poses sharply the question of the significance of descriptive sayings in the preaching attributed to Jesus, and the relationship of descriptive and imperatival sayings.

Lk. 22.26 is the only saying among them which actually employs an imperative form. Mk 10.31; Mt. 19.30; 20.16; 23.12; Lk. 13.30; 14.11; 18.14 all seem best understood as straightforward futures (indicative). Lk. 9.48 is a present indicative identification.

Other examples include: Mt. 20.26; Mk 10.43; Mt. 20.27; Mk 10.44; Mt. 23.11.

(2) Examples with doubling and identification between lines:

(a) Lk. 12.3

> Whatever you have said in the dark shall be heard in the light,
> and what you have whispered in the inner rooms shall be
> proclaimed upon the housetops.

Within each line the structure is causally contradictive, with the contrasts

'said'—'heard',	'whispered'—'proclaimed',
'dark'—'light',	'inner rooms'—'housetops'.

The relationship between the lines is identificational.

(b) Mk 4.22

> For nothing is hidden except to be revealed,
> nor has anything been secret, but that it should come to light.

Compare the variants Mt. 10.26; Lk. 8.17; 12.2.

The lines are causally contradictive, with the contradiction expressed in the opposites 'hidden'—'revealed', 'secret'—'to light'.

There is, however, identification between the lines 'as A, so B'.

(3) Examples of completion through reversed doubling (i.e. contrast).
(a) Mk 8.35

> For whoever wishes to save his life will lose it;
> and whoever loses his life for my sake and the gospel's shall save it.

Compare the variants Mt. 16.25; Lk. 9.24; 17.33.

The structure is causally contradictive within the lines, and contrastive between them. The contradiction is achieved through the opposites 'save'—'lose'. The contrast between the lines, 'A, but B', is achieved through the reversal of these terms, creating a chiasm.

(b) Mt. 10.39

> He who has found his life shall lose it,
> and he who has lost his life for my sake shall find it.

The structure is causally contradictive in the lines, with the opposites 'find'—'lose'. The contrast between the lines, 'A, but B', is achieved as above, through the reversal of terms.

Other examples include: Mk 10.31, Mt. 19.30; 23.12, Lk. 14.11, 18.14.

7. Antithetical Contradictives
(a) Mt. 5.14b

> A city set on a hill cannot be hidden .

The structure is antithetically contradictive: 'if a city is hidden, it cannot be set on a hill; if a city is set on a hill it cannot be hidden'.

There is a basic opposition between hidden—public.

(b) Lk. 13.33b

> It is not possible that a prophet should perish outside Jerusalem

The structure is antithetically contradictive. In Dundes' terms, 'being a prophet' and 'perishing outside Jerusalem' are mutually exclusive.

Other examples: Lk. 4.24, Mt. 13.57b, Mk 6.4; Lk. 9.62.

c. *Mixed Sayings*

8. Opposition, but with identification of 'means'

(a) Mt. 12.37

> For by your words you will be justified,
> and by your words you will be condemned.

There is both opposition and identification in the relationship of the two limbs. Opposition is emphasized by the contrastive semantic pair 'justified'—'condemned'. But there is identification through repetition of the means 'by your words'.

In this and the following saying, there is a necessary tension between the two sorts of structural features.

(b) Mt. 26.52b

> For all who take up the sword will die by the sword.

There is identification through the repetition of 'the sword'. But there is opposition between the limbs in 'take up'—'die', the contrast of actor—acted upon, in relation to the sword.

9. Miscellaneous transformations with mixed features

(a) Mk 4.25

> For whoever has, to him shall be given;
> and whoever does not have, even what he has shall be taken from him.

Compare variants Mt. 13.12, 25.29; Lk. 8.18, 19.26.

The structure of the first line is identification, A > B. The structure of the second line is oppositional, a form of causal contradiction, contrasting 'does not have'—'has'.

The relationship between the lines is contrastive, 'A, but B', contrasting 'has'—'does not have', 'given'—'taken'.

This seems to be a transformation of group 3.

(b) Mk 7.15

> There is nothing outside the man which going into him can defile him;
> but the things which proceed out of the man are what defile him.

Compare the variant form in Mt. 15.11.

The relationship between the lines is contrastive, 'A, but B'. This is reinforced by the contrast 'going in'—'proceed out'.

The first line is oppositional, A * B. The second line is identificational, A > B.

Note that in the first line there is also the contrast 'outside'—'going in'.

(c) Mt. 6.24

> No one can serve two masters;
> for either he will hate the one and love the other,
> or he will hold to one and despise the other.
> You cannot serve God and mammon.

Compare the variant in Lk. 16.13.

The structure is complex, but primarily oppositional.[36]

The first line is a transformation of the oppostion, 'A cannot B'. The final line is an expansion of this opposition, 'if A, then not B'. Lines two and three are chiastic and present contrast, both within the lines 'hate'—'love', 'hold to'—'despise', and between the lines, 'either A, or B'. However, this contrast between the lines is only achieved through reversal, and has a certain identificational force, 'as A, so B'.

(d) Mt. 7.13b, 14

> For the gate is wide, and the way is broad that leads to destruction,
> and many are those who enter by it;
> for the gate is small, and the way is narrow that leads to life, and
> few are those who find it.

Within the lines the structure is primarily identificational. But the relationship between the lines is contrastive, 'A, but B'. The contrast is reinforced by 'wide'—'small', 'broad'—'narrow', 'destruction'—'life', 'many'—'few'.[37]

4. *Summary and Conclusions*

We will now draw together conclusions from this analysis, and suggest some of the more important areas of interest that might reward further study.

1. Our analysis has shown the complex structure of some of the Synoptic proverbial sayings. We have been able, however, to analyze these sayings in a more satisfactory way, for the purposes of descriptive classification, than certain traditional analyses, which seek either to focus on the poetic features of the sayings, or reconstruct an 'original' or 'earliest' form of the saying.

The work of C.F. Burney on *The Poetry of our Lord* sought to analyze the sayings of 'Jesus' in the categories of Hebrew poetry; as synthetic, antithetic, or synonymous parallelism. Although we agree that many sayings of 'Jesus' have a poetic form, similar to some Old Testament poetry, which might be termed parallelism, or preferably doubling, Burney's analysis tended to obscure the fundamental nature of some of the sayings, and was therefore inadequate as a descriptive analysis.[38]

For example, Burney describes Mt. 10.24 as an instance of synonymous parallelism,[39] and it is certainly true that the relationship between the lines is identificational; but his description fails to include another primary feature of the saying, which is the contrast 'disciple'—'teacher', 'slave'—'master'.

Burney's analysis of Mt. 6.22, 23 describes it as antithetic parallelism.[40] Again, our analysis would agree that the relationship between the lines is one of antithetic contrast, but equally important is the identification structure of the lines themselves (A leads to B).

Our analysis, while recognizing and describing the poetic features of the sayings (particularly the types of doubling), also can describe other fundamental structural features which may be of equal or more importance to the structure and meaning, than the relationship between the lines. Perhaps the comparison of our approach with that of Burney is unfair, in that the aim of his work was a different kind of descriptive task. However, in attempting a classificatory system for proverbial materials we would argue that our approach allows for greater nuance in the comparison of material.

The recent work of J.D. Crossan on the 'aphorisms' of Jesus has been concerned with primarily historical questions, about the 'historical Jesus'[41] and the sayings attributed to him. A great deal of the book is concerned with attempts at reconstructing the different stages of the sayings, tracing the development of the sayings in the tradition. Crossan is aware of the oral nature of the Synoptic tradition, and discusses the issue of oral and scribal sensibility.[42] He notes that a concern with *ipsissima verba* is inappropriate with regard to oral sensibility, and prefers to speak of *ipsissima structura*. However, his analysis remains at the level of linguistic features, and focuses on questions of origin and development which are at times interesting, but often unpersuasive. Perhaps our analysis of the structure of the proverb would be a firm base upon which to build the sorts of historical questions which New Testament scholars have traditionally asked of the Gospels, since the minor linguistic variations in the different Synoptic versions of the sayings are of less significance in our approach. For although in some cases common structural patterns may be reflected in common linguistic patterns (e.g. Mt. 26.41b and Mt. 9.37), in other cases, the linguistic features may differ, but the basic structural features remain constant (Mt. 11.8c and Lk. 7.25b, or Mt. 7.18 and Lk. 6.43, or the family of 'first'—'last' sayings, Mk 9.35 etc.).

The structural study of proverbial sayings provides a means of classifying Synoptic material which, in view of the oral history of the tradition, is able to disregard slight variations in the written forms of the sayings.

2. Perhaps the most important feature of the sayings which our analysis has shown is the many basic oppositions which form the foundation of a significant number of sayings. It is obvious that this feature is in no sense unique to the Synoptic sayings, as Dundes' account of the proverb has shown, for it is the nature of the proverb to compare or contrast.[43] However, what is of interest is the nature of these contrasts and oppositions in our collection of sayings, and the fact that one can move from this important structural feature to some interesting observations about content.

The oppositions can be observed in contrasting semantic word pairs; contrastive pairs which are not exact semantic opposites; and contrasts of the voice of the verb, which create consequent contrasts between subject and object.

There are a number of interesting oppositions reflected in some of the contrastive word pairs:

(i) There are various categories for the division or grouping of people,[44] such as the moral one, based on positive or negative moral status, and expressed linguistically in the pairs: sinner—righteous, evil—good, righteous—unrighteous, good—bad, rotten—fine, faithful—unrighteous. There are divisions based on positive or negative status: disciple—teacher, least—great, slave—master, first—last, great—servant, first—slave, greatest—servant, exalts—humbles. There are pairs which reflect an internal—external division, whether you are in the group or outside of it: harvest—workers, many—few, against—for, with—against, gathers—scatters. There are some sayings which reflect the opposition, but not necessarily in a contrastive pair (Mt. 19.24). Also in this class, there is considerable overlap with other groupings of contrastive pairs, such as the moral division.

(ii) There are divisions of human nature and activity in an

internal—external opposition: spirit—flesh, heart—mouth, heart—treasure, tree—fruit, life—food, eye—whole body.[45]

(iii) There is an opposition between concealment and revelation: said—heard, whispered—proclaimed, dark—light, inner rooms—housetops, hidden—revealed, secret—to light.

(iv) There may be other oppositional patterns among the sayings, such as a numerical/quantitative one: great—few, many—few, one—ninety-nine, little—much, wide—small, broad—narrow.

The relationships between these forms of opposition probably involve a good deal more overlap than our comments show.

3. Having classified the material, we can now consider some of the implications of our analysis, as they may be worked out on two different axes, sociological and literary.

In recent years, the study of proverbial wisdom has been undertaken with more sophisticated sociological interests and questions. It has become clear that the folk wisdom of a people can give insights into their social world or symbolic universe.[46] The question presents itself whether our study of the structure of the proverb might provide the basis for insights into the kind of communities that preserved these traditions and found and expressed something of their identity in these sayings. Our observations about the kinds of oppositions which feature in many of the sayings, might give some help as to the social identity and setting of those who preserved them. These are a different set of questions to the traditional form-critical concerns with the Sitz im Leben of a particular form. We are not interested in tying the proverbial form to a particular social setting, indeed, that seems a rather fruitless task. Instead, our concern would be with the sociology of knowledge, and whether we can move from the structure of a community's wisdom to some understanding of their symbolic universe and their social setting. As an example of such an approach, we might mention the work of G. Theissen on the sociology of the early Jesus movement.[47] He characterizes his concern in 'Itinerant Radicalism' as being from the perspective of the sociology of literature, and involves: 'the question of the social conditions behind the behaviour that shaped the text' (p. 84). This means taking account of the wider life of the community than simply its overtly religious practice, which has traditionally been the focus of interest in form-critical studies. In a review essay[48] W. Stegemann explains Theissen's approach:

> He looks for and seeks to bring to light the connections between religious ideas and subject matters, on the one hand, and the sociological situation of those who hold these ideas, on the other (p. 149).

His particular thesis concerns the wandering radical life-style of Jesus and his earliest followers. In arguing for this, he is able to draw together: images of Jesus; ideas of discipleship; ethical injunctions; and the life-style of these wandering charismatics. As J.G. Gager explains:

> Each of these items reflects and reinforces the shape of the other. Furthermore, the life-style of these figures is in turn directly tied to socio-economic conditions of Palestine in the first century, conditions which are readily visible in other movements of the same period. . . . . Finally, he contends that it is no coincidence that we are able to uncover in the tradition a convergence between small conventicles regarding themselves as 'suffering outsiders' and a sharply dualistic and eschatological view of history.[49]

Theissen's work has not been accepted without criticism; indeed Stegemann offers a telling critique. However, Theissen serves as one of the few examples of a New Testament scholar prepared to look more fully at the social setting of the early Christian movement, its ideas, and its literary products, and to consider the broader sociological implications of the exegetical comments he will make. It is unfortunate that sociological study of the New Testament has remained at an early stage, often handicapped by little reflection on method.[50] There is a great need for a sociology of New Testament literature[51] asking about the production and consumption of our literature. We cannot escape the fact that our evidence is frequently severely limited and ambiguous with many key historical questions unresolved—modesty is called for in the face of such limitations. However, sensitivity to sociological issues can serve as a healthy corrective to the dominant 'history of ideas' approach to New Testament religion. For our work on proverbial wisdom there are too many prior questions (both in terms of method and historical evidence) which need to be addressed before a fruitful sociological study could be undertaken. The important place of proverbial wisdom in either the life of the early Jesus movement or the communities which preserved the Synoptic tradition should, however, form a part of any study of the social world of early Christianity.

The question of the function of proverbial wisdom remains an important one. In recent New Testament scholarship this has been approached largely in terms of a rather narrow view of rhetoric; it might be that a sociological interest could stand as a corrective to some of the conclusions drawn from such a narrowly conceived rhetorical inquiry.[52] Indeed, in Chapter 5 we will consider the rhetoric of the proverb from a perspective which combines certain sociological and linguistic concerns.

There are important questions to consider about the literary function of proverbs. How does one maintain the particularity of the self-contained proverbial saying, with its stark contrasts and oppositions, recognizing the close connection between form and content, and yet also realizing the importance of broader context in interpretation? What are the implications of the overall narrative context of the proverbial saying, in the Gospel as a whole, and with regard to the smaller narrative units in which many sayings are placed?

Our analysis of the proverbial materials in the Synoptics leads on to two sets of interests; the historical/sociological level, and the literary level. However, before we pursue these interests, our preliminary work on the proverbial sayings must be completed by a consideration of the history of interpretation of the material in New Testament research.

Chapter 3

ISSUES IN THE MODERN INTERPRETATION OF SYNOPTIC PROVERBIAL WISDOM

In this chapter we wish to sketch some of the recent history of the interpretation of our subject: this will not be an exhaustive study, but it is hoped that we will be able to touch on the most significant works in the field. Our aim is not primarily to describe the way in which research has developed, or to argue for the influence of one writer upon another (although we will in places draw attention to such factors), but to understand better what are the recurring questions and main points of interest in research on the proverbial sayings; why these have been considered important issues; and then to go on to formulate the main areas we will need to cover, both to give an adequate treatment of our topic, and to relate our work to the broader, ongoing interests of New Testament research.

1. *R. Bultmann*

The major critical treatment of the proverbial sayings is to be found in R. Bultmann's *The History of the Synoptic Tradition*, in a section on the 'Logia', subtitled 'Jesus as the teacher of Wisdom'.[1] Bultmann's work has been the foundation of most subsequent research, and as such, it is important that we offer a thorough account of it.

Obviously, his interests are primarily historical. He is in agreement with M. Dibelius' understanding of the aims of the form-critical task, as being:

> to rediscover the origin and the history of the particular units and thereby to throw some light on the history of the tradition before it took literary form (p. 4).

With regard to the proverbial material, Bultmann focuses on

questions of origin, and the history and tendencies of the tradition in transmitting and re-shaping the sayings. He has less to say about questions of Sitz im Leben, perhaps because of the difficulties involved in associating proverbial sayings with typical situations in the life of the community.

(i) *The history and tendencies of the tradition*[2]

The first tendency to which Bultmann draws our attention is that of *combining different but similar sayings.* This gives us a good opportunity to get at the heart of Bultmann's method in seeking to reconstruct the history of the tradition, and make judgments about particular sayings. The approach looks for what are considered sure examples of a tendency, and then works by analogy to make judgments about other sayings for which the evidence is lacking,

> In a whole series of . . . instances we are admittedly dealing simply with probabilities, or even bare possibilities. But it is a necessity of right method that we should be concerned with such possibilities, because the sure instances make the tendencies of the tradition clear, and we still have to reckon with the tendency even when the sources do not permit of an unambiguous judgement (p. 84).

Thus, he selects a cluster of sayings, such as Mk 8.34-37, for which there are a number of parallels elsewhere within the Synoptic tradition: in this case, Mt. 10.38-39; Lk. 14.27; 17.33. He then argues that because we have evidence from Matthew and Luke that the group of sayings in Mark did not always appear together in the tradition, we can go on to posit a tendency toward combining previously independent sayings. He claims that this could, if necessary, be backed up with arguments based on the contents of the sayings. Later on, Bultmann draws a comparison with Ben Sira for a collection of sayings which were obviously independent originally.[3]

There is certainly evidence that individual sayings are sometimes present in clusters, i.e. different but similar sayings may at times appear in combination, at times independently. There is a difficulty, however, with Bultmann's decision that movement is from independent saying to clusters. This judgment, in a number of places, seems to rest on a view of the priority of Mark, and the existence of 'Q' as another source for Matthew and Luke. Even if we allow these assumptions, which do not go unchallenged in contemporary New Testament scholarship,[4] Bultmann's claim to be able to determine the direction of the tendency of the tradition is still open to question from other directions.

W. Kelber criticizes Bultmann's commitment to the 'paradigm of linearity' (p. 32) which postulates 'a single directional course of transmission' (p. 32). He sees Bultmann's model for transmission of tradition as being based on the idea of evolutionary growth, from simple (earlier) to complex forms (later):

> it was a process as natural as that of biological evolution: simplicity grew into complexity (p. 5).

This linear development of tradition gives way in studies of orality to a much more complex and diverse picture:

> If orality is perceived as a speaking of living words in social contexts, a concept of the pre-canonical, synoptic transmission emerges that is at variance with the paradigm of linearity. In its entirety, the pre-Markan oral tradition diverges into a plurality of forms and directions. Variability and stability, conservatism and creativity, evanescence and unpredictability all mark the pattern of oral transmission (p. 33).

These comments tend to undermine the degree of certainty which Bultmann gives to his laws of transmission, and his ability to write a detailed history of the tradition. Thus E.P. Sanders notes,

> For the most part, students of folklore do not emphasize the kinds of laws of transmission about which Bultmann spoke (p. 18n. 4).

We will, however, continue to examine Bultmann's observations on the tendencies of the tradition; this provides a thorough treatment of the phenomena present, even if the historical judgments are not persuasive.

The second tendency noted is that *to a saying already in circulation a new formulation is added.* Thus for example, an originally simple saying is made more complex by the addition of a second line (doubling). Bultmann draws an example from Rabbinic literature, in *B.B.* 12b:

> if a man is in disfavour he does not readily come into favour; and if a man is in favour he does not readily fall into disfavour.

He notes that the first half of this double saying did circulate alone (Strack–Billerbeck, I, p. 661), 'and it would have existed alone in the first place' (p. 85). Here we see an instance of the important principle that the simpler or purer form is the earlier or original one.[5]

> If. . . we can succeed in identifying a particular literary type and its laws of style, we can then frequently distinguish an original tradition from secondary additions. We thus obtain a test for determining the age of a literary utterance by noting whether it appears in the original pure form belonging to this type of literature or whether it shows marks of further stylistic development.[6]

He cites Mk 9.43-47 as an example: here the hand, eye and foot are mentioned, but in Mt. 5.29 only the hand and eye are present, thus the saying about the foot can be seen as a secondary analogous formulation. The principle seems to be that as a saying is more complex, the later it can be placed in the history of the tradition.

The third tendency is *for a completed saying to be followed by a sentence which is only intelligible in the light of what it follows.* Thus, in Mk 9.50 we have the complete saying (in the form of a question) 'if the salt becomes unsalty, with what will you make it salty again?'; in Mt. 5.13 this same saying occurs, but added to it is the dependent sentence 'It is good for nothing anymore, except to be thrown out and trampled under foot by men'. For Bultmann, this represents a secondary expansion at the 'Q' stage of the tradition. Interestingly, Bultmann raises the question of genuineness at this point, noting that a secondary expansion does not necessarily mean that the saying is not genuine, for Jesus could have taken a saying already in circulation and enriched it. In the same way, the recognition of a cluster of sayings should not lead directly to a judgment about genuineness, for the tradition could have combined genuine sayings of Jesus. In this connection, Bultmann reiterates the point we noted earlier,

> The issue is not what judgment is made upon one particular instance, but only whether we have to reckon with a tendency of the tradition.[7]

A fourth tendency is *to expand an original saying by addition in the written stage of the tradition.* Bultmann cites the example of Mt. 17.20, which adds the words 'and nothing will be impossible to you', as compared with Lk. 17.6, and Mk 11.23. He notes that sayings are often expanded on account of their context, and this is particularly the case with metaphorical sayings, such as Mt. 10.25b; 7.16a; 7.20; Lk. 11.18b. However, this activity is not limited to the redactional work of the Evangelists, and Bultmann wants to use this observation about 'the general tendency of the tradition' (p. 93) to move further back into the history of the tradition:

> It is . . clear that we cannot confine our observations simply to those occasions where we can make a comparison with a source, but that we must push back even behind our earliest sources, Q and Mark, and in this way gain a glimpse into the growth of the tradition before it was fixed in the sources to which we have access (p. 93).

Here Bultmann is open to the major criticism of Kelber, that he insisted:

> on the irrelevance of a distinction between orality and literacy (p. 6).

One of the main presuppositions of Bultmann's work is that he can observe tendencies at the written stage of the tradition, through comparative studies of the Gospels, and by analogy posit similar tendencies in the earlier oral stage. Bultmann assumes continuity between the oral and the written phases of tradition: thus, in most cases, it was considered

> immaterial whether the oral or the written tradition has been responsible; there exists no difference in principle (p. 87).

Kelber is at pains to point out the distinction between the two media, and hence the mistake of moving back too easily from the written text to an oral tradition that is thought to lie behind it. On the distinction between orality and textuality Kelber explains:

> There is agreement to the effect that the circumstances of performance, the composition, and the transmission of oral versus written materials are sufficiently distinct so as to postulate separate hermeneutics.[8]

The final tendency to which Bultmann draws attention involves *transformations, as opposed to expansions*, for which various reasons can be discerned.

(a) A linguistic motive is present in Luke's tendency to avoid Semitisms and parallelism, e.g. 6.40; 11.17; 12.33f.; 13.23f.

(b) There is, more importantly, a dogmatic motive, such as the addition in Mk 8.35 of the phrase 'for my sake and the gospel's' (cf. Lk. 22.27; Mk 10.45), which Bultmann terms 'a christological expansion' (p. 93). This does not refer to the conscious introduction of particular dogmas, but what is for the most part an unconscious process, whereby Christian ideas are assimilated into the tradition. Bultmann gives examples from the extra-canonical literature, such as the transformations of Mt. 7.23 in the Nazarean version and in *2 Clem.* 4.5.

(c) Certain transformations occur on account of the inclusion of material in the Christian tradition.

> We are not simply concerned with editorial changes to which the traditional material was subjected, but we also find that without any such change some new light was often thrown upon material by its incorporation into the Church's tradition (p. 97).

Bultmann gives the example of Mk 8.36 as an instance of a saying paralleled in Jewish wisdom literature which is only given a Christian sense by its present context, which is to be considered secondary.

> Were Mark 8.36 to be by some chance among the proverbs or in the Book of Sira, no-one would misinterpret its meaning (p. 97).

He finds that the metaphorical sayings are most dependent on their contexts, and this leads him to raise the question of origin:

> For the great majority of metaphorical sayings we have to confess that we can no longer determine their original meaning, if it was anything more than general proverbial teaching . . . So we have to reckon on a certain amount of the stuff of the tradition having been secular in its origin (p. 99).

(ii) *Questions of origin and the genuineness of the proverbial sayings*
Bultmann is aware that his understanding of the tendencies of the tradition leads to a number of possibilities with regard to the issue of the genuineness of the material. By genuineness he seems to mean whether the saying can be connected with Jesus, or whether it derives from a later period in the transmission of material. Later in this section, he narrows the issue of genuineness to the sayings which 'can be ascribed to Jesus with any measure of confidence' (p. 105). This is an important distinction: the latter discussion is concerned with what can with the highest degree of certainty be considered 'characteristic of the preaching of Jesus' (p. 105).

Bultmann raises the issue of the secular/popular proverbs in the Synoptic tradition: they might have been quoted by Jesus (with or without some alterations), or coined by him, or treated as sayings of Jesus by the Church. He is keen to find some criteria for deciding between these options in particular cases. However, he offers no criteria for arbitrating; instead, he dismisses the idea that Jesus might have drawn on proverbial material already current with the following claim:

> In general it may be said that the tradition would hardly have preserved the occasional use of a popular proverb by Jesus (p. 101).

This is an assertion for which Bultmann gives no real support. In view of the long list of 'secular meshalim' which he gives (pp. 102-104), the question may be raised as to why the transmitters of the Synoptic tradition, who are unlikely to have recorded such proverbs if spoken by Jesus, would then incorporate into the tradition 'secular meshalim' from some other source. If these sorts of proverbs would not have been sufficiently interesting on the lips of Jesus to warrant their inclusion into the earlier tradition of his sayings, then on what ground were they brought into the later tradition? It seems that the criterion being used in this case does not have to do with the nature of the tradition, but with Bultmann's understanding of Jesus: this is a serious fault in his treatment of the issue of origin.

The idea that there are popular proverbs quoted by Jesus but with his alterations is also dismissed:

> it is also difficult to believe that the changes and revaluation of such meshalim as are to be found in the tradition have in fact retained some reminiscence of such changes and revaluations by Jesus. For these are most closely conditioned by their contexts, and they in turn are certainly secondary (p. 101).

He seems to ignore his own idea that Jesus might have himself coined popular/secular proverbs: this would not be in keeping with Bultmann's picture of Jesus as a preacher of repentance and the Kingdom of God.

The conclusion is drawn that these sayings were attributed to Jesus as the tradition of his sayings developed. He notes that the process may not have been intentional; these sayings may have originally found their way into the tradition as 'useful paranetic material' (p. 102). If this appears a valid reason for the inclusion of such material into the tradition of Jesus' sayings at a later stage, then on what grounds can we argue that such material, if uttered by Jesus, would have initially been excluded from the tradition? It seems that the only reason would be that such 'secular' or 'popular' material does not cohere with the picture of Jesus' message which we hold on other grounds.

Bultmann goes on to describe the nature of these 'secular

meshalim', as reflecting secular observations on life, or merely a popular piety. He also sees the fact that these sayings rely on context to make their meaning clear as an indication that they do not derive from Jesus, for if that was their origin, the Church would have ensured that they retained something 'characteristic' of him:

> most of these sayings, especially the metaphorical ones, do not have a specific meaning until they appear in a concrete situation (p. 104).

This is a surprising way of differentiating the 'secular' from the 'genuine' sayings. Perhaps Bultmann here betrays a rather narrow idea of meaning, which does not do justice to the range of legitimate meanings that a proverbial saying might have. Surely it is a characteristic of all proverbial sayings that their specific meaning is derived from the particular context, or performance. It might also be part of an individual's purpose in using proverbial speech forms that there should be a certain degree of ambiguity. We will address ourselves more fully to these questions at a later stage.

The issue of the 'popular' nature of the piety expressed in many of the 'secular' sayings is of increasing importance as Bultmann sharpens his understanding of the question of genuineness. He develops an idea of the 'characteristic' message of Jesus, which is closely tied to the idea of eschatology as the basis of Jesus' piety. Thus for example:

> not even the sayings about laying up treasure in Mt 6.19-21 have anything characteristic; they likewise have no eschatological frame (p. 104).

Again Bultmann introduces the possibility that Jesus might have drawn on 'secular' wisdom and made it his own: however, this suggestion seems for him to be a fruitless one, because he sees no grounds for making a positive decision in any particular case. The tradition has certainly taken up many popular proverbs; in some cases, this may be due to Jesus' use of the saying, but for Bultmann there is no way of distinguishing Jesus' use from inclusion into the tradition because of suitability to a specific sphere of the Church's interest. There are, however, criteria for making a positive judgment in some cases, and these have to do with

> the exaltation of an eschatological mood... the product of an energetic summons to repentance.... sayings which demand a new disposition of mind (p. 105),

and sayings which are not traditional to Jewish apocalyptic. There are only a few sayings which can actually meet these criteria, and they can be described as follows:

> All these sayings... contain something characteristic, new, reaching out beyond popular wisdom and piety and yet are in no sense scribal or rabbinic nor yet Jewish apocalyptic. So here if anywhere we can find what is characteristic of the preaching of Jesus (p. 105).

It is important to note that this is a positive criterion of dissimilarity, allowing for sayings to be affirmed as genuine, but apparently not intended as a means of determining secondary sayings, although the implication is there in Bultmann's work that all sayings are of dubious value unless shown to be genuine. It is also important to see that when Bultmann speaks of what is 'characteristic' of Jesus' message, he means what is 'distinctive'. In discussing the question of the origin of the proverbial sayings with Jesus, he comments:

> They furnish very little information as to the characteristic historical significance of Jesus, since we can discover no essential differences between them and Jewish 'wisdom'.[9]

Bultmann's equation of 'characteristic' material with what is 'dissimilar' or 'distinctive' has been a key feature of subsequent treatments.

In conclusion, we see that Bultmann is left with an absolute minimum group of sayings, for which he has a high degree of certainty as to their genuineness. He allows that other sayings may be genuine words of Jesus, but it is impossible to tell when their piety is popular, or their outlook secular. For him, it seems less likely that the tradition would have remembered such sayings as words of Jesus, and more likely that they entered the tradition at a later stage to address (unspecified) Church interests.

As a postscript to this section, it is interesting to see how Bultmann's thoughts on the proverbial sayings were developed, some thirty years later, in an essay entitled 'General Truths and Christian Proclamation'.[10] In this brief essay his concerns are explicitly theological; to relate the general truths of reason to the proclamation of the demand or word of God. He is interested both in the role of the twentieth-century preacher, and in the relation between general truths and proclamation in the New Testament presentation of Jesus.

He states the latter issue most clearly in the question:

> Is not the proclamation of Jesus rich in general truths, even though in its essence it is the eschatological proclamation of God's imminent reign? (p. 155).

He wishes to understand the relation between these very different levels of discourse.

Bultmann points out that even indicative sayings, which appear as general truths, can have the character of 'address', and issue a challenge or command; thus he cites the example of Mt. 6.24:

> All such sayings express an experience of life or wisdom about life that is understood to provide a rule for conduct (p. 156).

However, although the saying may have the character of address, if it is based on a general truth that is 'self-evident', it is not the address of Christian proclamation. What is distinctive about Christian proclamation has to do with Bultmann's existential understanding of Jesus' eschatology as a summons to decision in the present.

For Bultmann, the answer to the question of the relation of this material to the essence of Jesus' message lies in the fact that such general sayings:

> lose their character as general truths in a concrete situation. . . . All such proverbs become genuine address when they are spoken in the right moment by the right person (p. 157).

With regard to the New Testament picture of Jesus the context for wisdom that makes general truths into proclamation is the eschatological Kingdom of God.

This essay helps us to see again the central importance, for Bultmann, of eschatology as the 'essence' of Jesus' message. This is combined with his interest in historical certainty, and his quest for a minimum amount of material, the genuineness of which he can be sure, so as to provide a picture of what is distinctive about Jesus. We realize how distorted a picture may result from such criteria for historical reconstruction.

In considering subsequent work on the proverbial wisdom of the Synoptics, we can divide research into two categories. On the one hand, there have been those who have pursued Bultmann's interest in historical questions, whether their interest lies in the history of the tradition and transmission of sayings, or in the place of these saying in a larger attempt to reconstruct the message of Jesus. The other major interest in subsequent work has been a literary or rhetorical one, concerned with the function of proverbial wisdom. This concern has not been pursued without an interest in historical issues, but historical reconstruction has not been the stated goal of this category of studies. We will see that there has been a good deal of overlap between these approaches in both directions, but it will be helpful to introduce them separately.

2. *Literary/Rhetorical Approaches*
Beardslee, Crossan

W.A. Beardslee

There are a number of factors which appear to motivate Beardslee's work, ranging from his interest in literary criticism to process thought.[11] With regard to the place of proverbial wisdom within the Synoptics, his initial interest had to do with a dissatisfaction with the way the proverb is largely overlooked in New Testament studies, and a reaction against kerygmatic or confessional approaches to theology.[12]

A good deal of work has been carried out on the parable as a characteristic form of Jesus' speech; but the proverb, which at first sight appears simply as a general truth, has tended to be ignored. Beardslee sees this distrust of the proverbial form as the reaction against an earlier generation of New Testament exegetes who tended to focus on such material and thereby reduce Jesus' message to a kind of higher wisdom.[13] With the tide turning against the older liberal interpretation in favour of a message governed by eschatology, interest in the wisdom forms decreased. The parable, itself a wisdom form, only became the focus of much attention as it was seen in the context of Jesus' eschatology.

In Beardslee's introduction to *Literary Criticism of the New Testament*[14] however, a key place is given to an essay on 'The Proverb' (pp. 30-41). In this he initially attempts to introduce us to the place and function of the proverb in folk literature. The setting of this essay in the context of his book is important in understanding Beardslee's treatment of the particular form. Central to the whole book is the opposition between order and disorder, and this is also a key feature of Beardslee's work on the proverb here, and in his subsequent writings.

In the Preface he explains that it is the function of stories and of faith to organize experience into some kind of order. However, modern experience is marked by a crisis of faith and a crisis of coherent narrative. Thus, in his section on the Gospel as story, Beardslee draws attention to the lack of plot, resolution and character in much contemporary writing, with the explanation that this is:

> a sign that many contemporary artists cannot accept the conventional pattern of conflict between chaos and order (p. 18).

The Gospel story for Beardslee is a transitional form which derives from a tension between order and disorder. Its function is to bring order to experience by reenacting the past in a coherent way, while the disordering aspect involves moving the participant into an open future. It is most important to note, however, that this disordering function of the Gospel story is linked by Beardslee with the historical development of Jewish eschatology.

> Though the Gospels are strongly coherent narratives, and though they function as religious narratives to reenact the point of origin, the Gospels have in them a strong eschatological—revolutionary component that rebels against order imposed from the past (p. 28).

The function of the story in moving the reader into an open future can be seen in the way a Gospel comes to an end. The story of the resurrection shows that the story as a whole does not end with the ending of the book; rather the Gospel narrative is a story of how something began that is still in process and moving toward its future and conclusion (p. 21).

The structure of the Gospel story involves a tension or opposition between order and disorder, and this has to do, at the historical level, with the importance of eschatology. Throughout his book Beardslee continually draws attention to the break up in perceptions of order as expressed in contemporary literature, and he compares this to the functions of language and literature within the New Testament, in which order and disorder are a central structural feature. Unfortunately, this is at times confusing, for statements which at first sight appear to be general comments about the functions of literature and speech forms are in fact tied to particular historical phenomena.

When we come to the essay on the proverb, we find that the issue of order-disorder is central to his treatment. We will consider this work in some detail since it contains important ideas which are presupposed in Beardslee's other writings on the proverb, and in the work of those who have drawn on his insights.

Like the Gospel form there is a sense in which the proverb holds perceptions of order and disorder in tension. The proverb expresses a flash of insight which sees the 'order' in a certain kind of happening. This is a low level order; a fairly limited claim is being made. On the other hand, Beardslee can contrast the proverb with discursive thought which seeks complex interrelationships and is based on a vision of universal order. In contrast to discursive thought, the proverb expresses a fragmented vision: it is not antidiscursive, but prediscursive. Historically, Beardslee sees the proverb as a step on the way toward a systematic view of reality. However, he notes that in modern times the proverb has come into prominence because of the breakdown of the narrative form, and the rejection of coherent visions of order in the world. Thus, in modern times the proverb is self-consciously employed in the rejection of order, while in ancient times it was used to express low level claims of order, and was a step towards a larger ordered view of reality as a whole.

Beardslee is persuasive when speaking about the ordering of a particular tract of experience which is expressed in the proverb. Interestingly, he notes the narrative affinities of the proverb in the implied process which it describes:

> though it is not in any way a narrative, it implies a story, something, in fact, that happens, that moves through a sequence in a way that can be known.[15]

He also notes the heuristic function of the proverb, which although often taking the form of a declaration, compels insight on account of the compressed form, and the implied challenge to adopt the same view of the situation.

In the Old Testament, and in the Gospels, the moralizing context means that the proverb becomes also an expression of faith in God's just and orderly rule of the world. There are therefore two important motifs: the observation of a scene from life; and the expression of faith in God's moral order. Given this description of the proverb, Beardslee is at pains to explain the occurrence of such material in the Gospels, since the overall framework of Jesus' message was quite different from the world of the proverb. He rejects the characterization of Jesus as a wisdom teacher, but on the other hand he holds that the quantity of wisdom material prevents one from interpreting it in such a way that it serves as the vehicle for a non-wisdom perspective of faith. When he comes to look at the use of proverbial wisdom in

'Q', we find an answer to Beardslee's problem:

> The eschatological setting in which .... proverbial wisdom is set by Q has the effect of heightening the element of paradox in the proverb and even of effecting a reversal of common sense wisdom (p. 36).

Beardslee also shows how the macarism or beatitude, which in its present usage is present-oriented and world-accepting, becomes eschatological in the Gospels.

It is important to note that Beardslee's understanding of the eschatological context and character of such sayings is more subtle than appears from some subsequent treatments of the material.[16] In spite of the eschatological character of some macarisms, there is still a strong linkage with the wisdom background. There is no room for 'eschatological escape', for the subject matter of the sayings, the poor, the hungry, the persecuted, fixes the context as that of responsible human relationships.

> These sayings can be read as a pointed reversal of popular standards which valued strength, self-assertiveness, and prudence rather than the stance of the beatitudes. But the sphere of operation toward which the beatitudes are directed is the same as that of popular wisdom, despite their reversal of its standards. They deal with the concrete realities of man among men, and not with some 'heavenly world' (p. 38).

Beardslee returns to this theme in his later essays.

In concluding this review of the essay on the proverb, we should note how Beardslee returns to the theme of order and disorder in characterizing the function of proverbial wisdom in 'Q'. It reverses the usual function of wisdom which seeks to make 'a unified whole out of one's life',[17] by intensification through paradox and hyperbole. The eschatological setting leads to a disordering function, but the question remains how much this disordering or disorientation is an end in itself, or whether it should be seen within a larger context and as a step on the way to re-orientation or re-ordering.

In his essay on the 'Uses of the Proverb in the Synoptic Gospels'[18] Beardslee develops similar themes, considering in fairly general terms the function of the proverb, but also raising historical questions concerning the relation of the Synoptic material to Jesus. With regard to function he develops an argument for an element of confrontation in all proverbial wisdom, based on the necessity of choice in deciding which proverb fits which situation. However, this appears to be an argument which only works at the level of proverb performance, i.e. in oral practice, or in reading a collection of proverbs where one is forced to be selective. In the case of the literary use of proverbs, as in the Gospels, the situation is very different, for the choice has already been made by the writer, and any element of confrontation will work in a different way.[19]

When Beardslee raises the historical question, he is seeking to differentiate between proverbs which express a general folk wisdom, and those in which wisdom is immensely concentrated and intensified. The latter are considered 'the most characteristic Synoptic sayings' (p. 66), and as we have said, involve paradox and hyperbole. Although Beardslee does not explain what he means by 'most characteristic', it would seem that the idea here is of the most distinctive material, i.e. that which is dissimilar from traditional wisdom. At this stage Beardslee does not mention Bultmann's authenticating criterion, but he explains later that:

> The intensification of the proverb is .... related to the use of proverbs in an eschatological framework (p. 72).

The assumption that eschatology provides the basic framework of Jesus' message coupled with dependence on the criteria of dissimilarity and coherence are essential features of Beardslee's historical judgments about the relation of proverbial wisdom to Jesus, and the question of function.

In the article under discussion, Beardslee articulates well the issue of disorientation as an end in itself, or as part of a larger enterprise:

> To what extent can the disjunctive 'jolt' or reorientation demanded by the paradox be retrospectively seen in a larger coherent framework, and to what extent must it remain as an abrupt break in perception? (p. 69).

In answer to this question Beardslee draws attention to the use of familiar experience to jolt the reader into new insight:

> the strongly practical orientation of the bulk of the proverbs in the Synoptics is the context from which the paradox and hyperbole arise and from which their meaning is oriented (p. 70).

This does not, however, answer the question at issue. It shows a judicious rhetorical practice on the part of Jesus and the Gospel writers, but does not help us to understand better the nature of the disorientation brought about by the rhetoric. In this connection

Beardslee also mentions the presence of many sayings which represent the tradition of practical wisdom rather than intensification through hyperbole and paradox. He explains in an interesting way that:

> the Synoptic message does not always proceed by way of reversal . . . and continuity also has its place in this proclamation (p. 70).

Unfortunately, Beardslee is unwilling to allow continuity to stand alongside discontinuity in Jesus' message, and thus do justice to wisdom elements; it appears rather to be a mere rhetorical tool at the service of a more effective eschatological jolt.

Beardslee concludes his article by stating explicitly the importance of eschatology as the historical framework for his treatment of the proverb. He notes how radical eschatology has often been presented as world-denying: such a view is oversimplified, for, paradoxically, although eschatological urgency takes the direction of abandonment of the present, it produces a faith focused on the present, and making demands on it. As Beardslee also realizes, this is a key issue which we need to pursue.

There are a number of other articles by Beardslee which touch on similar issues in relation to proverbs in the *Gospel of Thomas*,[20] Plutarch's speech,[21] and with regard to the saying about saving one's life by losing it.[22] Before drawing together the most important insights from his work, we will consider one final article on the 'Parable, Proverb and Koan'.[23]

The aim of this article was to contrast:

> an earlier period when the words of Jesus were assumed to relate to God as an ordering factor, to a more recent period in which parables and proverbs are seen to open the hearer to a creative disruption (p. 151).

Again, Beardslee is returning to the relation of the proverb to perceptions of order; however, in this instance, this is part of a larger theological discussion of the relation of the transcendent and order.

In earlier studies of the parables and proverbs, particularly with regard to 'Q', these forms of speech were seen as condensing the continuities and order of life. Such studies were aware of paradox and surprise in the parables and proverbs, but this was part of a larger, coherent vision of order:

> They characteristically saw this element of surprise in a context of overarching meaning which could be re-established in fuller form after the moment of shock (p. 154).

With reference to Bultmann and others, Beardslee explains the shift from seeing disorientation as part of a larger process of growth in orientation, to seeing the function of disruption and creating discontinuities as standing on its own. This theological shift is to be seen as part of a wider cultural movement, based on an inability to find continuity and order in human experience.

At this point Beardslee introduces the work of J.D. Crossan as the proponent of a more extreme view of the disorienting function of proverbs: we will now consider Crossan's contribution to our topic. In his earlier work the most important contribution is his study of 'Comic Eschatology in Jesus and Borges' entitled *Raid on the Articulate*.[24] This work sees Jesus' proclamation as a comic eschatology, a playful rejection of the false securities of structure and order. With regard to the proverbial material he is concerned to show:

> the comic subversion of wisdom by counterproverb, that is, of proverbial aphorism by paradoxical aphorism (p. 69).

Crossan's dependence on Beardslee is acknowledged, and he speaks of Jesus' message as a rejection of the very order which wisdom seeks to describe, achieved through paradox. However, Crossan goes on to make some theological assertions which move him beyond Beardslee. For him, it is only in the destruction of order that one can experience God.

> it is liberation to realize that coherence is our invention, that there is beauty in the blackness, and that beyond coherence lies transcendence (p. 73).

In an earlier work entitled *the Dark Interval*,[25] Crossan speaks in a similar, and clearer way, of the parables:

> they are stories which shatter the deep structure of our accepted world and thereby render clear and evident to us the relativity of story itself. They make us vulnerable to God. It is only in such experiences that God can touch us, and only in such moments does the Kingdom of God arrive. My own term for this relationship is transcendence.

In his short book *Theopoetic*,[26] an exploration of 'Theology and the

Religious Imagination', Wilder characterizes Crossan's position as a kind of 'contemporary iconoclastic mysticism' (p. 77), which separates Jesus too radically from his religious environment, and, we might add, separates the parables too radically from other material which may derive from Jesus. Beardslee quotes Wilder's response to Crossan's work on the parables, which also relates to the latter's treatment of proverbial wisdom:

> Jesus' mythos of the Kingdom of God has more content to it than this kind of ontological reversal (p. 77).

We will have occasion to return to Wilder's helpful work on the language of Jesus at a later stage in our work, but it may be useful at this point to note some further implicit criticism of Crossan. Wilder is concerned to point up the failure to understand the complexities of mythological language on the part of those writing on the parables of Jesus. He is carrying on a dialogue with both contemporary writers and poets in their use of mythological language, and contemporary New Testament students, like Crossan, whose claims about Jesus' use of language appear overly extravagant. Although he does not introduce Crossan by name into the discussion at this point, the position to which he refers would seem to be similar.

> In our situation ....Many seek the life of the imagination passionately but draw back from any encompassing myth. The experience of transcendence is craved but no longer plot or world-story is hoped for .... At most they acknowledge a polytheism of fragmentary insights and look for no unifying pattern (pp. 80, 81).

He goes on:

> But true myth, involving language as it does, goes beyond any such momentary epiphanies and seizures, and pretends to order both experience and reality .... The poet today may, indeed, use only broken myths, may use the great myths of the past in only derivative ways, but since he uses language his work can hardly escape some sort of defining statements. Poets have never been able to turn poetry completely into music (p. 81).

The danger in Crossan's work is that it focuses attention on the rhetorical effect of the proverbial or parabolic material with little attention to the broader context of meaning.[27] The broader context is literary and linguistic, involving the myth or symbol of the Kingdom of God; and also sociological, involving the praxis and setting of

Jesus' activity. Beardslee is aware of these problems, particularly with reference to the importance of the content of the material itself:

> It is possible to interpret the message of Jesus about the Kingdom of God along a .... path of letting go of self and world, and to see the paradox and hyperbole of the gospel parables and proverbs in this context. The strong element in them of.... 'participation', of continuing re-entry into the human social context, may not be adequately represented by this line of interpretation, however (pp. 164, 165).

Crossan dismisses too quickly the content of the proverbial sayings, and this leads to the problem of the amoral nature of the experience of the transcendent, for it seems to be a rhetorical function of disorientation or disordering without reference to anything else.

Beardslee is unhappy with this; he is aware of the need for some 'ontological root' to the experience of disorientation. In Crossan's view it would appear that any rhetoric which shatters the hearer's accepted world would be appropriate, since the impact of Jesus' language is to destroy coherence, For Beardslee, there is more content to Jesus' language, with its controlling idea of the Kingdom of God, than mere subversion: thus, he relates the dislocation evoked by the paradoxical sayings to a transcendent reality characterized by 'rightness'. He warns against thinking in too simple a manner about the rightness of God and its disclosure in our life in the world. However, for Beardslee, after the moment of fracture or dislocation of the continuity of life, faith leads to a re-entry into the continuing social relationships of men and women.

On the one hand, Crossan represents a theological position which seeks 'a new imaginative grasp of the transcendent as a creative nothingness' (p. 172). For him the story begins and ends with the rhetorical effect of proverbial wisdom (and parables) as breaking up the continuities of life, shattering perceptions of order, allowing disorientation to be the end. The ultimate religious goal, and also the function of Jesus' language, is to show the transitory nature of coherence. On the other hand, Beardslee has come, albeit tentatively, to a position which seeks 'a fresh view of the transcendent as an ordering factor' (p. 172). The function of the proverb does not end with disorientation, but moves the hearer or reader on to a new order, less naive and self-centred, but ordered nonetheless. Sadly,

Beardslee does not pursue this issue much further.

We wish now to comment on this early work of Crossan, and also to draw together some of the insights gained from our review of Beardslee's important contribution.

It would seem that Crossan's position on the proverb in *Raid on the Articulate* involves a number of difficulties. He begins his work with a preface in which he states his debt to the new interest in literary approaches to the Bible, and, more specifically, what he terms 'structuralist literary criticism' (p. xiv). However, this work is based upon attempts at historical reconstruction of the authentic message of Jesus. Thus he explains that the book:

> presumes, acknowledges, and appreciates the results of historical investigation into the teachings of Jesus. It will never use texts except those supported as authentic by the vast majority of the most critical scholarship (p. xv).

Presumably, Crossan would be prepared to argue for the rationality of his method of reconstruction, for, on one level, and on the basis of his own argument, he would have to admit that the coherence of his historical reconstruction is his own invention. Crossan's discursive essay on Jesus' message, and the ideas which it presupposes, require a coherent and ordered understanding of human life and thought, as does any attempt at reconstruction. It is ironic that on this basis he argues for disorder and incoherence as ultimate goals/values. This shows up the difficulties of speaking and conceiving of disorder and disorientation as ends in themselves, without a broader ordering and defining system in which they can be understood. There is a link here with the philosophical position he adopts on the status of God. This is most clear in a passage from *The Dark Interval*:

> If there is only story, then God, or the referent of transcendental experience, is either *inside* my story and, in that case, at least in the Judaeo-Christian tradition I know best, God is merely an idol I have created; or, God is *outside* my story, and I have just argued that what is 'out there' is completely unknowable.... In all of this I admit most openly a rooted prejudice against worshipping my own imagination and genuflecting before my own mind (pp. 40, 41).

However, the fact that God is outside story requires a story about God; if God is outside language, how can we say that much. There are difficult philosophical issues at stake in Crossan's 'iconoclastic mysticism'; issues which certainly have not been fully treated in his often impressionistic work. In an interesting essay on 'A Theology of

Story: Crossan and Beardslee',[28] J.B. Cobb offers a helpful critique of Crossan's position, and raises the important question:

> Is the story that language does not contain a transcendent reference itself but one of the stories we can create for ourselves, or does it have a privileged position in relation to all other stories? (p. 156).

Cobb is unhappy with an understanding of Jesus' language that focuses on subversion alone, for 'no one lives without a story that makes some sort of sense of things' (p. 158). More importantly, he is not content to empty the Gospel of its ethical content:

> If we live by myths, then the judgment that only the disruption of myth is important means withdrawal from involvement in any effort to change the world by action... is this the last word of the gospel for the oppressed who long for justice? (p. 158).

An ethical content to the understanding of Christian faith is demanded both by the context in which we do theology today, and also by our attempt to do justice to the mission of Jesus as we know it from the Gospels.[29]

Our other major complaint about Crossan's work springs from his stated desire of building on *only* 'the most critical scholarship'. In our view, this can only result in a most distorted picture of Jesus' message. However, we will save our comments on this issue for our consideration of the historical aspect of Beardslee's work.

Beardslee's contribution to our subject is extremely valuable and stimulating, but there are two main areas in which his work is in need of revision.

First, the dominance of the opposition between order and disorder appears to have led to a rather simplistic characterization of traditional wisdom. As we have already noted, Beardslee's much quoted description of the presupposition of wisdom is: 'the project of making a continuous whole out of one's existence'. Thus, traditional wisdom is understood as a project of ordering one's life in a coherent way, and this is easily knocked down by the disordering function of Jesus' language. However, we must ask whether the 'wisdom project' can be described in such neat terms, or can we deconstruct the tidy oppositions between order and disorder, coherence and incoherence, orientation and disorientation?

Part of our problem results from the variety of settings for proverbial wisdom, and the use of the eclectic term 'the wisdom project' without specifying how or at what point in the literature we have access to the project. There is the proverb collection represented by the book of Proverbs; the literary use of proverbs;[30] oral proverb performance, of which we have examples in folklore studies; and the mixture of proverb use both as clusters and isolated sayings in the narrative context of the Gospels.

We have already made clear that the individual proverb involves a low level claim to order.[31] It is not a proposition that should necessarily be universalized, but describes the order in a particular repeatable incident or tract of experience; hence the importance of proverb performance. Ben Sira understood the importance of the appropriate time in relation to proverb performance:

> A proverb from a fool's lips will be rejected,
> for he does not tell it at its proper time (20.20).

A positive statement of this principle occurs at 18.29. Folklore studies teach us that in some African cultures points of law are debated and decided through the search for the most appropriate proverb for the case.[32] Indeed, we have in the New Testament an example of such proverb competition for the most appropriate saying, in Mk 7.24-30, the story of the Syro-Phoenician woman. This incident involves a proverb exchange between Jesus and the woman, in which Jesus tries to justify his reticence to act with the saying:

> it is not good to take the children's bread and throw it to the dogs.

However, the woman responds with an apt saying that counters Jesus' wisdom:

> even the dogs under the table feed on the children's crumbs.

It is a question of finding the appropriate saying to fit the setting, not an issue of competing truth claims, for both are 'true' to their appropriate setting. The incident does not demonstrate a shattering of the 'wisdom project' on the part of the woman, but it does show that 'making a continuous whole of one's life' is a rather grand claim for the function of proverb performance.

Aside from the low level claim to order with regard to a particular context, there is also a question of whether the function of a proverb is to make order or to observe it. Von Rad's work on wisdom in relation to Old Testament studies has been important in emphasizing the issue of order. This is bound up with his thoughts on the mentality of the ancient Israelite:

> These maxims will never be understood unless one presupposes as their background a mentality which still had vital questions to put to its environment..... to wrestle some sort of order from chaos.[33]

Von Rad sees the perceptions of order involved in proverbial wisdom as claiming a general and universal validity. He conceives of the ancient Israelite living in a world characterized by chaos, and the ability to capture the hidden order in what would otherwise be paradoxical events is the triumph of wisdom and order over chaos. This picture of the struggle between chaos and order as part of the structure of the ancient Israelite mentality is similar to the kind of characterization of the 'primitive mentality' which has been open to criticism from the work of anthropologists. Indeed, J.W. Rogerson in his *Anthropology of the Old Testament*[34] criticizes von Rad's treatment of the proverb on the grounds of his use of the concept of primitive mentality. Von Rad finds a contradiction in Prov. 26.4-5

> Answer not a fool according to his folly...
> Answer a fool according to his folly.

He sees this as an example of 'empiric gnomic' thought, for to the ancient Israelite no contradiction was involved. The two proverbs represent general and universal claims, but no attempt is made to connect them, because the ancient mentality did not reason in that way. Rogerson draws on Jack Goody's thesis concerning the implications of the move from orality to literacy which he applies to proverb use:

> It ... becomes (*with literacy*) possible to set one proverb against another in order to see if the meaning of one contradicts the meaning of another; they are now tested for a universal truth value, whereas their applicability had been essentially contextual (though phrased in a universal manner).[35]

For Goody, the literary setting of a previously oral speech form enables critical faculties to be developed; this seems to counter von Rad's notion of 'empiric gnomic' thought (taken over from A. Jolles) that suggested an uncritical acceptance of contradictory claims. Rogerson further cautions Old Testament students against making pronouncements about the differences between ancient Israelite mentality and modern modes of thought (p. 65). This may serve to reinforce our doubts about the characterization of wisdom deriving from a mental image of the battle between chaos and order.

Von Rad's understanding of wisdom, however, does contain some helpful insights when we disregard the more dubious comments on the primitive mentality. He emphasizes the order connected with the individual proverb, rather than speaking of a systematic coherence or order. This does some justice to the fragmentary nature of proverbial insight. However, he raises the claim to order of the individual proverb, from a low level to a universal one. If we drop the supposed limitations of the primitive mentality we soon see that the claim to universality is weakened.

On another level, the claim that the proverb involves the imposition of order on experience, whether or not it is in opposition to chaos, is open to question. Does the proverb impose or describe order? Is the function of the proverb to bring order to experience, or to bring order to expression in speech? The Nigerian writer Chinua Achebe has drawn attention to the pleasure involved in quoting an apt proverb:

> Among the Ibo the art of conversation is regarded very highly, and proverbs are the palm-oil with which words are eaten.[36]

It may be that proverb origin and use has more to do with delight or elegance in speech than the imposition of order. The artistry and poetic balance of the Hebrew proverb would be most appropriate in this regard. There are a number of sayings which draw attention to this idea of delight in speech. Prov. 15.23 is an example:

> A man has joy in an apt answer, and how delightful is a timely word.

Language and wise utterance is an essential feature of wisdom, both at the level of proverbial speech, and in the introductory chapters of Proverbs, where the images of the wise and the strange women focus on the importance of speech.[37]

Proverb performance involves an appropriate show of eloquence in fitting the saying and the setting. There is implied only a limited claim to order.

If we turn to a proverb collection such as the book of Proverbs, can this be characterized as an ordering project? We find in this work examples of paradox (13.24; 14.13; 25.15), contradiction (26.4-5 as discussed; cf. also 15.27; 21.14), and different advice with regard to similar subject matter (10.15, 29; 11.4, 28).[38] A reading of the book of Proverbs shows the need for greater nuance than Beardslee and Crossan allow in their description of the wisdom project as ordering.

When we introduce the books of Job and Ecclesiastes, we see that 'making a continuous whole of one's life' is too much to claim. Continuity and order are important to wisdom, but not in the sense of universal coherence implied by that quotation. The life of the individual includes surprise and unpredictability. As with other examples, the opposition between order and disorder is too simplistic. Proverbial wisdom makes low level claims to order, and on occasion disorder; but it is hard to see it as a project of making a *continuous* whole of life.[39]

Our second problem with Beardslee's work involves the historical reconstruction of Jesus' message which it presupposes. At this stage we will introduce our difficulties only in outline, since we must go on to look more fully at the work of Perrin in this connection.

Our main point is to note, however, that Beardslee and Crossan, although taking a primarily literary or rhetorical approach, nevertheless base their work on a critical reconstruction of Jesus' message which goes largely undiscussed. As we noted earlier, there are times at which comments that appear to be general statements about the function of proverbial speech forms are found to be dependent upon particular historical factors. In the case of Jesus' speech this is principally the issue of the eschatological basis of his message. Crossan is most explicit about his historical assumptions, although his comments are confined to the Preface of his book rather than the main text. We would not favour an ahistorical approach, but a more frank treatment of this aspect of their work, which may no longer be accepted as representing a critical consensus.

3. *Historical Approaches*
Perrin and Crossan

Norman Perrin's contribution to our subject is in the context of his wider interest in reconstructing the authentic message of Jesus, particularly with reference to his proclamation of the Kingdom of God. In his 1972 SBL Seminar paper 'Wisdom and Apocalyptic in the Message of Jesus' he gives us his most detailed treatment of the significance of the proverbial sayings. This essay involves Perrin's characterization of Jesus' total message as moving in a spectrum between proclamation and parenesis. Proclamation is understood to be 'the verbal announcement of something that determines the quality of human existence, something that effects one at the level of existential reality' (p. 546). On the other hand, parenesis (or sometimes teaching) indicates 'appropriate ways of expressing a response to the proclamation of the Kingdom of God' (p. 546). It is in the element of teaching that wisdom forms are generally thought to have their most natural function, however, for Perrin, there is something distinctive about the use of proverbial sayings in Jesus' speech.

Perrin's debt to Bultmann is of the utmost importance in understanding his section on the proverbial sayings, for he will accept as authentic only those sayings which Bultmann approves, and this forms the basis for all his work at reconstruction. He has also built on the insights of Beardslee, and thus it is no surprise when he speaks of our material that he sees their context not as one of 'faith in God's just and orderly rule of the world' (p. 562) but rather a strongly eschatological setting, involving an intensification of proverbial insight. It seems to come as a shock to Perrin when he discovers that:

> the most characteristic of the sayings which concern him (Beardslee) are on Bultmann's (approved) list; and better examples of sayings that would meet the criterion of dissimilarity it would be hard to imagine (p. 562).

Beardslee has not claimed to be attempting historical reconstruction, but for Perrin it is significant that his results, based on a literary critical approach, cohere with Bultmann's results, based on historical criticism. However, we have found that Beardslee's ideas are not achieved without presupposing important historical judgments. When Beardslee speaks of the 'most distinctive sayings' of Jesus we are not far removed from Bultmann's criterion of dissimilarity; and Beardslee shows much sympathy with Bultmann in coming to a characterization of the message of Jesus as eschatological challenge. Perrin's work on the proverbial sayings must be seen in the light of this dependence on Beardslee and Bultmann as an attempt to fit a very select group of sayings into a conjectural notion of the overall context of Jesus' message. There are therefore three important points for him with regard to this material: the intensely eschatological setting; the intensification of the normal proverbial insight; and the function of jolting the hearer out of making a whole of existence, and into passing a judgment on that existence.

With these points in mind Perrin goes on to claim that in the context of the message of Jesus most of the authentic proverbial sayings are to be seen as part of the proclamation of the Kingdom.

They lead to radical questioning of the accepted order (Lk. 9.60a; Mt. 5.39b), or they proclaim the eschatological reversal of the present, and so demand judgment upon it (Mk 8.35; 10.31; Lk. 14.11). A few sayings are seen to have a parenetic function in instructing the reader as to the nature of an appropriate response to the challenge of the proclamation.

It is an interesting reflection of Perrin's understanding of Jesus' significance that the only acceptable categories are proclamation (seen as eschatological judgment on the present), and parenesis. With such categories there is little room for a wisdom perspective of faith. As with Crossan's work, when a proverbial saying is considered proclamation, the focus seems to be simply on the rhetorical effect that can be produced by such a saying, and the significance of the content is lost. Thus, the saying about turning the other cheek, giving your cloak, and going the extra mile, is thought to be impossible; it then becomes a denial 'of the very fabric which makes possible communal existence in the world' (p. 563). The alternative for Perrin is to 'mellow them down' into extremely radical challenges barely possible of fulfilment. We are reluctant to give up the sense of this saying as a paradigm for the grace in human relationships which characterizes the Kingdom. Indeed, it becomes clear in reading Perrin's work that the issue of central importance for understanding his particular exegetical decisions is the sense in which the Kingdom of God is to be interpreted. This combines, on the level of historical allusion, an emphasis on the apocalyptic eschatology which the phrase Kingdom of God is thought to invoke; and at the level of language functions, Perrin continues in the tradition of Bultmann to interpret the eschatology of Jesus existentially.

One of the few dissenting voices which have been raised against the line of interpretation which we have been documenting, is that of C.E. Carlston. In an article entitled 'Proverbs, Maxims and the Historical Jesus',[40] Carlston draws attention to the key problem of eschatology:

> We must see Jesus' call to repentance as based on more than prudential escape from imminent judgment, understood as the shattering of all human history and hope. What is really characteristic of Jesus' eschatological teaching is its complex both/and character ('already .... and not yet') and the connection between the coming of the Eschaton and Jesus' own ministry. It is precisely this latter connection which prevents us from eliminating

> *a priori* the wisdom elements (if any) in Jesus' teaching as 'non-eschatological' and hence inauthentic (p. 103).

In our next chapter we must consider in more detail the method of historical reconstruction which has such an effect on the way in which the proverbial element in the Synoptics is understood, and this will involve focusing on the key issues of Kingdom of God and Eschatology. At this stage, however, we wish to introduce a concrete example of Perrin's treatment of a particular group of sayings, to show how his approach to the material is worked out in practice, and to begin to trace the direction of our criticisms and our own interpretation of the material.

We will consider those sayings which focus on a reversal of status (Perrin refers to these as 'Eschatological Reversal Sayings' in his 1972 SBL paper p. 564); these include Mk 10.31,

> many that are first will be last, and the last first.

and Lk. 14.11,

> everyone who exalts himself will be humbled, and he who humbles himself will be exalted.

Perrin's comments on these sayings are remarkably brief:

> the theme of eschatological reversal is one of the best attested themes of the message of Jesus. It proclaims the Kingdom as eschatological reversal of the present and so invites, indeed demands judgment upon that present (p. 564).

These sayings are seen as proclamation of the Kingdom. In an earlier work[41] Perrin gave further indication of his reading of these sayings, although his explanation is somewhat lacking in clarity. With reference to Mk 10.31, the saying speaks of the Kingdom as an activity of God in the present, which seems to be judgment; and a consummation which God will establish in the future through a reversal of human values. The responsibility of man is to respond to this judgment with complete self-surrender, which leads to a deepening experience of God. This is fairly representative of the current understanding of the authentic proverbial sayings which interprets them in a strongly eschatological setting, and sees their function as proclaiming a Kingdom which shatters human perceptions of order and value.

We will offer a re-examination of the treatment of these sayings by considering the motif of reversal from the viewpoint of tradition history. All the sayings in this 'family' revolve around the same structural opposition between negative and positive status; however, we will focus, for the most part, on the opposition expressed in the word group 'humility' and 'exaltation', as in Lk. 14.11, 18.14, and Mt. 23.12. Our concern is to see the types of contexts in which the motif traditionally occurs. This is obviously no substitute for exegetical study of the Gospel texts themselves, but it may be of some help in our critical consideration of Perrin's unhesitating adoption of an eschatological reading of these sayings.[42]

A brief survey of some of the relevant literature makes it clear that the motif of humiliation and exaltation is found in a variety of different contexts.

Prophecy

The book of Isaiah may serve as an example of prophetic literature where the motif is present in a number of ways.

1. There is the notion of man's humiliation in the light of God's exaltation: 2.11,

> the proud look of man will be abased, and the loftiness of man will be humbled, and the Lord alone will be exalted in that day.

This establishment of the appropriate status of man and God will happen on 'the day of the Lord'; however, the poem which follows (vv. 12-22) demonstrates that this activity of God is rooted in actual events—the day of the Lord concerns real human experience.

2. There are passages where someone or something experiences a reversal of fortunes, from humiliation to exaltation or vice versa. Thus at 9.1 the land of Zebulun and Naphtali although previously treated with contempt will now be made glorious. On the other hand, in 14.4-23 Israel taunts Babylon over the opposite reversal of fortunes: the one who once said 'I will ascend to heaven' (v. 13) now discovers that it will be thrust down to Sheol (v. 15). The Servant Song in chs. 52–53 expresses the same movement from humiliation to exaltation. The motif also presents itself in chs. 60–61; thus 60.22,

> the smallest one will become a thousand, and the least one a mighty nation.

Also at 61.7,

> instead of your shame you will have a double portion, and instead of their humiliation they will shout for joy over their portion.

3. There are passages which describe the reversal of roles where one in high office is transferred to a low status. 22.19-21 describes Shebna, a royal steward, who will be deposed from his high office and replaced by Eliakim. In 49.23 the rulers of other nations will become Israel's servants,

> and kings will be your guardians, and their princesses your nurses. They will bow down to you with their faces to the earth, and lick the dust of your feet; and you will know that I am the Lord.

Chapter 60 repeats the notion of foreign rulers serving Israel: v. 14 speaks of the sons of the oppressors bowing down to those oppressed.

There is one final passage of interest to our motif at 24.2. Here the notion is not so much of reversal, but of a levelling of status as an expression of God's devastation of the earth:

> the people will be like the priest, the servant like his master, the maid like her mistress, the buyer like the seller, the lender like the borrower, the creditor like the debtor.

The imminent catastrophe makes these status distinctions meaningless, because the fate of all will be the same. This is close to the interpretation of the reversal motif in the Synoptics offered by some critics, that in view of the imminent eschaton all status, and indeed all wisdom and order, is to be destroyed. We will argue, however, that this is to offer a rather limited account of Jesus' perception of God's activity.

Perhaps the main point to emerge here is that God is the one who humbles and exalts. This is brought home in the hymnic section of chapter 40 where the creative activity of God is set alongside his bringing down the exalted: verse 23,

> he it is who reduces rulers to nothing, who makes the judges of the earth meaningless.

Although the thrust of the book is toward a future activity of God, it is important to note that the motif is part of a general description of God's activity, apart from any temporal scheme; thus 26.5,

> for he has brought low those who dwell on high, the unassailable city; he lays it low, he lays it low to the ground, he casts it to the dust.

Wisdom

The wisdom literature offers many examples of this motif; we will draw principally from the canonical book of Proverbs and from Ben Sira.

The demise of the proud and the one who exalts himself is spoken of with a certain amount of inevitability: Prov. 16.18,

> pride goes before destruction, and a haughty spirit before stumbling.

The opposite is also claimed, often with wisdom and humility seen together, as in Ben Sira 11.1,

> the wisdom of a humble man will lift up his head, and will seat him among the great.

Injunctions against self-exaltation as an unwise path are offered at Prov. 25.6, 7, and in Ben Sira 7.4 this advice is given explicit theological content:

> do not seek from the Lord the highest office, nor the seat of honour from the king.

At various points God is explicitly included as the main actor in the process of humbling and exalting. Thus Prov. 15.25,

> the Lord will tear down the house of the proud, but he will establish the boundary of the widow.

And in the LXX version of Prov. 3.34,

> the Lord opposes the proud, but to the humble he gives grace.

The theocentric nature of the motif comes to clearest expression at Ben Sira 7.11,

> for there is one who abases and exalts.

There are examples of the reversal of fortunes, here seen as the consequence of wisdom; Prov. 12.2,

> a servant who acts wisely will rule over a son who acts shamefully, and will share in the inheritance among brothers.

In Ben Sira 11 such reversal of fortunes is seen in the light of the deceptiveness of appearances, such that those who appear exalted may not remain so, and those who seem insignificant may be exalted: verse 5,

> many kings have had to sit on the ground, but one who was never thought of has worn a crown.

This leads us to an aspect of the motif which occurs at several points in the wisdom literature: the idea of the one whose apparent humiliation is later seen to give way to exaltation. In some of these passages the wording and ideas are reminiscent of the motif in Isaiah 53. Thus Ben Sira 11.12, 13,

> there is another who is slow and needs help, who lacks strength and abounds in poverty; but the eyes of the Lord look upon him for his good; he lifts him out of his low estate and raises up his head, so that many are amazed at him (cf. also Wisdom of Solomon 2.12-20; 4.16–5.8).

The theme of a levelling of status, which we found in Isaiah, is also present at Wisdom 18.11 and Ben Sira 40.3. There are also passages where our motif appears as a reminiscence of God's past activity; Ben Sira 10.14-16.

> the Lord has cast down the throne of the rulers, and has seated the lowly in their place. The Lord has plucked up the roots of the nations, and has planted the humble in their place.

Finally, we would draw attention to examples of the motif where the form is similar to that of the Synoptic sayings; Prov. 29.23,

> a man's pride will bring him low, but a humble spirit will obtain honour.

Here and elsewhere in the wisdom literature the presence of a future tense would seem to indicate merely a logical future.

The wisdom literature displays a variety in the occurrence of the motif similar to that found in the book of Isaiah. Indeed, the distinction between wisdom and prophetic perspectives is difficult to establish at times, save for the occurrence of less specific referents, and a more individualistic emphasis. It is also interesting to note that what might appear to us a tension between explicitly theological statements and those from which God is apparently absent does not seem to have been a problem in the compilation of the wisdom literature.

Apocalyptic

If we turn our attention to apocalyptic literature we again find a variety of occurrences of the motif. In the *Testament of the Twelve Patriarchs* there are some interesting examples where the motif is seen in the context of Israel's history, particularly with reference to

Joseph. In *T. Zebulun* 3.1-8 Joseph's humiliation by his brothers was reversed so that they experienced humiliation at his feet. In *T. Joseph* 17.8–18.3 we read of Joseph's humility leading to his exaltation:

> I did not exalt myself above them arrogantly because of my worldly position of glory, but I was among them as one of the least (17.8).

In *1 Enoch*, the motif seems to occur most frequently in the prophetic sense of the demise of the mighty and the kings, see 46.3f., and 48.8,

> in those days, the kings of the earth and the mighty landowners shall be humiliated on account of their deeds.

The emphasis is on the bringing down of those who have exalted themselves: these are characterized as sinners. The destruction of the sinners shall result in blessedness for the righteous (ch. 53).

In the Qumran literature the question of status is an important issue, and represents a distinctive occurrence of the motif. For example, in the Community Rule there is a lot of space given to the relationships of men of different ranks. Rank describes position in the community; thus the priests are ranked highly and enjoy an exalted position 'according to the perfection of their spirit'. There is room for movement between ranks:

> they shall examine their spirit and deeds yearly, so that each man may be advanced in accordance with his understanding and perfection of way, or moved down in accordance with the offences committed by him (Vermes, p. 80).

Honour is given to those whose understanding and perfection of way is great.

In the War Rule, however, the familiar motif of reversal reappears,

> their kings shall serve you and all your oppressors shall bow down before you (Vermes, p. 140).

> thou hast raised the fallen by thy strength, but hast cast down the great in height .... thou givest to their honoured men a reward of shame (p. 143).

The reversal motif of humility and exaltation occurs in a variety of ways in this brief cross-section of literary traditions. It is interesting that the motif is not limited to any one temporal dimension—it has past, present and future aspects. There is one element of the motif which comes to expression repeatedly in all the literature, and that is the fact that we are here dealing with an activity of God—God is the one who humbles and exalts. Indeed as a reflection on past and present experience or as the expression of a certain occurrence in the future, the reversal motif bears witness to faith in the activity of God. In that sense we can best speak of it as a theocentric motif.

Although we would warn against a deterministic application of tradition history, we will see in this case that a study of the motif through a wider cross-section of literature helps us to appreciate that reversal cannot simply be assigned to an eschatological setting. When we come to the New Testament we find that the designation of the motif as *theocentric* does more justice to its diversity, and perhaps also to the essence of Jesus' message itself.

The motif is again apparent in its past, present and future aspects. In Lk. 1.51-53 Mary's hymn of praise focuses on God's past dealings with the humble and exalted, and expresses the faith that God acts in a just way in favour of the humble.

> He has done mighty deeds with his arm; he has scattered the proud in the thoughts of their heart. He has brought down rulers from their thrones, and has exalted those who were humble. He has filled the hungry with good things; and sent away the rich empty-handed.

The present perspective of this theocentric faith in which God reverses human status comes to best expression at Lk. 16.15b in Jesus' attack on the Pharisees' self-exaltation:

> for that which is highly esteemed among men is detestable in the sight of God.

The same understanding is present in the beatitudes which express blessing on the humble. The future aspect of the motif is seen in the reversal sayings such as Lk. 14.11, which have traditionally been understood eschatologically. The same aspect is present also in the epistles of James and first Peter. Both quote the LXX version of Prov. 3.34 (substituting Θεός for Κύριος) which describes God's attitude to the proud and humble. 1 Pet. 5.6 follows:

> humble yourselves therefore, under the mighty hand of God, that he may exalt you at the proper time.

Jas 4.10 reads:

> humble yourselves in the presence of the Lord, and he will exalt you.

Interestingly, James is quite concerned with this motif. In 2.1-9 he speaks of the sin of partiality, and the treatment of the humble and the exalted within the community. Again in 1.9-11 the motif recurs as proverbial reflection on present experience:

> let the brother of humble circumstances glory in his high position; and the rich man in his humiliation.

The motif occurs in this early Christian literature in the context of theological wisdom rather than eschatology.

We have seen that the reversal motif of humiliation and exaltation occurs within the New Testament and indeed within the Synoptics in a variety of ways. How are we to evaluate the treatment of the reversal sayings in the work of recent interpreters of Jesus' proverbial wisdom? We noted, both in the work of Beardslee and Perrin, the tendency to understand these sayings in the context of Jesus' eschatology, and that the function of such sayings is to call into question the attempts to bring order into our lives. Our study of tradition history raises a question over assigning the reversal motif too quickly to an eschatological setting. We found that the motif might best be described as theocentric, and we need to go on to consider further the issue of theocentricity and eschatology in Jesus' proclamation of the Kingdom. It is obvious that progress in the treatment of individual groups of Jesus' proverbial sayings cannot be made simply at the level of isolated exegesis. To a large extent, the interpretative tradition of New Testament studies directs the course of exegesis. A fresh examination of our material will involve a fresh examination of much broader issues in the historical reconstruction of Jesus' message.

Before we conclude this section, we need to consider briefly the later work of J.D. Crossan in which historical interests predominate. *In Fragments* is his most comprehensive work on the aphorisms of Jesus[43] and it brings us back, in some ways, to Bultmann's concerns with the history of the tradition. Crossan is interested in:

> how the aphoristic tradition works and what the aphoristic tradition does with its materials (p. ix).

However, the book can be divided into two parts: an initial discussion of the aphoristic genre; and a treatment of the history of the tradition, in which Crossan develops a 'basic generative model' for the aphoristic tradition. At this stage, however, it is worth observing that Crossan's use of 'aphorism' is extremely broad; thus, he includes such sayings as Mk 1.15, 9.1 and others which would not fit our description of the form. His work covers the shorter sayings tradition as a whole, as opposed to parables or narrative material, and therefore includes the sayings which we would consider examples of proverbial wisdom.

In his section on the genre, Crossan is concerned to argue for the heuristic function of the aphorism. He quotes with approval H.U. Asemissen:

> The aphorism in its representative form is the monument of its own process of thought. Whoever grasps its meaning is compelled to rethink and reflect, and goes through, in focusing the train of thought, the reasons behind the reasons which lead to the illuminating end result (Crossan p. 6).

He also notes that the heuristic function of the aphorism is often connected with contradiction, and the more perplexing the contradiction, the more it teases thought and insight from the hearer or reader. Hence, paradox is the aphorism's 'ideal form of action' (p. 6). The distinction between proverb and aphorism becomes a question of the traditional and authoritative opinions of the proverb being treated paradoxically in the aphorism.

Crossan also draws on the work of G. Neumann, who introduces the dialectic of Mimesis and Utopia with respect to the representational function of the aphorism. The aphorism is an 'in between' form, it is on the way from Mimesis to Utopia, and so the relationship of 'the representation of reality' and 'the projection of the not (yet) real' is expressed as conflict. The aphorism reflects:

> the conflicting relationship of reality and conception and challenges the reader continuously to this reflection (p. 12).

Crossan's case for the heuristic function of aphorisms is further developed through focusing on the debate over Francis Bacon's classic formulation:

> Aphorisms, representing a knowledge broken, do invite men to enquire farther; whereas Methods, carrying the shew of a total, do secure men, as if they were at furthest (p. 14).

Bacon is concerned with the effect of the aphorism on the recipient;

he finds systematic expression too final, and prefers to hark back to a time when thought was delivered in dispersed sentences:

> which did invite men, both to ponder that which was invented, and to add and supply further (p. 15).

In an interesting article 'On the Widespread Use of an Inappropriate and Restrictive Model of the Literary Aphorism',[44] R.H. Stephenson has criticized the Baconian or heuristic idea of the aphorism. The problem of the heuristic model is that it involves the idea that the content communicated is separable from the language and form. As J.G. Williams explains in a helpful comment on this debate:

> aesthetic concerns are deflected 'into a preoccupation with the message conveyed and with language as the means of its conveyance' (Williams, p. 75).

The heuristic model also favours new knowledge (this may result from Bacon's interest in science). Stephenson points out, however, that aphorisms often involve old ideas restated in new forms. He therefore proposes the epideictic model as more appropriate, for it is a form of oratory which defends traditional values, and focuses on subjects of common knowledge.

> As a literary model epideictic rhetoric would serve simply to account for the kind of discourse that seeks to please or delight the reader rather than to instruct or persuade (p. 76).

Stephenson proposes a dual structure for the literary aphorism: on the one hand, serving to communicate a thought, and on the other hand, wedding the thought to an aesthetic form. This is close to Williams' thesis that the aphorism should be viewed as both literary and conceptual, poetic and philosophical.

Crossan rejects Stephenson's arguments against the heuristic model. However, we have found the epideictic model useful in describing the aphorism. It is important to note that both heuristic and epideictic models have to do with the rhetorical effect of the aphorism, and this is inevitably dependent on the context and performance of a saying, and surely cannot be asserted on the basis of some inherent or essential feature of the aphorism as such. Some writers on proverbs in literature draw a similar distinction between proverbs as evaluative comments, which do not contribute anything new to the argument (epideictic), and affective proverbs which involve a significant addition to the argument (heuristic). This is a distinction at the level of function, and it is clear that one genre (the proverb) can perform a variety of functions, depending on a range of contextual factors.[45]

We would also favour the suggestion of a dual structure that does justice to both form and content. The aesthetic and conceptual features of the aphorism are important and not mutually exclusive: although it may be difficult, at a theoretical level, to explain their complementarity, it is even harder to argue for one aspect in favour of the other.

Crossan concludes his section on the genre with some comments on the aphorism and Jesus. His work focuses on the process and procedures of the Jesus tradition, and not with the question of the historical Jesus directly. The important question for understanding the tradition's process is this:

> Did proverbial materials generally enter the tradition at the original, transmissional, or redactional levels, or did it enter more or less evenly at all levels? (p. 29).

He explains his working hypothesis in this regard. The decision about the point of entry into the tradition will have to be worked out for each proverbial expression individually: there is no rule to solve situations automatically.

The main part of the book therefore involves detailed treatments of individual sayings with a view to understanding the diversity of aphoristic material, and developing a generative model for this aspect of the tradition.

Crossan makes a helpful distinction, which we noted previously, between *ipsissima verba* and *ipsissima structura*. To speak of the former is inappropriate at an oral level of communication, thus:

> the basic unit of transmission is never the ipsissima verba of an aphoristic saying, but, at best and at most, the ipsissimia structura of an aphoristic core (p. 40).

Thus, he can go on to distinguish 'performancial' and 'hermeneutical' variations: the former are simply linguistic variations which do not alter the structure or sense of a saying, whereas the latter give a different interpretation as well. Crossan gives as an example Mk 10.31.

> But many that are first will be last, and the last first.

of which Mt. 20.16 is merely a 'performancial' variation:

> so the last will be first, and the first last.

However, the version in the *Gospel of Thomas* 4b includes in the second half a 'hermeneutical' variation:

> For many who are first will become last,
> and they will become one and the last.

For Crossan, behind these examples of sayings there lies an aphoristic core, which we could describe as an opposition between first and last, although Crossan himself does not use this terminology. The core is the simplest unit in Crossan's generative model; in performance, however, the core becomes a saying: 'In oral sensibility one speaks or writes an aphoristic saying, but one remembers and recalls an aphoristic core' (p. 67).

An aphoristic saying is complete in itself, and isolated from its surrounding context. However, sometimes sayings come in pairs, or in Crossan's terminology, as Aphoristic Compounds. Of importance in the observation of compounds is the fact that the juxtaposition of sayings often creates new meanings, 'hermeneutical dynamics between the two aphorisms' (p. 120). Another feature of compounds is that 'verbal and thematic osmosis often occurs from one aphorism into the other' (p. 120). This leads Crossan to spend a good deal of space trying to establish 'the earliest recoverable saying'.

The next step on from compounds is the observation of Aphoristic Clusters, that is the juxtaposition of three or more sayings into a small complex. Clusters can be formed by word, form, theme, or structure.

The Aphoristic Conclusion involves a saying being used at the end of just about any other linguistic form imaginable, such as miracles, prayers, parables, dialogues, and stories. The Aphoristic Dialogue in its simplest form involves a minimal address to Jesus, often derived verbally from the saying's own content, and serving as a 'set-up' for the saying itself. The final unit to be observed is the Aphoristic Story, for the Gospels are narrative works, therefore sayings, however isolated, are always held within the overarching frames of the basic gospel story, and also shorter narrative units.

Thus Crossan is able to present his model for the possible transformations of the basic aphoristic core. Most of his aphoristic units are easily observable within the Synoptic tradition; however, highlighting such features is not in itself very enlightening. The bulk of *In Fragments* presents us with Crossan's, often idiosyncratic, judgments about the earliest form and the transmission history of particular sayings. It is therefore close to a fuller and perhaps more sophisticated version of Bultmann's work in *The History of the Synoptic Tradition*. One is left wondering how the earlier work of Crossan is related to this intricately argued historical-critical study. W. Kelber notes this incongruity:

> One is compelled to ask why this uncommonly creative literary critic, who has taken us to the edge of parabolic metaphysics, is now returning to hard-nosed historical criticism when dealing with the aphoristic tradition.[46]

Perhaps we would be wrong to fault Crossan for pursuing these historical interests, but, as we will go on to explain, it is difficult to see how such work can contribute much to our understanding of the significance of the proverbial material in the Synoptics, and our attempts to interpret that material.

4. *Conclusions*

In this chapter we have considered a number of critics whose work we regard as representative of the main themes in the modern interpretation of Jesus' proverbial wisdom. Obviously, we have had to exclude many books and articles on our topic which contain interesting and important insights,[47] and we will draw on some of these at a later stage in our work. However, we have been concerned to highlight the most important issues, and much that is written draws explicitly on the work of Bultmann, Beardslee, or to a lesser extent Crossan. Perrin's contribution[48] represents in clear form some of the most important principles in use in attempts at the historical reconstruction of Jesus' message, and the effects of such principles on the interpretation of the proverbial material.

As we have already explained, any attempt to move forward in our understanding of proverbial materials in the Synoptics must engage with some of the key issues in contemporary interpretation of the Gospels. Thus, we must now consider our method in attempting to reconstruct Jesus' message, and two of the key issues in that message, the questions of Eschatology and the Kingdom of God. Having reflected critically on the historical context of the wisdom materials, we may be in a better position to consider the function and significance of that material using insights from rhetorical and literary studies.

Chapter 4

PROBLEMS OF HISTORICAL RECONSTRUCTION: WISDOM, ESCHATOLOGY AND THE KINGDOM OF GOD

1. *Introduction*

a. *The Problem*

In this chapter we will examine some of the problems involved in attempting to reconstruct the message of Jesus; our attention will focus particularly on the difficulties raised by the juxtaposition of wisdom and eschatological material in the Synoptic record of Jesus' speech, and it will become clear that issues of history and meaning are inevitably intertwined. The historical decisions we make will affect our interpretive judgments.

We have already noted how the basis of most historical treatments of proverbial wisdom derives from Bultmann's analysis of the Logia, and the criteria which he applied to the material have been sharpened and applied most rigorously by Perrin. Doubt is cast on the value of the proverbial material for understanding Jesus' message on account of the continuity between this material and popular Jewish wisdom. This is often combined with a decision about the centrality of eschatology in Jesus' message, which in turn leads to a tendency to subordinate wisdom elements to this central idea, so that they either lose their character as 'wisdom', or are regarded as 'inauthentic'. C.E. Carlston gives a good summary of the historical problem with respect to 'Q': the problem is the same with respect to Jesus' speech:

> Why, if the Son of Man is to return soon as Judge... does one need to worry about the rules of conduct ordinarily associated with wisdom... If apocalyptic presupposes a world at its end and wisdom a continuing world; if apocalyptic thinks of God as active in bringing history to a dramatic close and wisdom thinks of human experience as the best guide to success and survival in an indefinitely extended history; if eschatology implies discontinuity and wisdom is based on thousands of continuities—how can a

> single document... hold to both views at the same time?... What is clearly called for is an understanding of wisdom and apocalyptic that will enable us to understand how Jesus and the early Christian tradition were able to keep them together.[1]

Our interest is here centred on the reported speech attributed to Jesus in the Gospel narratives, and it is this interest in speech which presents some of the most difficult problems in the historical study of traditions about Jesus. There are few sources outside the Synoptic Gospels which can be taken seriously as evidence for the speech of Jesus, and, on the whole, the value of these sources is judged by the degree of their consistency with what we already know about Jesus' message from the Synoptic Gospels. It is very difficult to add anything 'new' to that picture. Obviously the Fourth Gospel provides important material for comparison,[2] as do the so-called Apocryphal Gospels, particularly *Thomas*,[3] and there are also some parts of the remaining literature of the New Testament which may be of value. Of the little material deriving from 'non-Christian' sources that comment on Jesus there are no significant records of Jesus' message. Rabbinic treatments of Jesus are most probably dependent on the Christian sources.

The problems involved in the historical assessment of reported speech in any ancient text are obviously manifold. In ancient Greek literature, the speeches of Thucydides' characters are notoriously difficult to evaluate.[4] Early Jewish literature offers few examples of reported speech in narrative works for comparative study. History writing is usually concerned with a broader sweep of events than the reported speech of one individual; indeed, some historians would not attempt the sort of reconstruction practised in Gospel studies, particularly in view of the fact that access to Jesus' speech is largely limited to such a homogenous body of literature.

b. *Old Quest and New Quest*

In the nineteenth century, critics pursued an interest in the 'Life of Jesus'. The question of the miraculous was obviously of central concern, but aside from that, the attempt was frequently made to write the biography of Jesus, tracing the development of his personality and self-consciousness, his purpose and intent. This movement came under criticism toward the end of the century in the writings of, among others, M. Kähler, W. Wrede, and A. Schweitzer. Their insights were introduced to twentieth-century New Testament scholarship and developed most powerfully in the work of R. Bultmann.

In his important work *The So-called Historical Jesus and the Historic, Biblical Christ*, Kähler sketched out the two most significant lines of criticism which were to be levelled against the 'Life of Jesus' movement: these concerned issues of historical method and theological relevance. In regard to historical method, Kähler made a strong case for more honesty regarding the limitations of the sources:

> The cardinal virtue of genuine historical research is modesty. Modesty is born of knowledge, and he who knows the historical facts and sources acquires modesty in knowledge as well as in understanding.[5]

In the case of Jesus the sources for a biography are lacking, for the Gospels were not written with the purpose of describing how Jesus developed. In the light of the issue of theological relevance, these historical reservations are not, however, problematic for Kähler, for his interest is not in the reconstructed Jesus, but the biblical Christ as he is known to us through the witness and faith of the early Christians, and as he is known to us in our own history today.

> How can Jesus Christ be the authentic object of the faith of all Christians if the questions what and who he really was can be established only by ingenious investigation, and if it is solely the scholarship of our time which proves itself equal to the task? (p. 102).

We cannot encounter the biblical, significant Christ through the fluctuating results of biographers' disputations, but rather:

> within a tradition which possesses the inherent power to convince us of its authenticity (p. 122) . . . We want to make absolutely clear that ultimately we believe in Christ, not on account of any authority, but because he himself evokes such faith from us (p. 87).

The historical reservations evident in Kähler's call for modesty were carried further, in regard to knowledge of the historical Jesus, in Wrede's study of Mark, and most comprehensively in Bultmann's application of the form-critical method to the Synoptic Gospels. It is strange that the caution shown in making judgments concerning Jesus is not reflected in the degree of certainty with which Bultmann traces the history of the various aspects of the Synoptic tradition. However, problems raised by the presence of an oral tradition behind the Gospels and the implications of the early Christians' influence on the traditions about Jesus form the backbone of Bultmann's *History of the Synoptic Tradition*, and are still central to any historical treatment of Jesus.

On the other hand, Bultmann also developed more clearly and influentially the theological problems involved in the widespread interest in the 'historical Jesus'. For him, the kerygma was a call to existential commitment, and the original quest, with its desire for objective history writing, was a denial of the risk involved in faith. In fact, the scholarly reconstruction of Jesus' biography was the opposite of faith, namely righteousness by works, or worldly security. Although it need not occupy us now, arguments concerning the roots of Bultmann's theological position in Neo-Kantian epistemology and Lutheran theology have been carried on in several critical works.[6]

The importance of Schweitzer's contribution to the critique of the Old Quest is well-known, and his most distinctive contribution may be described as a hermeneutical criticism. He traced the history of attempts to write the 'Life of Jesus', and showed how each writer's understanding and hence his presentation of Jesus was shaped by the concerns and values of his own day. Along with this went a critique of the sources and evidence for a 'Life'. Interestingly, however, this did not lead Schweitzer to give up the task, for he offered his own account of Jesus' life. This was free of some of the worst excesses of psychologizing and rationalizing, but, nonetheless, it involved some bold historical judgments. Following the lead of J. Weiss,[7] Schweitzer stressed the central importance of eschatology to the historical understanding of Jesus life and message. He went to the opposite extreme of describing a Jesus quite different from the concerns and values of Schweitzer's own day. In some respects, the 'strangeness' of Schweitzer's Jesus may have contributed more to the impact of his work than the evidence he advances for his reconstruction.

Subsequent research may be, somewhat crudely, divided into those who have sought to take further the Bultmannian tradition along the lines of the so-called 'New Quest', and those who have built on the fundamental insight of Weiss and Schweitzer about the centrality of eschatology for Jesus, and have then pursued a more sophisticated form of inquiry along the lines of the 'Old Quest', with perhaps a more realistic understanding of the nature and limitations of the sources available. This does not describe all research on the historical Jesus, but gives an indication of the main streams of concern, although there is a good deal of overlap between the two, and in many respects they seem to have merged today.

What became known as the 'New Quest' seems to have begun with a lecture by E. Käsemann on 'The Problem of the Historical Jesus'.[8] He raised the question about the continuity between the historical Jesus and the kerygmatic Christ: a question which is forced upon the student of the New Testament by the nature of early Christian faith:

> Primitive Christianity is obviously of the opinion that the earthly Jesus cannot be understood otherwise than from the far side of Easter, that is, in his majesty as Lord of the community, and that, conversely, the event of Easter cannot be adequately comprehended if it is looked at apart from the earthly Jesus (p. 25).

If, with the proponents of the New Quest, we see a need for continuity between the faith of the early Christians and the concerns of contemporary theology, then the theological problems raised by interest in the historical Jesus can be temporarily suspended. However, the historical problems remained. There were no new sources for the life of Jesus to come to the aid of the new questers, but what did develop was a new understanding of history, which, apparently, made up for the inadequacies in the sources that had previously thwarted the Old Quest.

> If the possibility of resuming the quest lies neither in the kerygma, nor in new sources, nor in a new view of the Gospels, such a possibility has been latent in the radically different understanding of history and of human existence which distinguishes the present from the quest which ended in failure.[9]

The new understanding of history to which Robinson is here referring is an existentialist view. According to this view the historian should not concern himself with what actually happened, for that is of no interest by itself. The central concern is for 'historical encounter', thus:

> History is the act of intention, the commitment, the meaning for the participants, behind the external occurrence. . . it is the task of modern historiography to grasp such acts of intention, such commitments, such meaning, such self-actualization; and it is the task of the modern biography to lay hold of the selfhood which is therein revealed (pp. 67, 68).

This 'new' view of history means that:

> Jesus' understanding of his existence, his selfhood, and thus in the

> higher sense his life, is a possible subject of historical research (p. 72).

Whether or not we can evaluate this 'new' view of history from such an evasive presentation as Robinson offers, and whether or not it deserves the title 'modern historiography',[10] it is hard not to see some of the psychologizing tendencies of the nineteenth-century Quest returning in twentieth-century language. Robinson cites Bultmann's *Jesus and the Word*[11] as being 'prefaced with a classic statement of the modern view of history' (p. 70). Thus we see the apparent rejection of 'objective' knowledge about Jesus, in favour of the dialogue with history:

> no attempt is here made to render Jesus as a historical phenomenon psychologically explicable, and nothing really biographical, apart from a brief introductory section, is included.... Attention is entirely limited to what he purposed, and hence to what in his purpose as a part of history makes a present demand on us (pp. 6, 8).

'Purpose' and 'intention' are both essentially psychological categories. However, Bultmann seems unaware of this:

> In the case of those who like Jesus have worked through the medium of the word, what they purposed can be reproduced only as a group of sayings, of ideas—as teaching.... Little as we know of his life and personality, we know enough of his message to make for ourselves a consistent picture (pp. 10, 12).

Bultmann seems prepared to trust the record of Jesus' speech, albeit critically reconstructed, as an account of his intention and purpose, forming a consistent whole.[12] Apart from the fact that Robinson is using Bultmann, rather confusingly, as representative of a new view of history which underlies the 'New Quest' of which Bultmann does not approve; it is hard to see how this 'new' approach can save us from the difficulties with the nature of the sources which dogged the 'Old Quest', for our interest appears to remain the historically reconstructed message of Jesus. This observation is strengthened when one adds to the picture the work of writers such as E. Fuchs, who introduce an interest in the deeds of Jesus to our understanding of his 'purpose' and 'intention'. The New Quest is different merely in accepting a more fragmented picture of Jesus, rather than a full biography.[13]

Following further our rough division of research into two camps, we must consider the line of work which has built on the insights of

Weiss and Schweitzer in the tradition of the 'Old Quest'. What differentiates this approach from that of the 'New Quest' is a tendency to ignore the theological problems involved in seeking after knowledge of the historical Jesus, and to reject the idea of a new view of history which saves the day. In this tradition of research, there is an acceptance of the problems of the 'Old Quest' as historical problems. That is, previous studies were too ambitious and did not approach the sources carefully enough; however, the idea of history remains fundamentally the same, it is merely more sophistication and care that is called for. Thus C. Rowland in his recent work on *Christian Origins*:

> It was the half-hearted rigour of the quest for Jesus and his historical setting, which really emerged in Schweitzer's presentation.[14]

Rowland goes on to draw attention to the abiding value of Schweitzer's contribution to our knowledge about Jesus, namely, the 'centrality of eschatology' for understanding Jesus' idea of the Kingdom of God, and the need to view this in the context of first-century Jewish eschatological belief. Rowland is not interested in 'a new view of history', merely a better informed historical understanding and assessment of Jesus, hence, approximately one third of his book is devoted to 'Jewish Life and Thought at the beginning of the Christian Era'.[15]

We noted earlier that there is a good deal of overlap between adherents of the New Quest, and those who refine the Old. Bultmann provides an interesting example of one whose form critical work has been central to the latter interest, and yet whose theological reflections provide the background to the New Quest. Present research has tended to smooth over the boundaries of these different approaches, and this is perhaps not inappropriate, since we have seen that the common interest is in the historical reconstruction of Jesus' message. Today, such attempts at reconstructing Jesus' speech range from questions of authenticity for an isolated saying, to characterizations of the whole message. A number of principles for such historical judgments are employed fairly widely in Gospel studies, and these also form the basis for decisions about the origins of proverbial wisdom; some have been developed self-consciously, others are accepted as part of the critical 'common sense'. We distinguish three major principles which are, in fact, related.

2. *Principles for Historical Reconstruction*

a. *The Centrality of Historical Background*[16]

To understand a person, an event, or an idea is to understand what has gone before: questions of origin and influence are most important. In biblical studies, this interpretive principle is associated most explicitly with the 'History of Religions' school. H. Gunkel explains:

> The cardinal principle of historical study is this: that we are unable to comprehend a person, a period, or a thought dissociated from its antecedents, but that we can speak of a real living understanding only when we have the antecedent history. Historical understanding means an understanding built upon the historical associations.[17]

In relation to our interest, the problem of the nature and significance of the historical background of the Kingdom of God to an understanding of Jesus' use is to be considered. The work of Schweitzer must come within the category of a History of Religions approach to the Kingdom of God, for he introduced the important emphasis on the Jewish apocalyptic context for understanding Jesus' use.[18] Although dependent on Weiss' work, it was Schweitzer who focused attention on the apocalyptic background, whereas Weiss' primary aim, although only in his earliest work, was to understand Jesus' teaching on its own terms. In this respect, it is Schweitzer's work which has had the greatest influence on subsequent research.

In an interesting evaluation of his work, I.G. Nicol comments on the relation of Schweitzer to the History of Religions school:

> Despite his apparent rejection of the methods and approach of the history of religions school to the problems of the history of early Christianity, Schweitzer has in fact selected a principle of interpretation which presupposes the findings of this particular school. The discovery that the late-Jewish apocalyptic was the historically contingent framework within which early Christianity took shape is one which can be attributed to the work of this group of scholars and it is in part to them that Schweitzer is indebted for his principle of consistent eschatology. It would appear therefore that what Schweitzer refused to accept was not so much the approach of the *religionsgeschichtliche* school as such, but its obvious Hellenistic bias.[19]

However, it is Schweitzer's dependence on this school that becomes the basis of one of Nicol's criticisms, namely that 'Schweitzer allows Jesus no freedom of movement within this framework either to modify or transform it' (p. 54). Jesus is not only to be understood in terms of Jewish apocalyptic belief, but his outlook appears to be completely conditioned by that background. This is perhaps a slight overstatement of the case, since Schweitzer is careful to claim that the eschatology of Jesus (and John and Paul) differs from that of the texts which form the essential background to our understanding of his usage:

> The lines of connection which run backwards towards the Psalms of Solomon, Enoch, and Daniel, and forwards towards the apocalypses of Baruch and Enoch, are extremely important for the understanding of certain general conceptions. On the other hand, it is impossible to overemphasize the uniqueness of the point of view from which the eschatology of the time of the Baptist, of Jesus, and of Paul presents itself to us.[20]

In Schweitzer's case the historical background to the Kingdom of God is important and should be seen in Jewish apocalyptic. However, it is Schweitzer's notion of *consistent* eschatology which leads to most distortion. On the one hand, he observes the eschatological element in the preaching of Jesus; on the other hand, he also describes the Gospel narratives as a chaotic confusion. The only way forward for Schweitzer is to use eschatology as a key to pick a way through this confusion. Schweitzer assumes that Jesus' whole life, thought and action was determined by eschatology, and therefore our only hope for understanding the confusion in the narratives is to try to see how the various parts are consistent, or cohere with the eschatological outlook.

> we are .... justified in first reconstructing the Jewish apocalyptic of the time independently out of these documents, that is to say, in bringing the details of the discourse of Jesus into an eschatological system, and then on the basis of this system endeavouring to explain the apparently disconnected events in the history of his public life ('Quest', p. 366).

We will look later at the way a principle of coherence is commonly used in historical reconstruction. For now, we need to note the complexity (or perhaps confusion) of Schweitzer's position. However, there is clearly some relation between the History of Religions approach and Schweitzer's understanding of the Kingdom in Jesus' speech, and because of the problematic nature of the Gospel texts, Schweitzer is particularly dependent on the general context of apocalyptic thought which he sees lying behind Jesus' Kingdom concept. In respect of subsequent research, the tendency to allow the so-called background to an idea to constrain our understanding of its use in a particular text is an unfortunate legacy of the History of Religions school.[21]

The form in which this issue often arises concerns the notion of the hearer's expectations. It starts from the premise that Jesus offered no explanation of the phrase 'Kingdom of God',[22] he must therefore have assumed a certain common understanding existing in his hearers' minds. One therefore looks to the literature of Jewish apocalyptic to find what Jesus' hearers, and hence Jesus himself, would have understood by that phrase. However, the assumption that Jesus himself gave no content to the idea of the Kingdom of God would seem to rest on taking at face value the claim that his ministry began with the simple announcement that 'the Kingdom of God has drawn near'. If we assume the chronology of the Gospels to be unimportant (or wrong), and try to understand the term from the point of view of a reader (or hearer), we have a great deal of material (including parables and the record of Jesus' own activity) which gives content to the term: we can offer an explanation of Jesus' use without recourse to the supposed expectation of his hearers.

The appeal of the History of Religions type of approach is understandable. If one can define the correct understanding of a term from outside the Gospels, even if only in a broad sense, then one can use that understanding as a tool for making historical judgments about the material in the Gospels. If, however, we wish to confine ourselves to the Gospel texts themselves, it becomes difficult to see how we can untangle what is authentic from what is not, how we can arrive at a coherent and meaningful explanation of a term which takes account of the diversity in the Gospel material.

A further problem with relation to the emphasis on historical background and the idea of the Kingdom of God is the general question of what texts constitute the most important evidence for understanding Jewish belief and practice at the time of Jesus.[23] We cannot, at this stage, go into detail, but we should note on the one hand, the criticisms brought by T.F. Glasson and others[24] against Schweitzer's notion of a generally accepted apocalyptic concept of the Kingdom to be found in early Jewish texts; and on the other hand, the work of critics such as B. Chilton who have looked to other texts for an understanding of Kingdom language.[25] The further question arises of how representative any particular Jewish text might have been. In speaking of the phrase 'Kingdom of God' in the

Pss. Sol. 17.3, Perrin speaks of 'a typical example from a time very near to that of Jesus'.[26] But do the *Psalms of Solomon*, for example, give an account of the popular conception of the Kingdom? Or did that work influence the thinking of the sort of people who heard Jesus speak? Or are such texts representative of only minority opinion?[27]

It is quite clear that the situation would not be helped by a return to the kind of exegesis against which the History of Religions school was reacting. In the case of Weiss and Schweitzer, the ideas on the Kingdom of God, typified in the work of Ritschl, were far surpassed. The introduction of a more sophisticated historical interest was a great step forward. However, we would warn against going too far in allowing the so-called background of an idea to constrain our understanding of it in the speech or writing of an individual; as we will see, the possibilities for distortion are compounded when the tools for historical reconstruction are as flawed as is the case with the critical treatment of Jesus' message. Historical background can only be an extremely general guide in reconstructing Jesus' speech: what we say about Jesus should seem possible in a first-century context.

b. *Authenticating criteria*

Much has been written in recent years on the so-called 'Criteria of Authenticity'.[28] We wish to focus our attention on the two criteria which are most widely used, have the most potential for success, and bear most directly on our interest in the status of the proverbial sayings.[29] These are the criteria of Dissimilarity and Coherence (or Consistency), which form the basis of Perrin's attempts to rediscover the authentic speech of Jesus[30] and derive from Bultmann's form-critical treatment of the Synoptic tradition.[31]

The criterion of dissimilarity asserts that a saying can be regarded as authentic if it can be shown to be dissimilar to characteristic emphases both of early Judaism and of the early Church. It is also used negatively to claim that sayings similar to Jewish or Christian traditions are inauthentic, for it is presumed that their Sitz im Leben is in the life of the church, and not in the life of Jesus.[32]

Form criticism seems to provide the logic of this criterion, based on the principle that traditions about Jesus were retained and used only in so far as they met the needs and interests of the early church. However, this insight should not lead too quickly to a judgment about the origin of material. The concept of Sitz im Leben can be overworked. Sitz im Leben relates to the characteristic function of a tradition: a judgment about the function does not necessarily lead directly to a judgment about origin.

The form critical argument cannot so easily explain the rejection of material paralleled in contemporary Judaism. Indeed, in a recent article on 'The Dissimilarity Test' D.L. Mealand offers a different account of the function and purpose of the criterion:

> The point of the test as I see it is to recognise that earliest Christianity arose out of Judaism, and that the transition from Judaism to Christianity is a complex matter, but that if we can be reasonably sure of anything about Jesus of Nazareth it is that his teaching and his activity seem to have contributed substantially to that transition.[33]

This sounds like an important point; that any account of Jesus must help us to understand the transition from Judaism to Christianity. However, it is difficult to follow Mealand's argument that the Dissimilarity test will assist us in this respect:

> this tool attempts to isolate those sayings and deeds attributed to Jesus which would help to account for the transition from Judaism to Christianity (p. 45).

It would seem that sayings dissimilar from both Judaism and Christianity are the least likely to help explain the transition from the one to the other. Sayings in continuity with Jewish teaching, and those which modify traditional ideas, would seem most helpful in understanding how Jesus as a Jew came to be seen as the founder of a renewal movement in first-century Judaism.

Perhaps the most common criticism of this criterion concerns the goal, as expressed by Perrin,[34] of finding the most 'characteristic' teaching of Jesus through the use of this tool. By focusing our attention on what is dissimilar from the religious environment, we are left with what is distinctive in the sense of 'unique', but not necessarily in the sense of 'characteristic', which is what we are interested in.[35] Thus, Downing suggests:

> it begs the question entirely to suppose that 'the most characteristic' is 'the most distinctive'. You might find it to be so. You might equally well find that Jesus was characterized by a distinctive ability to be indistinguishable, the epitome of ordinariness in first-century Judaism, quite typical.... Perrin is using a Christian apologetic motif ('Jesus is unique') as a standard of judgment.[36]

Unfortunately, Downing may have pushed a valid point too far, since it would be difficult, although perhaps not impossible, to offer an account of the rise of Christianity based on a founder who was 'indistinguishable' from his religious environment.[37]

Our problems in employing this criterion are compounded when we compare it with our previous comments on the centrality of historical background in understanding. On the one hand, we find a tendency to stress the understanding of Jesus' use of ideas in terms of their relation to ideas in early Jewish literature; and on the other hand, a tendency to reject ideas which have parallels in early Jewish literature. R.S. Barbour attempts to salvage something worthwhile from the confusion by claiming that:

> Sayings of Jesus, or other pieces of tradition, which exhibit formal characteristics that are consistent with Palestinian first-century Judaism—poetic parallelism etc.—but have a content that is distinctive can claim genuineness or originality.[38]

Apart from the problematic use of a distinction between form and content, and the fact that this principle can only prove originality, Barbour's rescue attempt does not help with the central issue of Jesus' Kingdom language. Here, the interest in the Jewish background of the term is at the level of content. The clash between principles of historical reconstruction is quite clear.

The dissimilarity criterion is often used in conjunction with the principle of coherence. Thus, Perrin explains:

> With the criterion of dissimilarity as our starting-point, and with the results of the application of this criterion as the only foundation upon which we can build, the next step is to find a criterion by means of which we can move carefully into areas of tradition where this criterion would not be applicable. Here we propose a second criterion, which we will call 'the criterion of coherence': material from the earliest strata of the tradition may be accepted as authentic if it can be shown to cohere with material established as authentic by means of the criterion of dissimilarity (p. 43).

We have seen this criterion at work in many of the works on the proverbial sayings in the Gospels, where wisdom material is interpreted eschatologically so as to 'cohere' with what is considered to be the 'characteristic' emphasis in Jesus' preaching. The combination of dissimilarity and coherence has been widely criticized:

> When one adds the coherence principle to that of dissimilarity, then any errors in the results obtained by that method are liable to

> be magnified by the use of this second criterion. If the core of material upon which we build our reconstruction of the teaching of Jesus is inaccurate, then the addition of material which seems to be consistent with that core is likely to reflect those same inaccuracies.[39]

Although this is certainly true, the combination of these two principles would lead to another form of distortion even if the 'core' were accurate. The problem arises from allowing one element of the tradition, even if it is considered the most distinctive, to act as an unquestioned judge over the remainder. Our present critical principles dictate that in the case of material which appears to be unnaturally juxtaposed—as Perrin would say of popular wisdom and eschatological ideas—the sayings which do not pass the dissimilarity test are considered inauthentic, because they fail to cohere with 'characteristic' material. There is an alternative, however, and that is to see how material which is 'unnaturally' juxtaposed might cause us to change our understanding of the whole picture: that is, for example, how the presence of wisdom material might cause us to modify a purely eschatological understanding of the Kingdom of God in Jesus' language. This calls for a suspension of our negative judgment, until we have seen what the whole picture would look like, were the popular wisdom material to be authentic. Sanders points out that:

> the remaining material (after dissimilarity has been applied) does not interpret itself or necessarily answer historical questions. It must still be placed in a meaningful context.[40]

Should that context be other aspects of the reported speech of Jesus in the Gospels, or, as Sanders would have it, the suggested 'background' of eschatological belief in Jewish literature. At present, the context for understanding Jesus' Kingdom language is often Jewish apocalyptic literature, rather than the, albeit tendentious, material recorded in the Gospels, which could give a different content to the Kingdom language.

The worst aspects of a History of Religions approach are compounded when used in conjunction with the criteria of dissimilarity and coherence. The central Kingdom language of Jesus is understood through a study of its supposed background in Jewish apocalyptic texts, rather than through its broader context in the reported teaching of Jesus in the Gospels. We would favour an attempt to describe Jesus' idea of the Kingdom in the broadest possible terms, taking into account as much of the Gospel material as possible. This would be at least as valuable as the present practice, and although the historical authenticity of this reconstruction would be open to question, it would give a fresh, and potentially more accurate picture of Jesus' Kingdom proclamation. By not making a prior decision about the whole we would be able to allow the particularity of the parts to speak for themselves. This is to turn on its head a standard critical procedure typified again by E.P. Sanders:

> Enough evidence points towards Jewish eschatology as the general framework of Jesus' ministry that we may examine the particulars in the light of that framework (p. 10).

We are suggesting that it would be helpful, for reasons of historical interest, *to re-examine the framework in the light of the particulars.*

We will go on to consider further the principle of coherence in our next section, but let us first draw some conclusions about the authenticating criteria.

The criteria we have been discussing possess an uncanny ability to survive in spite of some fundamental faults. Most of the critical essays written on the criteria in recent years end with a list of misgivings and a reaffirmation of the criteria in a slightly altered form.[41] There is a feeling, as Mealand makes clear, that it is better to argue with criteria than without. This appears to be a reasonable position, but only if the criteria are theoretically sound, and this does not seem to be the case.

Our study so far suggests that the dissimilarity test should be abandoned, unless one is self-consciously setting out to assess the uniqueness of Jesus—even then, the results of such work would always depend on an argument from silence. However, we have found, on the positive side, that any account of Jesus' teaching (as part of his overall impact) must help to account for the transition from Judaism to Christianity. This is a very general principle, some might say a blunt tool. However, it is better to admit the limitations of the authenticating criteria, and look for other means of progress in our attempts at historical reconstruction of Jesus' message, than to continue working with tools that have an inbuilt tendency to distort. Our emphasis should be on understanding Jesus in continuity with his Jewish environment, while being aware that we need to give some account of the strong opposition to Jesus, and the rise of the early Christian movement with its eventual break from Judaism. This is obviously a large task, and moves well beyond the strict confines of

Gospel studies, but that is the context in which we have to operate.

c. *Coherence as a broad principle of historical reconstruction*
Coherence is a somewhat confusing term. On the one hand it can be used in the sense of intelligibility, and so any attempt at historical description or explanation requires some degree of coherence. However, coherence is generally used in the material we are considering in the sense of consistency or compatibility. In this sense and as a tool for historical reconstruction it can be conceived and employed in a number of ways, particularly when we are dealing with the reported speech of an individual, as is the case with the Gospels.

At present, the principle of coherence seems to be applied in a somewhat arbitrary fashion. A critical reading of the Gospels unearths a number of inconsistencies in the reporting of Jesus' speech. This observation is then used as the basis for historical judgments, whereby material considered inconsistent with the 'characteristic' message of Jesus is labelled inauthentic, and attributed to later stages in the development of the tradition. There is therefore an assumption of coherence on the part of Jesus, while the Gospel writers, and presumably their first readers, were capable of accepting a high degree of inconsistency and incoherence. To make historical judgments on this basis seems 'inconsistent'.

We will now consider some of the possible ways of formulating and applying a principle of coherence:

(i) Coherence and Dissimilarity
As generally employed in conjunction with dissimilarity, the criterion of coherence raises a number of questions.

First, we may note how some New Testament critics have sought to explain the apparent inconsistencies in the Synoptic picture of Jesus' message through recourse to the idea of development. This kind of argument has usually been discredited on two counts. The tendency toward psychologizing explanations; and the unreliability of the Synoptic chronology. It has been argued that the sources do not allow us to trace development in Jesus' thought. We would agree with this assessment of the sources, but that surely does not preclude theories of development which restrict themselves to the 'text' of Jesus' message alone, and eschew attempts at precise chronological or psychological explanation.[42]

Second, an alternative approach would have to admit the historical possibility that Jesus was inconsistent. A refinement of this would be the suggestion that his idea of God, and hence his message, was fragmented rather than systematic. Such a view would place Jesus firmly in the tradition of wisdom, where the proverbial outlook concerns low-level truth claims, based on limited, and often contradictory, tracts of experience. If it is inappropriate to expect coherence from a collection of proverbial wisdom, and if the possibility exists that, at least in part, Jesus drew on the resources of Jewish wisdom, then it would be wrong to expect a simple coherence in Jesus' message. How would a criterion of coherence be applied to any thinkers who have utilized the aphorism as their main means of communication (e.g. Lichtenberg, Pascal, or Kafka)? It is interesting to observe that many of the most influential philosophers such as Kierkegaard and Wittgenstein adopt a style which is often aphoristic and resists systematic restatement.

This leads to a final question, namely, 'whose idea of coherence?' What sort of consistency should we expect from someone who was above all else a popular preacher? One way of refining our idea of coherence would be to look at the possible overlap between wisdom and eschatological 'traditions' in other early Jewish literature. Is the apparent inconsistency we observe in the Gospels really significant, or do we find examples of such 'traditions' juxtaposed elsewhere? This is a question we will take further in our final chapter.

(ii) Coherence in Literary Studies

The previous position relies upon an idea of the primacy of coherence which could be developed more comprehensively.

If we take as our starting point the assertion that Jesus' message is our 'text', whether derived in its 'final form' from any one Gospel, or as some kind of construct or harmonization from the Synoptic tradition, then it will be instructive to look at the notion of coherence as it is construed in the realm of literary studies.

Uncovering Coherence. The apparently common-sense idea has usually prevailed that the most coherent reading should be considered the most persuasive reading. Thus in *Validity in Interpretation* E.D. Hirsch states that:

> Faced with alternatives, the interpreter chooses the reading which best meets the criterion of coherence. Indeed, even when the text is

> not problematical, coherence remains the decisive criterion, since meaning is 'obvious' only because it 'makes sense'.[43]

The most persuasive reading is the one that gives the fullest possible account of the work so that 'all the parts fit'. The assumption of coherence in a literary work is therefore a common convention:

> Until he has established clear evidence of its inadequacies, a literary critic does well always to proceed on the assumption that the author has done the best job possible with his work.[44]

Cases of deliberate irony, paradox, or ambiguity require a temporary suspension of coherence on a small scale, but must still fit into a larger coherent account of the work. In his important study *The Act of Reading*, W. Iser notes the importance of these temporary inconsistencies to New Critical theory, which was based on what Iser calls 'the classical norms of interpretation' where each work was a unity that demanded harmony between all the different elements. However, that ideal of unity should not be too easy to observe:

> The value of the work is measured by the harmony of its elements... this means that the more disparate those elements are at first, and the harder they are to relate to one another, the greater will be the aesthetic value of the work when, at the end, all its parts are joined together in a harmonious whole. The harmonization and eventual removal of ambiguities—this is the unacknowledged debt of New Criticism to the classical norm of interpretation.[45]

Perhaps students of the Gospels have not been good enough at observing the 'real' coherence that lies behind the apparent inconsistencies in the 'text' of Jesus.

This charge is borne out in some recent 'literary' studies of biblical texts where there are often attempts to explain apparent intrusions into the text as meaningful parts of the whole. Where once sections of the text that did not readily cohere with the rest were seen as editorial, redactional or secondary, the tendency is now to try to explain how they contribute to our appreciation of the literary artistry of the author.[46] M.E. Stone offers an interesting example of such principles in his essay 'Coherence and Inconsistency in the Apocalypses: the case of "the End" in 4 Ezra'. *4 Ezra* is considered the carefully crafted work of a single author, but the term 'the End' is used in this work to denote two different eschatological events. Hence, the question arises of the consistency of the author's use of terminology, and also the coherence of his thought.

> The preliminary hypothesis must always be that the author's thought was coherent. If so, then when analysis of a term uncovers prima facie contradictions or inconsistency, it is possible that the meaning assigned to it is not exact. Alternatively, there may be an unstated premise, view, or feature lying outside the text that actually provides the author's thinking with coherence. For, unless the author was weak of mind, or the book a jumble of miscellaneous literary remains, it made sense to the author; and the task of the modern analyst is to attempt by a combination of careful historical, philological study and empathetic exegesis, to discover how that was so. This must be done while bearing in mind that the documents of apocalyptic literature are religious compositions of a non-Aristotelian type, and consequently the application of a criterion of rigid logical consistency within them is not appropriate.[47]

A major presupposition in Stone's work is the assumption of coherence on the part of the author of a literary work: he therefore goes on to criticize the usual path taken by historical criticism:

> the first resort on the discovery of an 'inconsistency' is not to accuse the author of an inconsistent combination of consistent (but quite hypothetical) sources, sources whose existence is often posited only because of the supposed inconsistencies. Nor is it appropriate, somewhat less naively, to charge him with the unsuccessful integration of structures of thought or schemes of eschatology or other such entities having no better claim to existence than did the sources. Instead, we should question the criteria by which the 'inconsistencies' are detected. Has the content of the terms been adequately described? Has the structure of the thought been carefully studied? If something seems to be inconsistent, but the ancient author wrote it, what enabled him to do so? (p. 242).

Stone realizes that it would be wrong to propose that ancient authors always wrote coherent works; some may have made contradictory statements, and indeed whole books could be incoherent,

> This assumption should be, however, a hypothesis of the last resort, and will be strongest when supported as well by other features of the writing than conceptual 'inconsistencies' (p. 243).

The position here outlined would suggest that the critic should be persistent in seeking coherence in Jesus' 'text', and not resort too quickly to assigning material to other sources on the grounds of apparent incompatibility. We should bear in mind, however, that this sort of reading is a more easily defensible enterprise when applied to the texts of each evangelist than as an attempt to read the 'text' of Jesus' message as a means to historical reconstruction. That is not to say that the latter interest is not legitimate, it is simply more problematic.

Deconstructing Coherence. In literary studies, however, the principle of coherence is not always considered the key to the most persuasive reading. We noted earlier W. Iser's description of the New Criticism in terms of its basis in what he called 'the classical norm of interpretation': this forms the ground of his criticism of the primacy of coherence and unified meaning. Iser wants to reject the claim, implicit in the New Critical enterprise, that art represents 'the appearance of truth'. He also wishes to argue that the coherence required in interpretation is not something inherent in the work itself, or in the mind of the author, but something constructed by the reader. Iser wants to shift the focus from the text to the reader.

> the uniform meaning of the text—which is not formulated by the text—is the reader's projection rather than the hidden content (p. 17).

Iser describes the reading process as one of 'consistency-building', which has recourse to the classical norms of totality, harmony, and symmetry of the parts being dealt with. A coherent system is constructed by the reader as progress is made through the text, and the various elements of the work are either fitted in to the system, covered over, or they lead to modifications. Iser stresses that with the model of 'consistency-building' the emphasis, with regard to the notion of coherence and unity, is on the reader:

> As a structure of comprehension it depends on the reader and not on the work, and as such it is inextricably bound up with subjective factors, and, above all, the habitual orientations of the reader (p. 18).

For Iser, the process of harmonization, or the placing of a coherent system over a work is a way of coping with the unfamiliar, and indeed the uncontrollable aspects of a text.

A suspicion about the value of coherence as a key to literary understanding is also a feature of deconstructive criticism. The move from structuralism to deconstruction involves a shift from seeing the text:

> as a closed entity, equipped with definite meanings which it is the critic's task to decipher, to seeing it as irreducibly plural, an endless

> play of signifiers which can never be finally nailed down to a single centre, essence or meaning.[48]

Paul de Man adds his weight to the critique of New Criticism and its notion of organic unity and coherence, showing how it deconstructs its own claims. He finds a discrepancy between the theoretical claims and the actual practice. The obsession with 'organic' form was undermined by the very 'ambiguities' and 'tensions' which were sought out. Thus he concludes:

> This unitarian criticism (i.e. New Criticism) finally becomes a criticism of ambiguity, *an ironic reflection on the absence of the unity it had postulated*[49] (italics mine).

De Man's criticism goes on, like Iser's, to see the coherence and unity as the product of the reader, rather than as something inhering in the text. Deconstruction seeks out tensions and contradictions within a text, not to delight in reconciling them (as with the New Criticism) but to expose them and hence to avoid the attempt to dominate the text by imposing the reader's ideology (what Johnson calls 'integrative violence'[50]) or to undermine the ideology of the text.

Without trying to arbitrate between the merits of New Criticism and Deconstruction, we can observe that the location of unity and coherence in a text is not the unquestioned aim of all literary theory:[51] the observation of irreconcilable tensions and inconsistencies in a text may be just as significant. This, of course, has implications for the way we treat the 'text' which Jesus authored. As this is a text which, in a very real sense, the critic constructs, our leanings toward new critical or deconstructive principles will have an important effect on our work and its conclusions.

(iii) The Mythology of Coherence

We have considered the principle of coherence from the perspective of literary studies, but criticism of its use in Gospel studies can be supported from other sources, and it is perhaps necessary to give some suggestion as to why the problematic nature of the appeal to this principle has been largely overlooked.

In an interesting article on 'Meaning and Understanding in the History of Ideas',[52] Q. Skinner discusses what he calls the 'mythology of coherence'. Skinner explains how classic writers are often not altogether consistent, or they fail to give any systematic account of their beliefs. It then becomes easy for the historian to conceive of his or her task as that of supplying or finding in each text the coherence which appears to be lacking:[53] this constitutes the mythology of coherence,

> it remains hard to see how the whole enterprise of looking for the 'inner coherence' of a given writer's doctrines can yield anything except a mythology of coherence—a mythology .... in the sense that the history written according to this methodology can scarcely contain any genuine historical reports about thoughts that were actually thought in the past (p. 22).

The problem with the principle of coherence is that it is an ideal, which is frequently inappropriate for judging the report of the thought of an individual. History written according to this principle becomes a series of abstractions, a history of thoughts at a level of coherence which may never have been attained. The principle of coherence may be useful at the level of historical generalizations and the construction of types and models, but at the level of individual thought, it is often overworked. In a similar way I.G. Nicol (1974) quotes from G. Florovsky's essay on 'The Predicament of the Christian Historian' in his critique of Schweitzer's notion of 'consistent' eschatology:

> The historian is never content with a fragmentary vision .... He endeavours for the sake of intelligibility, to substitute 'an orderly vision' for that 'dust of small facts' of which the actual happening seems to consist .... A historian tends to overcome, in a synthetic image, the empirical complexity and often confusion of individual bits, and occurrences, to organize them into a coherent whole, and to relate the multiplicity of occurrences to the unity of a character .... It is by this method that all the major generalizations of our historiography have been created: the Hellenic mind; the mediaeval man; the bourgeois; and the like .... They are, as it were, valid visions, like artistic portraits, and, as such, they are indispensible tools of understanding. *But 'typical men' are very different from real men of flesh and blood* [*Religion and Culture, Essays in Honour of Paul Tillich*, ed. W. Leibrecht (London: SCM, 1958), pp. 152-53 (italics mine)].

Again we see that the principle of coherence is indispensible to historical study, but when applied to the reported speech of an individual, it seems inevitably to distort. This forces the question of whether the reported speech of an individual is, in itself, a proper subject of historical study. It is the nature of the sources which forces us to pose this question. If, instead of the three Synoptic Gospels, we had three independent sources—one Christian Gospel; one Jewish polemic against the false Messiah; and one Roman life of the Galilean—all reporting similar sayings of Jesus, then the prospects for historical study would be better.

(iv) Possible ways of construing Coherence

Our inquiry into the principle of coherence would seem to leave three possibilities, between which it is difficult to arbitrate.

First, we could continue to use a principle of coherence as the tool for historical judgments, perhaps refining our idea of coherence in the light of some of the problems we have raised. This method offers the best possibilities for making 'historical' judgments, but, in the light of our previous comments, it is the most problematic way forward on theoretical grounds.

Second, we could stop resorting to apparent inconsistencies as the grounds for assigning material to a later stage of tradition, and try to become more skilled at seeing the 'unity' that was, or could have been there all the time.

Third, we could admit that imposing our own idea of coherence on the 'text' of Jesus' message is not necessary or desirable. We should content ourselves with highlighting the inconsistencies in this 'text', as in any other.

This treatment of the theme of coherence will, it is hoped, show the tenuous and at times arbitrary nature of our attempts at reconstruction.

3. *Concluding Comments*

In the light of our criticisms, we would suggest that there are two basic alternatives with regard to the historical reconstruction of Jesus' message.

Either we admit the present difficulties of the task, and focus our attention on a comparison of the three presentations of Jesus we have in the Synoptic Gospels (the Fourth Gospel and non-canonical Gospels would provide other interesting accounts). As we have seen the multiplicity of literary theories would no doubt lead to a broad variety of 'readings'. It is doubtful, however, whether historians or theologians will be prepared to accept such a limitation on their work. However, it must be said that there are theological movements developing which clearly accept as one of their starting points the need for a sceptical attitude to our ability to perform historical reconstructions on the basis of the biblical texts.[54]

Alternatively, we may acknowledge that our interest in the message of Jesus will have to be pursued without the aid of any sure criteria, and in the light of the several possible ways of construing the coherence of that message mentioned above. We would, however, be able to carry on our work in the context of certain broader principles which concern the activity of Jesus, and the impact of his life, as we know it from other evidence. These will be blunt tools, and will yield many competing reconstructions, but that will be better than the unreal certainty achieved through working with invalid or arbitrary criteria.

We have seen in this study that our historical judgments affect the way that we construe the meaning of material in the Gospels. Each saying or theme is understood in relation to some broader context whether derived from Jewish literature construed as 'background' to the Gospels, or with reference to some decision about the 'characteristic' message of Jesus. We have criticized both these notions, and introduced the idea of reversing the usual critical procedure whereby the reconstructed framework is used to interpret the parts, so that our understanding of the 'whole' of Jesus' message could be more informed by the diverse parts of the Synoptic tradition. This is no guarantee of greater historical accuracy, but would seem to be at least as plausible as the standard critical practice—if it does not lead to a certain historical reconstruction of Jesus' speech, it would at least provide a better understanding of early Christian perceptions of Jesus' message.

In his article on the historical Jesus, W. Walker contrasts the 'atomistic' approach, based on the criteria of authenticity, with a more 'holistic' approach, which he favours. He conceives this shift of emphasis as a return to a 'sobered version' of the Old Quest; something that has, in the past, been suggested by a number of critics.[55] Walker admits the limitations of this move:

> it must be conceded that the results of such a quest will be far from satisfying to one who demands certainty regarding the authenticity or inauthenticity of each particular pericope, but these results will be much more adequate for the historian who is attempting to understand the origins of Christianity.[56]

This inquiry is guided by three tests against which any attempt at reconstruction must be measured:

1. It must set Jesus convincingly within the context of first century Palestinian Judaism.
2. It must show why his life ended in execution at the hands of the Roman authorities.
3. It must account for, or at least illumine, the birth of the Christian community.

As Walker points out, such an inquiry moves away from focusing on the authenticity of aspects of Jesus' message, to questions more accessible to historical investigation. Interest in the message of Jesus will not come to an end, but it will be set within the context of these broader questions, which will act as a useful control on some of the more esoteric descriptions of that message.[57]

These suggestions are similar to the section on method in E.P. Sanders important study on *Jesus and Judaism*. He also poses the above 'tests' as historical questions which should guide our interest in the historical Jesus. He is critical of studies which focus exclusively on the teaching of Jesus, and fail to account for the results of his ministry and its impact on the developing Christian movement and its relationship with Judaism. Sanders seems to suggest a twin basis for his historical study. First, he sees the general context for understanding Jesus as Jewish eschatology:

> enough evidence points towards Jewish eschatology as the general framework of Jesus' ministry that we may examine the particulars in the light of that framework (p. 10).

As we noted earlier, this is a dubious starting point. Questions arise about the nature of Jewish eschatology, and from whose attempt at reconstruction we should work. These issues receive little critical reflection in Sanders work. The second prong of his work concerns a list of 'facts' which he considers indisputable, and hence, sure ground to begin his investigation.[58] These 'facts' are activities of Jesus and events in his life, and the trouble with such 'facts' is that they always require interpretation. In a review of Sanders' book M. Hooker observes:

> it is noticeable that although he deliberately avoids beginning with the teaching of Jesus, it is nevertheless his assessment of that teaching which determines his interpretations of Jesus' actions.[59]

Sanders, however, does provide a helpful corrective to much previous work, in admitting the difficulties involved in basing one's inquiry on an 'atomistic' reconstruction of Jesus' speech, and he emphasizes the more tangible questions which form the overall context for any historical study of Jesus.

Many problems remain. The questions posed are extremely general, and there appears so much scope for different kinds of answers. Sanders admits, for example, that there may be no connection between Jesus' intention and his death. He may have been put to death accidentally, or on a misunderstanding. However, Sanders thinks he can offer a good explanation for a causal thread between Jesus' life, his death, and the Christian movement. In the end, we will have no sure criteria for settling disputes such as this one; the most persuasive case that takes account of the most evidence and answers the most questions should prevail.

The study of Jesus' speech would become a subsection of the study of Christian origins. Unless placed in a broader context like this, the reported speech of an individual is not a legitimate subject for inquiry, and the sort of precision sought by some critics in judging the authenticity of individual sayings and pericopes has led to the establishment of doubtful criteria. The more precision is sought on a small scale, the more scope there seems to be for distortion.

We must place Jesus convincingly in his contemporary environment, without allowng that context to constrain our understanding of his thought, since we must account for a new historical movement. We must offer an account of his ministry which shows the continuity with both Judaism and the early Church, and helps to account for the development from one to the other. We must account for opposition to his ministry and his death.

Our study cannot hope to answer all these questions, but any attempt at reconstruction must contribute to answering these questions. There will be a variety of ways of characterizing the message, and hence the significance of Jesus, based largely on the ways in which we may construe the coherence of that message. Some will look harder for the underlying unity of the reported speech; others will argue that there are tensions and inconsistencies that undermine a coherent ideology; and others will appeal to varieties of historical explanation, such as the idea of development or the influence of later stages of tradition, from anonymous oral voices to the creative role of the evangelists themselves.

With regard to the initial impulse for this inquiry, we would suggest that the work of many critics who have sought to reconstruct the essence of Jesus' message as a basis for their treatment of the proverbial wisdom material reveals a misplaced confidence in the tools and criteria for their historical judgments—and perhaps a lack of understanding as to how much their historical decisions affect their interpretive ones. We can at least be sure that it is mistaken to make a negative judgment on material merely on the grounds of its continuity with other Jewish proverbial wisdom, or to force the interpretation of the remaining material into line with eschatology. After looking, in our next chapter, at the question of the rhetoric of the proverb in its literary setting, we will go on to offer a fresh account of the relation between wisdom and the Kingdom of God in the reported speech of Jesus. How useful this proves to be to the task of historical reconstruction is not an easy question to answer.

Chapter 5

THE FUNCTIONS/RHETORIC OF THE PROVERBIAL SAYING IN THE SYNOPTIC LITERATURE

1. *Introduction*

In our review of the work of Beardslee and Crossan we noted an interest in the rhetorical function of the proverbial saying in Jesus' speech. At that stage we raised some questions about what we saw as a rather one-sided account of this rhetoric, based largely on the author's understanding of the historical context of Jesus' use of wisdom language. Having criticized their work of reconstruction, particularly with regard to the dominant significance which they there give to eschatology as a controlling idea, we wish to reconsider the rhetoric of the proverb.

In recent folklore studies attention has focused on the issue of proverb performance, and increasing stress has been laid on the importance of contextual factors for understanding the workings of the proverb.[1] In our concern with the way the proverbial sayings functon in their literary setting, the issue of context is obviously of central importance. We will differ from the student of folklore, whose interest in context would lead to a consideration of an extremely broad range of factors; our understanding of context will be limited by the information provided in the text.[2] This could involve the immediate context of a saying, e.g. such details as the participants in a conversation, or context could be conceived as broadly as the literary work as a whole.

In general terms we can describe two types of immediate context for proverbial material in the Synoptics. First, there are many examples of the conversational use of proverbial sayings in the Synoptics, e.g. Mt. 9.10-13, Mk 7.24-30, and Mt. 19.16-26. In many cases the conversation and saying are related to a narrative event which brings about the conversation, such as Mt. 9.10-13 where it is Jesus' action of eating with the tax-gatherers and sinners which leads to the question and Jesus' proverbial response.[3] The significant event may be an implied one, such as the healing requested in Mk 7.24-30.[4]

Second, proverbial sayings also occur in more extended discourse of a didactic nature; see, for example, Lk. 12.22-34.[5] Again, such discourse will often be related to narrative incidents; see, for example, Lk. 11.10, where the whole incident and the saying stem from the disciples observing Jesus at prayer (also Mt. 10.10c).

We have previously mentioned the narrative qualities of the proverb, and it is interesting to note that some proverbial sayings, e.g. Lk. 14.8-11[6], occur at the conclusion of parables, or in close connection to them. Here the extended narrative of the parable is mirrored in the miniature narrative of the proverb; the close relation between parable and proverb becomes apparent.

With regard to the question of rhetoric or function, perhaps the most interesting feature of the material we have selected for study is its descriptive quality. The proverbial sayings on which we have focused as a significant aspect of the spoken material in the Synoptics are mostly in the form of indicative sentences. This has led some to argue that such indicative sayings may actually function in an imperative way e.g. Bultmann's treatment of Mt. 6.24 as 'address',[7] or Mk 9.35 and similar sayings. In Beardslee's work, some descriptive sayings which are paradoxical in content are said to function to disorient the hearer/reader. We wish to develop a more comprehensive account of the function of such sayings, and we propose to show that one of the most fruitful sources for such an account will come from recent work in linguistics. An approach to the function/rhetoric of the proverb through *pragmatics* offers an account of language use at a more public level than the sometimes theological or esoteric approach of some New Testament critics.

2. *How to do Things with Proverbs*

Within the realm of linguistics, pragmatics has been defined as 'the study of how utterances have meanings in situations'.[8] As a field of study, pragmatics is relatively new. Its main concerns can be derived, in large measure, from the work of the philosophers of language J.L. Austin and J. Searle.[9] If the scope of semantics can be described as having to do with the 'sense' of an utterance, then pragmatics may be said to include a concern with the 'force' of an utterance. To give a full account of the meaning of an utterance one has to describe its force, and this involves contextual factors which move beyond the purely semantic, phonological or syntactic level. Thus, from the point of view of linguistics, an utterance may have an indicative form but its force may be more than just descriptive of a state of affairs.[10]

The sentence 'There is a bull in this field' is in the indicative mood, and its sense is not difficult to understand at the semantic level. However, when we think of this as an utterance within a particular situation the force may vary depending on contextual factors. Thus, the sentence may be spoken by a farmer as he approaches a family about to set up a picnic on the grass. In this instance, the force would be that of a warning. On the other hand, should the farmer be approached by an irate prospective bull-purchaser, the force of the utterance would be to reassure the person that the visit had not been in vain. One could conceive of a situation where the utterance was spoken to both sets of people at once: the tone of the utterance might indicate the pragmatic force of a warning, but there would also be the additional 'implicature' of a reassurance.

In his helpful introduction to pragmatics[11] Leech offers some other examples of a pragmatic analysis of utterances which will inform our study of the rhetoric of the proverb. He relates the sentence uttered by an American hostage in Iran in 1980:

> Considering that I am a hostage, I should say that I have been fairly treated.

This is a highly ambivalent utterance which was, however, presumably intended to convey some information. The speaker had to hold in balance several factors, namely, a desire to tell the truth, to reassure people at home, and not to offend the hostage-takers. To classify the utterance simply as a declaration or as reassurance would be overly simplistic, for the speaker wishes to perform a number of goals which compete with one another. Leech finds this a good example of the indeterminacy involved in some conversational speech:

> The indeterminacy of conversational utterances .... shows itself in the NEGOTIABILITY of pragmatic factors; that is, by leaving force unclear, s (speaker) may leave h (hearer) the opportunity to choose between one force and another, and thus leaves part of the responsibility of meaning to h (p. 24).

Another example would be the sentence:

> If I were you, I'd leave town straight away.

This could be interpreted as a piece of advice, a warning, or a threat, depending on contextual factors. Again, the utterance 'Sit down' could have a variable force, and in different circumstances could be called an invitation, a suggestion, or an order.

It can be seen that the study of pragmatics takes account of important contextual factors which are essential to an adequate understanding of an utterance. In some ways, a pragmatic analysis of an utterance could be said merely to spell out the obvious. Indeed, Austin admits this point in his initial work on speech acts and performatives:

> What I shall have to say here is neither difficult nor contentious; the only merit I should like to claim for it is that of being true, at least in parts.[12]

Pragmatics has become a somewhat contentious area of debate at a theoretical level, but the practical insights it offers are often quite clear and uncontentious. It shares a good many of the concerns of what is elsewhere called rhetoric—the effective use of language in communication. However, pragmatics is concerned with the use of language in the most general sense, whereas rhetoric is often conceived of in terms of artful and persuasive speech. The issues of negotiability and indeterminacy, which we have already touched on, would stand on the borders of both subjects.

An approach to proverb performance through pragmatics is hinted at in N.R. Norrick's study, *How Proverbs Mean*, and in an earlier essay on nondirect speech acts.[13] Norrick distinguishes two sorts of nondirect speech acts. First, there are figurative speech acts in which a speaker says one thing and means another, that is, the literal meaning of the utterance must be rejected. Thus, the utterance 'the fishing boats danced in the harbour' conveys the idea that 'the fishing boats moved rhythmically in the harbour'. Second, there are indirect speech acts in which a speaker says one thing and means it, but conveys a different speech act by virtue of the first. Thus, the utterance 'I'm almost out of paper' is an assertion at the literal level, but may also convey the request 'Please get me some paper'.

Norrick argues that such nondirect speech acts are used in situations involving a double bind, i.e. where the speaker is involved in a clash between the principle of truthfulness and politeness. For example, you meet an acquaintance wearing a hideous hat. That person asks your opinion of the hat. The situation is a double bind, with truthfulness conflicting with politeness,[14] and the solution is generally to produce a nondirect speech act, 'an utterance with multiple interpretations',[15] such as 'I used to have a hat like that when I was a teenager' or 'What a useful hat, I'm sure it will keep the rain off'.

Double binds produce ambiguous speech acts. Such nondirect speech acts occur when speakers want to disguise their true feelings, to leave themselves escape routes, or to offer hearers choices. Such acts are performed when speakers feel 'the intended action is too offensive, prying, pushy, or embarassing, to approach directly'.[16] Norrick mentions several kinds of nondirect speech acts used to resolve double bind situations, one of these is the use of proverbs. He suggests several reasons for this strategy:

a. The traditional nature of proverbs is an important factor. On the one hand, this aspect of the proverb allows speakers to express opinions without strictly being accountable for them: they are not just their opinions. This leads on to the sense of authority which a proverb carries. It is probably true that the same qualities are present in sayings which are proverbial in style, but are not in common use, they may be the creation of an individual (aphorism). The formal qualities give the same impression of an idea somewhat detached from the speaker.
b. Proverbs are commonly intended to convey something more or something different than what they directly express. Thus, the saying 'like father, like son' may simply express a belief about fathers and sons, but it more often functions as a compliment to the father or son, or as a warning to the father. The speaker is able to hide his or her personal intention behind the anonymity of the proverb's literal statement.
c. Proverbs give responsibility to the hearer for deciding on the contextual meaning. Various contextual factors are involved in moving from the literal sense of the saying to a concrete application or applications. The figurative nature of many proverbs (like other metaphors) requires interpretive decisions on the part of the hearer, which again distances the speaker.

Proverbs, then, may be considered as nondirect speech acts,[17] which distance the speaker from the idea conveyed,[18] and give greater responsibility to the hearer in terms of interpretive choices. We wish now to consider some of the Synoptic proverbial sayings from the point of view of a pragmatic analysis, hoping to give a more nuanced account of the rhetoric of this important speech form.

First, there are several instances, mostly in conversation, where a proverb is used with the effect of resolving a situation of conflict without the speaker (usually Jesus) having to issue a direct command, comment or a denial of another person's position. This may involve an implicit appeal to the authority of tradition, or a degree of ambiguity which forces the hearer(s) to make interpretive choices.

We return to the incident involving the Syro-Phoenician woman (Mt. 15.21-28; Mk 7.24-30) as a good example of this strategy, which also illustrates the importance of extra-linguistic factors in a pragmatic analysis of proverb performance. Both speakers employ the strategy of indirection[19] on account of the tension involved in the situation: the woman's performance is the more successful in every way.

In Mark's account, Jesus is seeking privacy, and enters a house hoping that no one will find him (v. 24). The woman does find him, however, and her request for healing for her daughter is therefore delivered in a situation which is already charged with difficulties. The text goes on (v. 26) to introduce another complicating factor in addition to her sex, namely her country of origin. Jesus' comment to her (v. 27) is introduced with an imperative command 'Let the children be satisfied first' (absent from Matthew's version), followed by the figurative saying, which has the force of a refusal of her request. In Matthew's version of the incident, the woman's arrival on the scene is a noisy one. This irritates the disciples and receives no immediate response from Jesus; instead it results in a minor conflict between the disciples and Jesus.[20] When the woman is able to confront Jesus directly with her request for help (v. 25), Jesus' proverbial response stands alone—the strategy of indirection is intensified. Speculation as to the theological implications of the saying may be overworked, and there is often an unfortunate tendency among commentators to soften the opposition between 'children' and 'dogs'.[21] The force of the saying in this context is a refusal (by Jesus) to act on behalf of this woman.

Rather than arguing directly against Jesus' rejection of her request, the woman uses the same device of indirection, and the same figurative labels, to argue forcefully, and at the same time tactfully, that Jesus should act on her behalf. The force of the woman's saying is somewhere between a request and a demand. Thus, both speakers employ the rhetorical strategy of citing descriptive proverbial sayings which derive their force from the context.[22]

The incident at Nazareth, recorded in Mk 6.1-6 and Mt. 13.54-58, includes Jesus' use of a proverbial saying ('A prophet is not without honour except in his home town *and among his own relatives* and in his own household') in a situation of conflict. The crowd observe on the one hand the remarkable gifts which Jesus has, and yet on the other hand they know of his humble origins. The narrative in both cases records the offence that this caused. Jesus' proverbial comment has the force of an indirect and mild rebuke, as the hearers connect Jesus with the 'prophet' and see their behaviour described as a failure to give honour.

It is interesting that Luke's account (4.22-30) involves a variant of the same saying, but the situation develops into a much greater conflict as the rebuke involved in the saying is employed in a way that provokes the crowd to violence. Indeed, the force of the proverbial saying is a much stronger rebuke than in the case of Matthew and Mark, for it plays on the inconsistency in the implied demands of the crowd (v. 23) and the expectation of an unfriendly treatment of the 'prophet'. Prior to this saying there is no evidence that the people were taking offence at Jesus, their response was favourable (v. 22). Thus, the use of the saying in this context has the effect of provoking offence, rather than a tactful handling of a situation of conflict.[23] In v. 23 there is some suggestion that Jesus has misinterpreted the force of the question 'Isn't this Joseph's son?'. Where Luke seems to imply that this question has the force of praise or is at least a neutral observation, Jesus seems to take it in a negative way, and so the incident develops into a confrontation. In terms of rhetorical strategy, in Luke's account, Jesus does not let the proverbial saying in v. 24 stand on its own with its ambiguous implicatures, instead he cites examples from history which push the point home quite explicitly, rather than giving 'responsibility to the hearers' for the force of the saying (as do Matthew and Mark).[24]

A second rhetorical strategy based on the indirect nature of the proverbial saying concerns what Leech called 'the negotiability of pragmatic factors', and can be seen most clearly in sayings involving opposition or doubling. In these cases the force of the saying will vary principally on account of the audience. the use of proverbial sayings in this kind of situation gives some responsibility for interpretation to the hearer(s) and gives the speaker the chance to perform more than one task in one utterance. In some cases in the Synoptic literature the force of a saying may be determined by the context, but the form of the saying leaves open other possibilities and implications.

In an earlier note we referred to the issue of various illocutionary forces with regard to the saying concerning the 'first' and the 'last'. There is a whole family of sayings which concern the opposition between negative and positive status (e.g. Mt. 19.30; 20.26, 27; 23.11, 12; Mk 9.35; 10.31, 43, 44; Lk. 9.48; 14.11; 18.14).

In Lk. 9.46-48 an argument occurs amongst the disciples over the issue of status. Understanding what is going on, Jesus takes a child and says: 'Whoever receives this child in my name receives me; and whoever receives me receives him who sent me; for he who is least among you, this is the one who is great'. We have previously discussed how the common interpretation of this family of sayings takes them as eschatological reversal sayings which disorient the hearer. But in fact the saying is concerned with a reversal of status in the present. The negotiability of the saying lies in the fact that the hearer could identify with the 'least', in which case the force of the saying is affirmation: the saying encourages the humble person. Alternatively, the hearers might consider themselves 'great', so that the force of the saying would be to challenge their position. The actual content of the terms for negative status (here 'least') and positive status ('great') is somewhat vague. The preceding action and comment concerning the child suggest an interest in and care for the weak—a practical attitude of humility. In other instances the context of the sayings gives more precise content to the terms. In Mt. 19.30 the contrast between the first and last has to do with material well-being. (Although the context is a question about the future for the disciples, and the reply refers to the time of glory of the Son of Man, the force of the saying is one of promise, with an implicit note of judgment against those materially 'first'.) In Mt. 20.26, 27 the issue has to do with the exercise of authority over one another, as is also the case in 23.11, 12.

In Lk. 14.11 the parabolic setting makes it difficult to know how to give content to the terms 'humble' and 'exalt'. In much parable research there is a tendency in interpretation for the content of the parable to fall away in the face of the one theological (or often eschatological) point being made. The text is considered in terms of a dichotomy between 'worldly wisdom' and 'theological insight'. Thus Jeremias questions:

> Is Lk. 14.11 .... intended to be a piece of practical wisdom, a rule of social etiquette? Surely not! The comparison with .... 14.14b, with 18.14, and with Mt. 23.12 shows that Lk. 14.11 is speaking of God's eschatological activity, the humbling of the proud and the exaltation of the humble in the Last Day. Hence the direction in Luke 14.11 about the desirability of modest behaviour in a guest becomes the introduction to an 'eschatological warning', which looks forward to the heavenly banquet, and is a call to renounce self-righteous pretensions and to self-abasement before God.[25]

Jeremias' exegesis is dominated by a concern with the opposition between the portrayal of Jesus as a teacher of wisdom, which he sees as the corrupting influence of the early Christians on the Gospel tradition, and the 'authentic', historical picture of Jesus as the eschatological prophet. This forbids any subtlety in his reading of the text, or much attention to the function of the proverbial saying. I.H. Marshall reflects the same stark choice between worldly wisdom and theology in his comment on this verse, and this is coloured with the apologetic motif of demonstrating the superiority of Jesus' thought to that of 'the rabbis':

> This could be simple, worldly advice to guests, and it is amply paralleled in Jewish writings .... But it is presented here as a parable .... This is confirmed by the conclusion in v. 11 which speaks of the humiliation and exaltation of men by God. Hence the advice given (while good and valid on a worldly level) is a parable of how men should behave over against God (p. 581) .... whereas for the rabbis the saying was merely a piece of worldly wisdom, for Jesus it is an expression of God's verdict upon men.[26]

We would suggest that the text of the parable in Luke does not necessitate such a choice between wisdom and theology. The saying in v. 11 has some theological content, namely, the idea that exaltation and humiliation is God's work and reflects God's values—as we argued in Chapter 3, the theme is theocentric. However, there is no indication that the teaching is not to be worked out in the realm of human relationships. The context (v. 7) suggests that the teaching should in some way address the needs of the situation. The parable uses this situation as its main image, and the final saying does not close off a traditional wisdom concern with behaviour towards others. The saying's primary function in the context is to challenge the behaviour of the guests, but it does so in a way that opens up the possibility of endorsing the one who acts humbly. The saying possesses a certain vagueness—i.e. it does not simply condemn the proud guests—but it provides a generalizing reflection on a specific situation which invites further applications. And so it is that the saying appears again at 18.14, where a slightly different content is given to the terms 'humble' and 'exalted'.

In this case (Mt. 18.14), it is the religious dimension which is stressed, but this is again understood with reference to relationships between people (v. 9). The context and the parable itself contrast the attitude of the Pharisee, both to God and his fellow man, with the attitude of the tax-gatherer. Again the saying at the end of the parable has the dual force of judgment and promise. The context and the parable give one possible point of reference for the saying which could be re-applied elsewhere, with different content being given to the terms 'humble' and 'exalted'.

The use of the proverb as a nondirect speech act in these contexts means that the hearer/reader has some responsibility for interpretation and application. The point of judgment, challenge, promise or affirmation could often be made much more explicitly, and in a way that ties the speech act more directly to the incident. However, the use of the proverb, with its quality of indirection, and the relative vagueness of the key terms, means that the saying has multiple applicability. Luke's use of the same saying at 14.11 and 18.14 gives slightly different content to the main terms, and the whole family of sayings concerning positive and negative status demonstrate something of the potential of the proverb as a nondirect speech act.

We now move on to some other examples of proverb performance. In Mt. 12.34b and Lk. 6.45c we have a good case of a descriptive proverbial saying which can be analyzed as a nondirect speech act. Both Gospels have here the cluster of proverbial material concerning the opposition between good and evil, and using the metaphors of 'tree' and 'fruit'. Matthew's account has a direct condemnation which appears (v. 24) to be of the Pharisees, thus v. 34: 'You brood of vipers, how can you, being evil, speak what is good? For the mouth speaks out of that which fills the heart'.[27] Here the explanatory proverb has the force of a judgment on those addressed, but the text goes on in v. 35 to mirror the opposition in v. 33 between the good and evil, so that the saying may also have the force of an affirmation, commending the character of those who speak well. Luke's version of these sayings does not include the specific attack on the 'evil', but the twofold force of the saying is more clearly balanced: 'The good man out of the good treasure of his heart brings forth what is good; and the evil man out of the evil treasure brings forth what is evil; for his mouth speaks out of that which fills his heart'.

The comparison of these two versions of the same proverbial saying brings home the problem of the relationship between the specific context of the proverb and its generalizing nature. In the case of Luke's version, the context is a long section of didactic material (6.20-49) addressed to the disciples. There may be a critique of the disciples intended in vv. 39-42, but the sayings in vv. 43-45 are only loosely related to these preceding verses. The problematic question of where to apply these sayings, and how broadly to conceive their claim, is brought home by the juxtaposition with vv. 46-49. If v. 45 concerns the importance of speech as an indicator of the inward tendency, then vv. 46-69 stand against that claim. Speech alone can be deceptive, the important issue is what a person does. Earlier in our study we mentioned the low level claims to truth involved in proverb performance. The key issue is using the appropriate proverb at the appropriate time (cf. Mt. 12.30 and Mk 9.40 which are only formally contradictory, but are appropriate within their particular contexts). Verses 43-45 stress the importance of speech: vv. 46-49 are critical of the value of speech in favour of action.

Another example of this aspect of proverb performance can be seen in the treatment of the 'good' and the 'evil'. In Mt. 5.45b the opposition between 'good' and 'evil' is dissolved: both receive the same treatment under God. This saying is used to serve the command to love enemies, for if this distinction is abrogated in the sight of God, then the disciple of Jesus, who wishes to be called a son of the Father should love both neighbour and enemy: there should be no distinction between 'good' and 'evil' in the way the disciple treats other people. However, this same distinction between 'good' and 'evil' is asserted in 7.15-20 and 12.33-35, in the service of a denunciation of 'false prophets' as 'bad trees' producing 'rotten fruit', and the 'brood of vipers' as 'evil'.

The truth claim involved in a proverbial saying is limited by contextual factors, but sometimes, particularly in longer sections of discourse, the contextual factors are lacking, and it becomes difficult to see how to apply such a saying. The juxtaposition of material in Lk. 6.43-45 and 6.46-49 is a good example of the problem. Certainly one of the effects of the juxtaposition of these sayings is to bring out the limited nature of the claims that they make.

It is also perhaps not surprising to find that one proverbial saying (or more accurately several variants of one core saying) may occur in different contexts within the Gospels, sometimes giving different sense or force.[28] Mt. 10.24-27 includes two groups of sayings paralleled elsewhere. First, there are the sayings concerning the disciple and teacher, the slave and master, which are found in a slightly different form and context in Lk. 6.40. In Matthew these sayings have the force of a judgment upon some disciples, with an implied challenge; thus Gundry:

> Matthew directs these statements against falsely professing Christians who exalt themselves above their persecuted Teacher and Lord by evading persecution through keeping quiet (cf. vv. 26-33).[29]

In the Lukan version the context is not persecution, and the force of the saying is less clear. Fitzmyer sees a reference to instruction in the Christian community,[30] while Marshall lists four possibilities[31] though favouring the idea that the disciples should not behave in a different or superior fashion to Jesus, who did not judge others (v. 41).

Second, the sayings concerning what is hidden and will be revealed (vv. 26, 27) are paralleled in Mk 4.22; Lk. 12.2, 3; 8.17. This group of sayings shows even more clearly the strongly contextual nature of proverb meaning. In his *History of the Synoptic Tradition* Bultmann argues that the proverb in Mt. 10.27 and Lk. 12.3 was 'originally .... a warning from folk-lore to tell someone a secret' (p. 95). He compares it to the German saying 'The sun will bring it to light', and therefore favours Luke's version as the original, with Matthew modifying and misinterpreting it. However, to call the saying a warning is to make a judgment about its pragmatic force which is dependent on context. There is no doubt that Bultmann's German saying could also have the force of a promise in another context. It seems inappropriate to talk about the 'original' force of a proverb. It might be possible to show that a particular saying is traditionally (i.e. more often) found in a context where its force is warning, but to use the same proverb in a different context where its force is promise is not to misinterpret it—the misinterpretation is in Bultmann's misunderstanding of proverb performance, which is then used as the basis for a dubious historical judgment (cf. our treatment of Bultmann in Chapter 3).[32]

In Mt. 10.26 the saying 'for there is nothing covered that will not be revealed, and hidden that will not be known', functions as a promise to encourage the disciples not to be afraid. The ambiguity lies in what exactly is 'covered' and 'hidden', but perhaps the following verse gives content to that, namely, what Jesus has told them in secret (perhaps the mystery of the Kingdom; cf. 13.11). In Lk. 12.2 the saying appears to function as a judgment on the Pharisees who are guilty of hypocrisy. However, the link with v. 3 is problematic, unless the 2nd person plural verbs refer to the Pharisees. Fitzmyer sees a break after v. 1 which completes the attack on the Pharisees: vv. 2, 3 in that case address the disciples as general teaching on the dangers of hypocrisy in their experience, and so have the force of a warning.

In Lk. 8.17 and Mk 4.22 a similar saying occurs in a different context, following the parable of the sower and the saying about the lamp. Although some of the details are different, the function of the saying in both cases seems to be that of a promise, either directed specifically to the disciples, or in a more general sense. Commenting on Mark's text, Anderson finds the promise of the full manifestation of God's kingdom to be limited to 'those who can open themselves completely to receive God's gift of understanding';[33] this is made clear for him in vv. 23, 24a. Lane is quite specific about the nature of the disclosure of v. 22: 'The reference is to the parousia'.[34] With reference to Luke's version, Fitzmyer claims:

> In the present Lukan context the contrast [secret/public, hidden/ made known] emphasizes that even the secrets of the kingdom can be divulged (p. 720).

Marshall, on the other hand, seems to see the force in Lk. 8.17 as a command to the disciples:

> Here the context refers to the disciples making known publicly what Jesus has told them secretly (cf. Matt 10.26f) (p. 330).

Again we see that when a proverbial saying occurs in extended discourse it is often difficult to be certain about the specific force of the saying: its generalizing form leaves open a degree of ambiguity.

In our first chapter we mentioned the interpretive problems surrounding Lk. 7.35 and Mt. 11.19b, particularly with respect to the question of a possible allusion to the figure of personified Wisdom in the Old Testament and early Jewish literature. However, when we consider the rhetoric of the saying in terms of its force, the question of a possible allusion need not be our primary concern. In Matthew's version, the assertion of the wisdom of Jesus' actions serves as a judgment against this generation. In Luke, there may be an ironic linking of 'wisdom' and 'children' such that the wisdom of the children of this generation may prove to be folly. The opposition between the 'people and the tax-gatherers' in v. 29, and the 'Pharisees and the lawyers' in v. 30 suggests that the saying in v. 35 may also serve to commend/affirm the former group. This is reinforced by the repetition of δικαιόω in vv. 29 and 35: those who justified God will be justified (vindicated) by God on account of their wise action. Whether the metaphor in 7.35 and 11.19b alludes to the Wisdom of God or her envoys is difficult to know: however, positing such an allusion is not necessary for understanding the saying. A metaphorical personification of wisdom in this context would seem to be an appropriate way of commending wise action, or ironically rebuking those whose actions were foolish.[35]

3. *Summary*

We have seen how a study of the proverbial saying in its literary settings suggests a variety of functions. Pragmatic analysis has helped us to appreciate the nondirect force of the proverb, and the importance of contextual factors in its interpretation. As a conversational strategy its use is readily explicable; however, it is often difficult to understand the force of a saying in a more extended discourse, and some of these discourses take on the form of a list of wisdom sayings in a way which is hard to relate clearly to the narrative of the Gospel.[36]

We have also seen how one particular saying (or family of sayings) may be used within a variety of contexts within the Synoptic tradition, and we have reinforced the point that it becomes extremely problematic to see how a historical judgment could be made about the 'original' use(s) in the ministry of Jesus.

In our final chapter we will draw together insights from this study, and comment on the significance of proverbial wisdom elements in the Synoptics for the picture of Jesus and his ministry, with particular attention to the proclamation of the Kingdom of God.

Chapter 6

WISDOM OF THE KINGDOM: THE SIGNIFICANCE OF PROVERBIAL WISDOM IN THE SYNOPTICS

In this concluding section we will address the question of the significance of proverbial wisdom sayings in the Synoptics. Having considered historical and rhetorical issues we will offer some constructive comments on the place of 'wisdom' in the reporting of Jesus' message. We cannot hope to give a detailed consideration of the issues involved, but will offer some pointers towards a more positive evaluation of the place of proverbial wisdom in the Synoptics. Our comments cannot be taken as a direct attempt at reconstruction, but should be seen as an essential step on the way to such a project. It is hoped that they may also serve as an aid to those critics seeking a literary appreciation of the work of each evangelist in presenting the story of Jesus to his community.

1. *Arguments based on Compatibility*

There are a number of ways that we might proceed in this section, but first, we should mention the work of those who have sought to give historical accounts of Jesus' message which give significance to wisdom materials by arguing for the compatibility of wisdom and eschatology.[1] The value of such work for historical reconstruction will be open to question in the light of the points made in Chapter 4.[2] Even if we can show that the previously problematic juxtaposition of wisdom and eschatology is not really a problem, we are not necessarily any nearer being able to claim a firm historical basis for this material in the speech of Jesus. However, attempts to demonstrate the compatibility of Synoptic material and the falsity of the antithesis between wisdom and eschatology may be instructive for our reading of the Gospels.

Several writers have questioned this opposition and have suggested a more coherent account of Jesus' message. Such work usually involves the idea that in Jewish literature wisdom and eschatology/apocalyptic may be connected,[3] and then proceeds to draw out the connections with specific reference to Jesus' message. A number of such studies have been undertaken with respect to the hypothetical source 'Q'. For example, C.E. Carlston argues that for many in the ancient world—Jesus included—the will of God (wisdom) does not change in spite of the approaching end (eschaton). Wisdom teaching remains appropriate, but the consequences of wise or foolish behaviour will not be seen in this life.

> The time for the awarding of appropriate rewards and punishments has been shifted from this life to the next. Hence God's justice cannot be disconfirmed by the ambiguities of temporal experience.[4]

This is a neat way of resolving the difficulty, but again relies heavily on allowing one aspect of the message to determine our understanding of the other parts: it would be difficult to argue that every example of proverbial wisdom is to be understood in terms of the future life. When we look beyond 'Q' we see that Jesus' understanding of God's justice is seen in his present activity, for Jesus is an activist, healing, feeding, exorcizing etc.

R.A. Edwards seems to see the role of proverbial wisdom on a par with the idea of an interim ethic, providing guidance for behaviour in the present in the light of the imminent end. Thus, he talks of 'the intensification of the awareness of the importance of the present'.[5] He stresses the importance of being aware of what God is doing and responding to it as central to prophecy and wisdom.

> the right time for an activity (a prominent theme in wisdom) is compatible with an eschatological approach to life. Those who discern the signs of the times are those who have seen the relationship between a variety of experiences (p. 148).

The role of the wise person is to be attentive to experience, and in the light of Jesus' proclamation and activity, that experience is of an imminent action of God. However, the proverbial wisdom attributed to Jesus in the Synoptics is not overly concerned with the temporal questions on which Edwards concentrates. Nor does the reflection on experience in his teaching appear to be tied to the idea of an imminent eschaton. There is a danger of thinking in terms of wisdom as an abstraction, and often a homogeneous one, rather than starting from the nature of Jesus' wisdom. In Chapter 1 we drew attention to some of the ways of conceiving of wisdom, and we saw that wisdom is a diverse phenomenon. We must be careful to focus on wisdom as it is seen in Jesus' message, not on wisdom as an abstract tradition from which we can choose an aspect that seems to fit the needs of the point we wish to argue.

The most comprehensive attempt to relate wisdom to the common view of Jesus' message is the work of R.L. Jeske, *The Wisdom Structure of Jesus' Eschatology*.[6] This relies on a review of the phenomena of wisdom and apocalyptic in Jewish literature, and then goes on to argue that Jesus' appropriation of apocalyptic ideas undergoes what Jeske calls a 'wisdom corrective'.

There are two key points in Jeske's argument. The first concerns the attitude of wisdom to the future.

> Man has no control over it (the future). He can have no pride over against it. Indeed, pride is resolved by it, because in the framework of the future lie the factors which limit man and destroy all pride: failure, misfortune and death. In the face of the future—whether imminent or remote—man does not have the ability to calculate events or to map out a definite schedule upon which he can plan with certainty .... Only God stands over the future (pp. 30, 31).

In this connection Jeske quotes Prov. 27.1 'Do not boast about tomorrow, for you do not know what a day may bring forth'; Ben Sira 10.10 'A long illness baffles the physician; the king of today will die tomorrow'; also Prov. 11.4, and Ben Sira 10.5; 11.14; 19.12f.; 33.15; 51.6f. From this Jeske maintains that the wise person is one who refrains from speculating about the future, while folly involves the belief that future events are accessible to human beings.

The second main aspect of Jeske's work is his attempt to show the compatibility of wisdom and apocalyptic. A great deal of this material[7] focuses on wisdom as understanding (mantic wisdom). While it may be possible to argue the case that Jesus is at times presented as the wise man of understanding who reveals mysteries (concerning the Kingdom of God), that does not help account for his use of proverbial wisdom sayings. In his article on 'The Court-Tales in Daniel and the Development of Apocalyptic',[8] J.J. Collins makes a helpful distinction between two types of wisdom:

> Within the profession of 'wise men' we must distinguish proverbial wisdom, which makes up most of the OT wisdom books, from

> mantic wisdom, as practised by Joseph and Daniel, which includes the interpretation of dreams, signs, and visions. (Proverbial wisdom leaves little trace in apocalyptic. Mantic wisdom, especially if it is considered to include the interpretation of Scripture, is a phenomenon of basic importance for apocalyptic. Mantic wisdom, however, especially when concerned with political oracles, is closer to prophecy than to proverbial wisdom (p. 232).

The failure to distinguish these two types of wisdom frequently occurs, particularly in discussions on the origins of apocalyptic.[9]

However, Jeske does go on to address the further question of whether the proverbial form is found in apocalyptic, and he argues that although the wise man becomes seer, traditional forms still abound.

> The preponderance of wisdom forms and styles supports the observation that the seer maintains his role as sage (p. 91).

He does offer some examples of the use of proverbs in apocalyptic literature, but it is perhaps an overstatement to speak of this as a 'preponderance'. In *4 Ezra* 7.58 we find a proverbial saying in an apocalyptic context, 'what is plentiful is of less worth, for what is more rare is more precious'. This saying serves as an illustration in a longer discourse on the small number of people who will be saved. There is also a proverbial saying in 7.25—'empty things are for the empty, and full things for the full'—this is used in an apocalyptic way to suggest that those who lack goodness in this life ('the empty') will not be rewarded at the coming judgment. Jeske goes on to try to link this with a group of sayings in the Synoptics.

> In vv. 25-44 (of *4 Ezra* 7) this teaching is brought into direct connection with the future, specifically the judgment at the End-time. Those who lack the wisdom to obey God have an empty future; the future of those who obey him is full. The popularity of this idea in apocalyptic circles can be seen from its use in Mark 4.25 (Mt. 13.12, 25.29/Lk. 8.18, 19.26), in the context of Jesus' words concerning the secret of the basileia (4.11) and of the coming manifestation of the presently hidden secrets (4.22) (p. 101).

However, the question remains open whether Mark's use of a similar saying should be termed apocalyptic; and even if it is considered an apocalyptic context in Mark, it may not be in the temporal sense which *4 Ezra* reflects, but in the sense of special understanding. Jeske cites a few other examples, some of which cannot really be considered proverbial sayings[10] and then draws his conclusion.

> These examples should suffice to show how a neutral wisdom saying can be employed by the apocalypticist for his own purposes. It undergoes an 'apocalypticization', in that the element of the *future* is introduced, specifically the future judgment, or the End-time (pp. 101, 102).

We would not disagree that on a few occasions apocalyptic writers have used proverbial sayings to illustrate their points. However, with regard to Jesus' use of proverbial sayings it would have to be argued for each example that the 'element of the future is introduced'. The problem is that in many of Jesus' sayings the idea of the future is absent, both from the saying, and we would argue from the context. There are examples of sayings which involve the future tense, but it is unwise to suggest that the occurrence of such a linguistic feature necessarily indicates an apocalyptic or eschatological concern. Jeske's work, thus far, does not really help to address this issue.

Finally, in his section on proverbial exhortations, Jeske seems to link the 'mantic' and proverbial aspects in his understanding of wisdom in apocalyptic:

> The authority behind these sayings is not the wise man who has sought solely to find order in the world and in one's life, nor the sage who has attempted to relate everyday living to the creating and redeeming activity of God. The seer has done these things, he possesses this knowledge; but he has done and therefore knows more. The authority of the seer is the authority of one who has been divinely appointed to witness the divine secrets, the things now hidden, and to discover the final future. By direct revelation he has received access to the heavenly facts, which will at the time appointed become earthly reality. He has been chosen to learn about the new aeon, which will come into being upon the passing of the old (p. 109).

In this figure of the sage-seer (who can speak with confidence about the future, sometimes employing proverbial forms) Jeske finds evidence for the compatibility of wisdom and apocalyptic and on this basis suggests a more positive assessment of their juxtaposition in Jesus' message. However, for Jeske, the function of wisdom in Jesus' message is the opposite of that described above in the sage-seer figure, for the wisdom corrective in Jesus' message is a refusal to speculate about the future. Wisdom and apocalyptic are considered compatible in Jewish literature 'after the subject of the future became established as a legitimate concern of the wise' (p. 111); however,

Jesus' relationship to wisdom and apocalyptic traditions involves a wisdom corrective against the speculative apocalyptic idea of the Kingdom of God, which Jeske sees as the common expectation. Thus, Jesus' Kingdom language and parables with their emphasis on man's response and the lack of future speculation correct the widespread view derived from apocalyptic tradition:

> Concentration on and speculation about future cosmic developments are futile and must give way before the recognition of God's rule *even now* and man's integrating reponse to it (p. 17).

For Jeske it seems that wisdom corrects apocalyptic in Jesus' language, whereas apocalyptic transforms wisdom in the Jewish literature reviewed as background to the New Testament.

Unfortunately, when Jeske moves on to give exegetical support to this idea of a wisdom corrective to apocalyptic (or the wisdom structure of Jesus' eschatology) the evidence is very slight. He reviews four parables in which he sees the corrective most clearly. The first is Mt. 7.24-27/Lk. 6.47-49 concerning the house built upon the rock. He argues that the foolish man is guilty of speculating about the future, and thus limiting its possibilities, while the wise man resists this danger and acts wisely in the present. Thus,

> It is wisdom to realize that man does not have the future within his power, but can structure his present in view of the wide potential of that future. It is folly to speculate about the future, i.e. to limit its possibilities, thereby judging one's present to be secure (p. 120).

In response to Jeske one could argue that the story does not give explicit details about either men's attitude to the future, and, if anything, it is the wise man who shows foresight (which is necessarily to be understood as a concern with the future). Alternatively, one might say that the wise man speculates that a flood may come, and the foolish man speculates that one will not come: the foolish man was unlucky, or he speculated poorly. It is hard to see this as a wisdom corrective to apocalyptic: the story can more naturally be seen as an illustration of the importance of action as the way of wisdom.

The parable of the faithful and wise servant in Mt. 24.45-51/Lk. 12.41-46 is a better example of the wisdom corrective. 'It is the wise servant who does not speculate about the future, over which he has no control' (p. 121).

In the case of the parable of the wise and foolish maidens (Mt.

25.1-13), Jeske sees the mistake of the foolish maidens as trying to speculate too precisely about the time of the bridegroom's arrival. However, it can be argued that the main quality of wisdom demonstrated is not really a reluctance to speculate about the future, but again, better foresight.

Jeske's final parable is the rich fool of Lk. 12.16-21, and he again makes the temporal issue central:

> the rich man prides himself in his present wealth, which in turn makes him pride himself in his future security. He refused to sense his own limitations, and claims lordship over both present and future (p. 123).

In order to support this reading of the parable Jeske has to remove it from its context (esp. v. 15) and also remove the final verse (v. 21) as secondary. The temporal issue is certainly important in the parable, but it is not an apocalyptic concern with the future, rather the way that the future constrains the present has to do with the unpredictability of death—a common theme in Israel's wisdom.

We would suggest that there are at least two distinct themes in these examples and in the logia which Jeske considers.

On the one hand, in the case of Mt. 24.45-51/Lk. 12.41-46 and Mt. 25.1-13 the theme seems to be that if there is going to be 'speculation' about the future, then the message is that it will be longer than might be imagined, hence, foresight is a virtue in the stories we looked at. This would tie in with other aspects of Jesus' reported speech which suggest that precise descriptions of the future are inappropriate or futile (e.g. Lk. 17.20, 21 and Mark 13, especially vv. 32f.).

The other theme, in the parable of the rich fool is that if someone is living wrongly in the present (i.e. self-sufficiently) then the fact that the future may be shorter than expected should cause them to change their ways. As we noted above, the shortening of the future does not seem to involve the expectation of the eschaton. This ties in with the critique of self reliance in some of the other logia which Jeske cites (e.g. Mk 10.15 par, 10.23b, 25 par).

Jeske offers some good insights on a number of other sayings[11] and perhaps his most convincing comments are on Mt. 6.25-33/Lk. 12.22-31 as displaying a wisdom corrective. He argues that the point of the discourse is that:

> confidence in the future does not begin with the question of how and what one can do to secure his existence; confidence begins with the acknowledgement that it is God who secures one's existence,

which happens when one seeks his rule and will (p. 132).

Jeske's work is based on the assumption of an apocalyptic background to Jesus' Kingdom usage, with a consequent stress on the element of futurity, and a central focus on temporal questions. It is from this starting point that he traces the (somewhat limited) contours of a wisdom corrective. However, if we begin with Jesus' message, it might be simpler and more accurate to say that his Kingdom preaching is non-apocalyptic, at least in the sense of not encouraging speculation about some future event or events. The non-apocalyptic aspect of Jesus' message is more widespread than the 'wisdom' passages. Some of the wisdom material which Jeske has treated would contribute to a much broader Kingdom proclamation on the part of Jesus.

There are two lessons to be learnt from Jeske's work. First, wisdom and apocalyptic may be connected, and it is possible that the latter is in some ways a development of the former. However, the connection has to do with what we have termed 'mantic' wisdom, that is the stream of wisdom which is primarily concerned with special knowledge and understanding—perhaps about future events. It remains an open and an interesting question whether the Synoptic presentations of Jesus reflect this stream of wisdom, but there does not appear to be any simple connection between such mantic wisdom and the sort of proverbial wisdom with which we are concerned.

Second, Jeske has taken one wisdom theme, namely that the future is beyond man's control, and has used that as a key to the understanding of the place and significance of wisdom in the Synoptics. It may be true that this theme is of some importance in Jesus' message, but the nature of the proverbial wisdom attributed to Jesus is more diverse than this, and the problematic aspects are where sayings seem to have no connection with future temporal issues.

2. *Rethinking the Kingdom of God*

In posing the question of the significance of wisdom elements in the Synoptics our work has shown the reluctance of New Testament critics to treat the common view[12] of the Kingdom in Jesus' message as a negotiable factor. Our study on the problems of historical reconstruction of Jesus' speech has shown that the route to the common view of the Kingdom via Jewish apocalyptic is problematic, and also that the method whereby such a view of the Kingdom is largely non-negotiable and is used as a fixed point to judge other material is arbitrary. The way forward in Gospel studies must involve a reconsideration of the Kingdom concept, as, arguably, the central focus of Jesus' message in all three Synoptics. In strict terms this should begin with the study of Jesus' message in each Gospel as the least problematic field of interest—however, in spite of the difficulties of method, it will probably not be long before interest shifts to the question of the historical Jesus, even though this can only be in the form of tentative speculation.[13]

We wish to make a number of observations concerning the Kingdom of God in the Synoptics.

a. *The Diversity of Kingdom Language*

If we come to read the Synoptics without a prior decision about the significance of the term Kingdom of God we find that a number of different metaphors are used in relation to the Kingdom, and this leads on to the question of whether it is correct to think of a single coherent ideology behind the Kingdom language, and it also becomes clear that the material does not easily fall into the present–future structure with which so much research is concerned. This is not to deny that around the phrase 'Kingdom of God' there is often a verb in a present or future form: we would merely suggest that this is not often the central concern being emphasized. The temporal question may be asked, but it may not be the writer's main interest.

We cannot here offer a constructive statement of each Evangelist's presentation of Jesus' proclamation of the Kingdom, but we can explore some of the variety of language and context. In this we are not concerned to draw a distinction between tradition and redaction, for a writer's use of traditional material may be of equal (or more) significance to the points at which he departs from his sources. However, comparative study of the three Synoptics may at times be helpful in drawing attention to significant emphases—the significance of any 'redactional' alterations would have to be argued in each case.

The Kingdom in Mark[14]

There are only fourteen examples of the phrase 'Kingdom of God' in Mark's Gospel, of the four remaining uses of the noun 'Kingdom', 6.23 is on the lips of Herod, presumably a reference to his wealth. In 13.8 it seems to be similar in meaning to 'nation', while in 3.24 and

11.10 the term has more theological significance. At 3.24 'Kingdom' like 'House' seems to be a metaphor concerning the rationale of Satan's activity, while at 11.10 the reference seems to be to the rule of the Davidic Messiah.

The most important use of the phrase 'Kingdom of God' occurs at 1.15, as it introduces Mark's presentation of Jesus' message. The literature on this verse, and particularly the verb ἤγγικεν, is enormous.[15] It seems to be commonly accepted that, at the level of philology, the discussion has exhausted itself,[16] and for our purposes it is most important to look more closely at the context of the verse to understand better what the force of the phrase might be. Thus, leaving behind discussions about the possible Aramaic precedents for ἤγγικεν, it might be argued, as M. Black seems to imply,[17] that the parallelism with 'fulfilled' suggests the translation 'the Kingdom of God *has come*'. This may be a rather heavy-handed use of the idea of synonymous parallelism. There are also good reasons for rendering the phrase 'has come near', and the other two uses of the verb in Mark (11.1; 14.42) are used in a spatial rather than a temporal sense, suggesting that there may be a contrast here between temporal fulfilment and spatial nearness (cf. the two senses of ἐγγύς at 13.28, 29). Perhaps this sort of ambiguity would have been acceptable to an author who was not overly concerned with precise temporal issues. Rather than signalling the inauguration of some eschatological programme, the context seems to suggest that the focus is on an activity of God. Mark introduces his Gospel with reference to prophetic announcements that God is about to act (Isa. 40.3 and Mal. 3.1, although Mark understands the citation as Isaianic). Verses 1-13 are concerned with preparation for God's activity: the language of fulfilment in v. 15 recalls this emphasis on preparation and readiness. In Isaiah it is preparation for the coming salvific rule of God which is announced, and this is worked out in God's action of bringing the exiled Israelites out of Babylon. Here in Mark it is also preparation for the rule of God, but at this stage we have only an announcement, it is not clear what the content of God's activity will be. However, as Mark's first chapter continues it becomes clear that Jesus is not merely a messenger of God's activity, but is in some sense a major actor in this Kingdom, teaching in a novel way (vv. 21, 22) and performing miraculous deeds (vv. 23-27) causing a stir (v. 28). The remainder of the Gospel gives further content to this activity of God's rule, both in terms of the remarkable actions and teaching of Jesus, and in specific references to the Kingdom which give more depth to this focus of Jesus' concern.

It is interesting that as one reads on in Mark the question arises as to whether it is possible, and indeed necessary, to find a unifying theme to the Kingdom sayings, or whether the Kingdom of God is a much more flexible concept than has sometimes been assumed.

Mark has few parables in which the Kingdom is compared to some fictional narrative. However, in 4.26, and 30 there are the parables of the seed and the mustard seed, introduced in terms of the Kingdom. In both parables the emphasis seems to be on the movement from small beginnings to the grand conclusion. The image is of a radical transformation, and might be seen as a movement from low expectations to an impressive fulfilment. These parables would fit best with the understanding of the Kingdom which seems to be implied at 1.15, i.e. God's activity is something which moves from small beginnings to grand conclusions.

At several points the spatial metaphor of 'entering' is used (9.47; 10.23, 24, 25), and this clearly raises the question of the unity of the Kingdom concept, for the emphasis seems to have shifted from the Kingdom as God's activity of ruling, to the metaphor of the Kingdom as a place. In 9.47, 'entering the Kingdom' is used in parallel with 'entering life' and in opposition to 'going into' or 'being cast into hell'. The whole section is difficult to use as evidence for Jesus' Kingdom concept because of the exaggerated imagery, but the main concern of the section seems to be with right behaviour. The opposition is between the Kingdom (or life) and Hell: to enter God's Kingdom is to win his favour, and this is not an eschatological concept, at least not in the sense of God's decisive intervention in history. In ch. 10 there is the possibility that 'entering the Kingdom' should be seen in parallel with 'inheriting eternal life' (v. 17), and perhaps also 'having treasure in heaven' (v. 21); however, it may be that Jesus is keen to distinguish these terms. The whole section focuses on the apparent incompatibility of wealth and entry into the Kingdom, and v. 27 stresses the opposition between God and man. However, the following verses (28-31) shows that the opposition is not simple, for those who have lived sacrificially for Jesus' sake are on God's side.

The spatial metaphor is continued in 14.25, where Jesus speaks of 'drinking wine in the Kingdom' (apparently a reference to the period after his death), and in 12.34, where one of the scribes, who is in agreement with Jesus' understanding of the tradition, is described as 'not far from the Kingdom'. However, in 15.43 another Jewish leader, Joseph of Arimathea, who is also presented as a sympathetic figure is described with the temporal metaphor of 'waiting for the Kingdom'. Again in 10.14, 15 the Kingdom is spoken of with metaphors of possession: the Kingdom can belong to someone, and it is something which can be received. The point being made here has to do with the importance of modelling behaviour on that of a child. In Lk. 18.15-17 the context emphasizes the importance of humility, while in Mt. 18.1-4 this is made explicit in a similar saying comparing the attitude of a child and the requirement for Kingdom entry. In all these sayings involving spatial metaphors and metaphors of possession, the emphasis seems to be on how human beings receive God's approval: temporal questions are here of secondary importance.[18]

Thus far, the Kingdom may be described as an activity of God's ruling; a place to be entered, in which to drink wine, or to be considered near; something to wait for; something to be possessed through receiving or belonging.

The saying at 9.1 has been much discussed,[19] but in the context of Mark the reference seems to be to what took place on the mountain. In what precise sense this can be described as an experience of 'seeing the kingdom of God after it has come with power' is not clear, although what happened on the mountain was certainly perceived to be an unusual experience of God's activity.

The final reference in Mark is at 4.11, where Jesus speaks of the disciples having been given 'the mystery of the Kingdom of God'. Whatever this special insight is, it does not help the disciples a great deal, for they are soon found wanting in regard to understanding (v. 13) and faith (v. 40). This parallels the dubious value of the special insight in Mark's 'Little Apocalypse' in ch. 13, for the elaborate detail given is immediately taken away in vv. 32, 33, 35.

Mark's Kingdom language is difficult to fit into the common eschatological view of the concept. There are few references to the Kingdom, as there is also little teaching material recorded. The so-called 'Little Apocalypse' certainly suggests future events of national (catastrophe) and personal (judgment) significance. However, the time of these events is not known: they are neither imminent nor far off. Temporal issues do not determine the nature of the Kingdom teaching (cf. e.g. 10.17f.). Neither does the expectation of future events seem to be the most decisive factor in Mark's overall presentation of the content of Jesus' ministry.

The Kingdom in Luke[20]

Luke has thirty-two explicit references to 'the Kingdom of God' in his Gospel, three which omit 'of God', and four which refer to Jesus' Kingdom.[21]

His first use of the phrase in 4.43 is quite significant, for unlike Matthew or Mark he does not record an initial announcement of the Kingdom's nearness, but implies that what Jesus has done at Nazareth and Capernaum was preaching (εὐαγγελίζασθαι) the Kingdom, and this is what he will go on to do in the other cities. At Nazareth, Jesus read from Isa. 61.1, 2 and spoke of the Scripture being fulfilled as he read. Here, apparently, the Kingdom involves the announcement of good news to the poor, release to the captives, recovery of sight to the blind, freedom for the downtrodden, and the proclamation of the year of the Lord's favour. This picks up themes which stand out most clearly in Luke's presentation of Jesus' ministry. In Capernaum Jesus also teaches, but the emphasis in Luke's narrative is on his activity of exorcism (vv. 33-36, 41) and healing (vv. 38-40). In this early reference to the Kingdom in Luke the main emphasis is on help for the disadvantaged.

The Kingdom is also 'proclaimed' and 'preached' in the summary at 8.1 (κηρύσσων—εὐαγγελιζόμενος), in the commission at 9.2 (κηρύσσειν), and the command at 9.60 (διάγγελλε) while in 9.11 Jesus is reported as 'speaking about the Kingdom'.

The theme of help for the disadvantaged is further developed in Luke's beatitude concerning the poor (6.20), where the metaphor of possession is used. As with Mark, a similar metaphor is used of the Kingdom in 18.16—'the Kingdom belongs to such as these', and in v. 17 'whoever does not receive the Kingdom'; the latter involves an injunction to childlike behaviour, while in the former case it is not clear what the connection is between access to Jesus and possessing the Kingdom. The Kingdom is spoken of as something given in 12.32, where the context concerns God's care for the disciples in the face of life's anxieties and the demands of discipleship.

The use of spatial metaphors is quite widespread. A number of instances involve eating and drinking in the Kingdom; see 13.28, 29; 14.15; 22.16. In 16.16 the difficult saying about forced entry involves a spatial metaphor. Mark's entry sayings are paralleled at 18.17, 24, 25. It seems most likely that the use of ἤγγικεν at 10.9, 11 involves spatial nearness rather than the temporal sense. At Lk. 21.31, however, the use of ἐγγύς seems to suggest a temporal nearness. Again at 17.21 the Kingdom is spoken of in a spatial sense as 'in your midst', but the context (the Pharisees' question) concerns the time of the Kingdom. In 23.51 Joseph is described as 'waiting for the Kingdom', while in 12.31 the Kingdom is something which can be sought. The variety of such spatial metaphors makes it difficult to see the phrase 'Kingdom of God' as evoking a transcendent and final act of God.

At 18.29 the disciples' behaviour is described as being 'for the sake of the Kingdom', while at 9.62 certain behaviour is not considered 'fit for the Kingdom'. In 19.11 there is an expectation that the Kingdom will 'appear immediately': this is Luke's narrative comment on the attitude of the crowd. As in Mk 9.1, Luke records a saying about 'seeing the Kingdom' in the context of the Transfiguration. In 8.10 the disciples are able to know 'the mysteries of the Kingdom'. The parables of the mustard seed and the leaven (13.18, 20) are offered as similes for the Kingdom. Finally, there is talk of the Kingdom's 'coming', at 22.18, 17.20, and in the Lord's prayer at 11.2.

Again, in Luke, Jesus' language about the Kingdom does not seem to evoke a coherent ideology of the eschaton. Perhaps more than the other Gospels, Luke's use of Kingdom language is many-sided (cf. 12.31; 21.31). By this we mean that it seems to speak of God's nature and activity, and their implications, conceived of in quite broad terms. Luke also seems to go farthest in developing Jesus' distinctive view of God and its bearings on human relationships and behaviour.

The Kingdom in Matthew[22]

Matthew uses the phrase 'Kingdom of Heaven' thirty-three times, and 'Kingdom of God' four times, he also has a number of other relevant phrases: 'Gospel of the Kingdom' (4.23; 9.35; 24.14); 'his Kingdom', referring to God (6.33), and to the Son of Man (13.41); 'your Kingdom', referring to God (6.10, 13); 'your Kingdom', referring to Jesus (20.21); 'the Kingdom' (13.19; 21.31); 'Kingdom of my Father', Jesus speaking of God (26.29); 'the Son of Man coming in his Kingdom' (16.28); 'Kingdom of their Father' (14.43); 'Kingdom prepared for you' (25.34); 'sons of the Kingdom' (8.12; 13.38). There are also five other uses of the term Kingdom (4.8; 12.25, 26, 28; 24.7).

Spatial metaphors are used relatively frequently in Matthew: thus he speaks of 'entering the Kingdom' at 5.20, 7.21 (in the context of practising righteousness and doing the Father's will), 18.3, and 19.23, 24; of 'reclining in the Kingdom' at 8.11; of 'drinking in the Kingdom' at 26.29; of 'preceding into the Kingdom' at 21.31; the phrase 'in the Kingdom' is used in connection with status at 20.21, 5.19, 11.11, 18.1, 4, and of the position of the righteous at 13.43; we might also mention reference to the 'keys of the Kingdom' at 16.19, and also the phrase 'gather out of his Kingdom' at 13.41, and the description of the scribes and Pharisees as those who 'shut off the kingdom' 23.13. Many of these examples are used to influence behaviour with little indication of an eschatological basis. Some seem to speak of the Kingdom as the experience of God's blessing in some form of existence after death. In an important article on 'Apocalyptic Eschatology as the Transcendence of Death',[23] J.J. Collins argues, among other things, that Jewish apocalyptic literature is not characterized by a future expectation of a 'definitive End' or a distinction between two ages requiring the destruction of the world in between. Instead, he sees a concern with heavenly, supernatural realities providing the possibility that human life can transcend death:

> It is this hope for the transcendence of death which is the distinctive character of apocalyptic over against prophecy (p. 68).

Collins rejects the idea of apocalyptic being distinguished by an ideology of the eschaton as the End of the present world order. His view of apocalyptic's future expectation has similarities to some of the emphasis in Jesus' teaching on the Kingdom in Matthew and the other Synoptics. Such an understanding of apocalyptic 'eschatology' removes many of the problems of compatibility with wisdom and ethical material in Jesus' speech. However, it would be wrong to reduce Jesus' idea of the Kingdom to the 'transcendence of death', or to imagine that such a reformulation of the issue solves all the problematic Gospel texts. Collins' work does offer the possibility of some continuity between apocalyptic concerns and an aspect of Jesus' teaching on the Kingdom of God—this is perhaps the main point of interest for those concerned to compare Jesus' speech and Jewish apocalyptic texts.

Metaphors of possession are also used in Matthew's Kingdom sayings: the righteous will 'inherit the Kingdom' 25.34; the Kingdom can be 'taken away' 21.43; the Kingdom 'belongs to' those like children 19.14; for the poor in spirit and the persecuted righteous 'theirs is the Kingdom' 5.3, 10.

Matthew has the largest number of parables of the Kingdom: the wheat and the tares 13.24, the mustard seed 13.31, leaven 13.33, hidden treasure 13.44, the costly pearl 13.45, the dragnet 13.47, the

King settling accounts 18.23, the labourers in the vineyard 20.1, the wedding feast 22.2, the ten virgins 25.1. Again, the parables do not present a single view of the Kingdom as evoking an eschatological act of God. Unless one follows the approach typified by Pamment, whereby one's core understanding of the Kingdom, as a unified whole, is used to interpret each of the difficult references. Thus:

> Those scholars who have argued that the first evangelist understands the kingdom of heaven as a present as well as a future reality have cited the parable of the mustard seed, 13.31f, and that of the leaven, 13.33 in support of their view. These simple parables, taken out of context, lend themselves to a variety of interpretations. This makes it all the more necessary to interpret them in context. In 13.31f, the sowing of the seed must refer once more to the preaching of the kingdom's imminence ... The parable of the leaven, 13.33 .... The key to the parable's meaning is the word ἐνέκρυψεν. The imminence of the kingdom is a μυστήριον, 13.11. Most people do not recognize the truth of the preaching. The reality of the imminence of the kingdom is hidden from them as leaven is hidden in meal (pp. 219-20).

We would prefer to allow the variety of the parables to remain, thus, the different emphases include the judgment, the nature of God's activity (small beginnings, hiddenness), the absolute claim of God on a person's life, forgiveness, God's graciousness and the reversal of value that involves, and the wisdom of foresight and being prepared for God's activity.

Matthew speaks of the 'gospel of the Kingdom' at 4.23 and 9.35 in narrative summaries in connection with teaching and healing. At 24.14 the context is the proclamation of the gospel, presumably by the disciples, to the whole world before the end comes. In the context of the parable of the sower we find the expression 'hearing the word of the Kingdom' (13.19).

Matthew also uses the verb ἐγγίζω to describe the Kingdom's nearness at 4.17 and 10.7, and the context has usually been thought to suggest temporal nearness, but there may be intentional ambiguity, involving a spatial metaphor as well (cf. 21.1; 26.46). The temporal note is also sounded at 6.10, but the context suggests that the coming of the Kingdom is connected to the doing of God's will (the theocentric vision expressed in the opposition between 'earth' and 'heaven' determines behaviour). Matthew differs from Luke and Mark in the saying which precedes the Transfiguration story (16.28), for here it is 'the Son of Man coming in his Kingdom'.

Various people are described in their relation to the Kingdom, thus 'sons of the Kingdom' in 13.38 are seen in a good light in opposition to 'the sons of the evil one'; however, in 8.12 the 'sons of the Kingdom' are seen in a negative light as those who will be cast out from the Kingdom of Heaven. At 13.52 we read of scribes who have 'become disciples of the Kingdom', while at 19.12 Matthew speaks of those who have made themselves 'eunuchs for the sake of the Kingdom'.

As with Luke, Matthew speaks of the 'mysteries of the Kingdom' at 13.11.[24]

Matthew uses the unique expression 'the kingdom of Heaven suffers violence' at 11.12, to describe the recent history of the Kingdom.

Again, the idea of the Kingdom is complex, and involves a number of different emphases which are sometimes difficult to reconcile. In Matthew's Gospel, the theme of judgment is quite prominent, and this has left its mark on the Kingdom language. There is also an emphasis on hiddenness, especially ch. 13. In general, temporal issues are probably more prominent in Matthew's Gospel than in Mark and Luke, but there is no straightforward pattern of temporal concerns linked to the Kingdom language, and there are many other strands to Matthew's presentation of Jesus which prevent us from making these wholly determinative.

Conclusions

We wish now to draw together some of the insights that this analysis has generated.

First, because the background to Jesus' Kingdom language has been Jewish apocalyptic literature the temporal question has dominated.[25] It is obvious that if one poses such a question then every text can be squeezed into one or other of the temporal categories, but that is not to say that it is the most important issue in Jesus' Kingdom preaching. We would suggest that none of the Gospels presents a coherent ideology of the Kingdom of God as God's final and eschatological act. There are obviously themes of judgment, death, and the eschaton, but these are not unambiguous, particularly in their relationship to one another, and do not dominate reference to the Kingdom. The idea of the Kingdom as concerning blessing or judgment after death often seems more appropriate to the material than the idea of the eschaton as a decisive disruption in history or the end of the world.

Alongside the problem of the dominance of temporal questions is the use of the term transcendent to describe the Kingdom. The idea of transcendence is invoked to counter the suggestion that the Kingdom is in any sense a human achievement: instead it is claimed that the Kingdom is God's work alone. However, the use of the term transcendence is somewhat confusing,[26] for in theological studies it is most often used in opposition to immanence, to stress the otherness and separateness of God from his creation. In regard to the Kingdom in the Synoptics this entirely misses the point for the Kingdom of God is surely about God's closeness and involvement in human affairs. It is also questionable whether the emphasis on the Kingdom as an act of *God* is really faithful to the picture presented in the Synoptics. It is obviously the case that the Kingdom is strictly speaking God's rule, but in much of Jesus' teaching about the Kingdom the emphasis is on human activity. We would prefer to describe the Kingdom as theocentric.

Third, we would question whether it is helpful to think of the Kingdom as one specific entity, or whether it is much more many-sided than generally imagined.

Perrin has suggested that we should not think of the Kingdom as a concept but as a symbol evoking a myth.[27] Drawing on the work of Wheelwright and Ricoeur he distinguishes between steno- and tensive symbols, claiming that the Kingdom should be considered the latter. A steno-symbol has a one-to-one relationship with what it represents, while a tensive symbol has a set of meanings that can neither be exhausted nor adequately expressed by any one referent. This is quite a helpful distinction, and a great improvement on Perrin's earlier work, but one wonders whether Perrin's use of ideas about symbol and myth is not merely another attempt to bring in the History of Religions background which can determine our understanding of Jesus' language. When Perrin talks of the myth evoked by the symbol that in itself introduces the problems of historical background and hearers' expectations which we have already discussed. It tends to move the focus of interest from the actual content of the reported speech to some hypothetically reconstructed myth which would have come to the minds of Jesus' hearers or the Gospel readers. However, Perrin's work does open the way to a more flexible idea of the Kingdom.

Should we look for some unifying idea or statement that can hold together the diversity of language observed, or should we be content to explore the diversity of the language used, allowing the context of each utterance to determine meaning, without attempting a synthesis? We have discussed the methodological issues involved in studying Jesus' speech, particularly with reference to the problem of how to construe the argument about coherence, and also the question of the relationship between the whole and the parts. At this point, the traditional historical-critical way forward would be to argue for different streams of tradition within each individual Gospel. Thus we might seek to highlight material peculiar to an Evangelist, and from that reconstruct his particular emphasis; and then posit other stages in the tradition (perhaps based on source analysis) with their emphases; and finally make some comments about which aspects of the material might represent Jesus' message. Such a procedure is fraught with difficulties. It is not necessarily the case that the earliest stages of tradition are closest to historical accuracy, nor that later stages, which have been amended the most, are necessarily of less value as historical evidence. The question of understanding an Evangelist's point of view is not necessarily helped by distinguishing 'tradition' and 'redaction' for, as we have already noted, the greater significance might lie in the use of traditional material. It is also a problem knowing whether to proceed on the assumption that an Evangelist held, for example, a coherent or unified view of the Kingdom, or whether his view was, strictly speaking, incoherent or merely more diverse.

We are most interested in reading the Synoptics as integrated, though not necessarily unified, narrative accounts of Jesus. That is to say that the appeal to earlier stages of tradition should not be made to explain problematic texts, but neither should we necessarily expect to find a unified or coherent ideology in the narrative. The same would be true if we had access to Jesus' actual words, or any other stage in the tradition: it may be mistaken to assume a fully unified use of Kingdom language.

We now offer some constructive points about the presentation of Jesus' message about the Kingdom and the significance of the proverbial wisdom material.

b. *Kingdom Language and Apocalyptic Imagery*

Even if we reject the idea of a significant apocalyptic background to Jesus' Kingdom concept, and the need to understand his message and impact in an eschatological context, that does not mean that we would deny the presence of apocalyptic/eschatological imagery in the Synoptics. However, the question should be raised as to how such imagery would have been understood in the first century. How literally did early Judaism, early Christianity, or Jesus take their own metaphors? One of the few critics to take seriously this issue is A.N. Wilder, who has written extensively on the language of early Christianity, particularly the issue of apocalyptic/eschatological imagery.[28] In an essay on 'Eschatological Imagery and Earthly Circumstance' he poses the following questions:

> Did the writer mean his words to be taken literally—including references to immediate fulfilment? . . . Are we to take the figurative discourse as a 'clothing' of otherwise incommunicable revelation or vision? Is the cosmic language supposed to refer to 'spiritual', that is super-mundane realities; or to such realities seen as paralleling earthly phenomena; or is it rather an imaginative version of the earthly phenomena themselves? At what points are we to recognize more or less transparent historization of older myth and symbol? Does the eschatological imagery of Deutero-Isaiah represent merely a poetic idealization of a mundane New Age while that of the late apocalypses denotes the absolute end of all created existence? Does this later dualistic eschatology signify in fact the end of the world and a sheerly miraculous future state, or does it teach by hyperbole the transformation of the world? (p. 229).

Wilder goes on to explore the relationship between eschatological language and its social setting.

This is a point taken up by Borg[29] in his efforts to trace Jesus' involvement in the political and religious destiny of his people. Thus he notes that the question of the threat of historical destruction for Israel is usually subordinated to the expectation of the end of the world. However, rather than subordinate everything to the imminent end theme, which he argues has a very small exegetical base,[30] Borg wants to start from the fixed point of Jesus' unambiguous threat of the end of Israel. If Jesus threatened the imminent destruction of Israel what language and imagery would be capable of conveying such a catastrophic message:

> The religious loyalties of any first-century Jew suggest that only the imagery of cosmic disorder and Weltgericht would have been adequate to speak of the destruction of Israel (p. 216).

Borg's work is just one example of how Synoptic imagery can be taken seriously in a non-literalistic way.[31]

The question of how we read apocalyptic imagery in the Synoptics is important and problematic, and requires further investigation, but even if we wish to take such language literally, we find that there is much language about the Kingdom which does not involve such imagery. Indeed, it might be appropriate to start by separating the questions of Jesus' Kingdom idea(s), and instances of apocalyptic language and eschatology. Having gained a preliminary view of the Kingdom, we might then be in a better position to judge its relation to other themes in the reported speech of Jesus.

c. *Theology vs. Eschatology*

Some New Testament critics have begun again to question whether the centre of Jesus' message should not be seen in terms of theology, with the eschatology derived from Jesus' view of God. Thus, in his essay 'Eschatological or Theocentric Ethics?'[32] Hans Bald reviews the debate between Schürmann and Vögtle[33] on the relationship between eschatology and theology in the message of Jesus, and he also mentions the work of critics such as Windisch,[34] Conzelmann,[35] and Goppelt,[36] who have stressed the central importance of Jesus' conception of God. Interestingly, in his introduction to Schweitzer's *The Mystery of the Kingdom of God*[37] W. Lowrie asserts the theological basis for Jesus' eschatology:

> 'Thoroughgoing eschatology' is surely not incompatible with the recognition of a deeper intuition in Jesus which is necessary to explain the intensity of this very eschatology itself. It would be a rigorous extreme indeed which would exclude the recognition of Jesus' God-consciousness—his consciousness of God as Father—as the primary and all-controlling fact of his religious experience (p. 40).

Unfortunately, the legacy of Schweitzer in New Testament studies has been the tendency to see eschatology rather than theology as all-controlling.

Perhaps the best treatment of the relationship between ethics, eschatology and theology can be found in A.N. Wilder's *Eschatology and Ethics in the Teaching of Jesus*. Although Wilder does not want to deny the presence of eschatological material, he does want to argue that much of Jesus' teaching and ethics is not eschatologically determined. The ethics ignore an imminent catastrophe, and find their true sanction for Wilder in the fact of God, his nature and his will for people. It is the new apprehension of God and his will which compels a new ethics.[38]

Another factor in the exclusion of theology from characterizations of Jesus' message is the common claim that 'Scholars are generally agreed that Jesus introduces no new concept of God'.[39] It is obviously the case that Jesus was concerned with Yahweh, the God of Israel, and this goes some way to explaining his heated disputes with other religious leaders. Jesus, the scribes, and the Pharisees shared a belief in the same God, and a desire to live faithfully before him: what was disputed was the question of what this God was like, and consequently how this would effect human behaviour and relationships. How one conceived the nature of God would effect how one behaved and expected others to behave. In view of the situation in which Israel found herself, the Jewish leaders depicted in the Gospels, probably consciously and unconsciously, emphasized certain aspects of their shared traditions about God, while Jesus emphasized others. Thus, Jesus did not introduce a new God, but it would be strange to deny that he had anything new to say about the nature of God, even if it were only a change in emphasis; and that is surely the ultimate basis of his disagreements with his contemporaries.

For our purposes, we do not need, nor are we able, to answer every question about Jesus' expectation of future events. The evidence in the Synoptics is often ambiguous and complicated, and is open to many interpretations. We can, however, say with certainty that in some of Jesus' language about the Kingdom, and in other aspects of his speech and activity, the emphasis is on the centrality of God (theocentric), on reforming people's view of God (often in opposition to other views apparently current at the time), and on how this affects human relationships (proverbial wisdom) and should affect people's behaviour (ethics and proverbial wisdom).

An example of this theocentric emphasis can be seen in the common theme of opposition between the things of God and the things of men. We have already seen this opposition in our study of the structure of the proverbial saying. Thus, Lk. 16.15b expresses the idea clearly: 'that which is highly esteemed among men is detestable in the sight of God'. This saying comes in the context of Jesus' critique of those who put wealth before God. A similar instance would be Matthew's opposition between 'heaven' and 'earth' in his teaching on wealth (6.19, 21). In Mark the opposition can be seen in the incident with the Pharisees in chapter 7, and particularly the proverbial type saying at v. 8: 'neglecting the commandment of God, you hold to the tradition of men'.

The opposition between God and man is also fundamental to the structure of many of the proverbial sayings which oppose positive and negative moral status, or group affiliation (cf. Chapter 2 above).

This opposition of God and man should not be misunderstood. It is not a question of a transcendent God in opposition to a sinful world: rather it should be seen in terms of whether God is acknowledged and taken account of, or whether God is effectively ignored and absent from human affairs. To be on God's side is to act rightly (e.g. in Luke 16 not loving money) or to be in one of the privileged groups (e.g. in the status sayings, the humble are opposed to the exalted). Thus, the impact of Jesus' view of God is worked out in human terms, and this often takes the form of a proverbial wisdom comment (or parable) which may merely describe the new state of affairs which Jesus sees, or may have the pragmatic force of suggesting a certain form of action. We cannot, nor would we wish to, explain all the proverbial sayings in this way: some will have a less significant role in Jesus' speech. However, it is thought that a theological or theocentric focus does more justice to the wisdom nature of much of Jesus' speech, and also to other elements which are either ignored or transformed by the desire for consistency in his message.

Since the work of Dodd and Jeremias, the parables have been forced into an eschatological mould, but many resist such an interpretation, and are better seen as examples of teaching which gives more content to Jesus' idea of God and his Kingdom, and content to the nature of the impact of these ideas on human relationships and behaviour. The parable of the labourers in the vineyard in Mt. 20.1-16 can be seen essentially as teaching about the nature of God, while the concluding proverbial saying opens up the implications of this view of God in the field of human relationships and behaviour. Traditional views of status are challenged on the basis of God's values and behaviour. This draws us into the question of the significance of Jesus' activity.

d. *The Activity of Jesus*

One of our criticisms of the dominant line of research on proverbial wisdom (Bultmann, Beardslee, Crossan, Perrin and others) was that the emphasis on the purely rhetorical role of intensified wisdom (based on a particular view of Jesus' Kingdom proclamation) failed to connect Jesus' message with his activity. It is surely the case that Jesus' Kingdom preaching is to be seen in connection with his activity of healing, exorcizing, table fellowship with the marginalized, etc. There is also often a clear connection between Jesus' wisdom sayings and his activity.

Beardslee's question whether the 'jolt' brought about by Jesus' attack on conventional wisdom also led to a 're-entry' into the sphere of human responsibility, becomes rather strange when we take into account the things which Jesus is reported to have done (e.g. Mt. 4.23; 9.10; Mk 1.39; 2.15; Lk. 4.40; 5.29), and to have commanded his disciples to do (e.g. Mt. 10; Mk 6; Lk. 9; 10). Jesus' understanding of God and his Kingdom had implications for his own behaviour, and that of his followers; implications which brought him into conflict with other Jewish religious figures, who disagreed with him. And, as we noted earlier, any 'jolt' brought about by Jesus often seems to have been at the level of his activity, with his speech reinforcing the idea to be derived from his behaviour. This perception takes the emphasis away from the narrowly conceived rhetorical effect of proverbial wisdom.

An understanding of Jesus' concern for the Kingdom of God divorced from his activity will always be deficient.[40] It seems quite plausible that the things Jesus did were elucidated by what he said, and vice versa. Thus the sayings about status reversal, the parables on the same subject (e.g. Lk. 14.7-14, 16-24; Mt. 20.1-16), and Jesus' explicit teaching (e.g. Mk 2.15-17; Mt. 9.10-13; Lk. 5.29-32), all help to explain and confirm Jesus' action of eating and befriending the marginalized (tax-gatherers, sinners, women). This serves to fill out Jesus' view of God, and show how the emphasis and implications are different from other streams of Judaism. Practical action and wisdom teaching are important ways in which Jesus' experience and view of God are explicated: there is no claim to uniqueness here. Jesus operated as many other religious figures have done and still do.

The importance of stressing the activity of Jesus is that it gives content to Jesus' view of God: both in terms of what God is doing and will do (through the agency of Jesus), and in terms of what God requires in the behaviour of his people (through the example of Jesus).

e. *On not seeking a neat fit*

One of the main aspects of Jesus' Kingdom proclamation was his concern to bring before the Jewish people a fresh vision of the nature of God, his promises to them, and his demands upon them, both individually and corporately. There is also undoubtedly a strong sense of urgency which takes several forms, and seems to have several motivating forces behind it. This would include the fate of the Jewish people (as emphasized recently by Borg), and also the ultimate destiny of people, again both individually and corporately. It would seem impossible, from the evidence of the Synoptics, to sort out the precise nature of Jesus' belief about future events. It may be that he taught no single, consistent view. He certainly is reported as having, at times, made claims about future acts of God, but it is questionable whether these were determinative of his whole message and activity, or the main content of his concern with God's Kingdom.

It may well be that, at times, aspects of the reported teaching of Jesus are strictly irreconcilable. However, we would suggest that there is much material, both speech and activity, which is not conditioned by, for example, belief in the imminent eschaton, but is rather concerned to place Jesus' view of God at the centre of things, with everything which that implies for human beings, and it is in this respect that Jesus' proverbial wisdom draws its significance.

Our comments on 'Rethinking the Kingdom' have been brief, and many problems remain. However, we have been concerned to show that the Kingdom of God is a more 'slippery' phenomenon than is sometimes supposed—both in each of the Synoptics, and most likely in the speech of Jesus himself. We would not deny that in each Synoptic Gospel Jesus is reported as, at times, speculating about future events of great seriousness. The idea of the eschaton as the single most important aspect of Jesus' message and activity, determining the nature of all other material, cannot, however, be easily substantiated from the Gospels: it is particularly difficult to see this scenario as 'the meaning' of the phrase 'Kingdom of God' on the lips of the character Jesus, or in the minds of his hearers or readers of the Gospels. Among other factors to be considered, there is more theological content to Jesus' message, and this also influences his activity. Jesus' idea of God, and the implications of it in human affairs are important: it can be seen to have affected his behaviour, and to have been at the basis of much of his teaching. Whether or not it is possible to go on to solve the problems of the relationships between the different parts of Jesus' message and ministry, at the level of each Synoptic Gospel, or at the level of the historical Jesus; a recognition of the importance of his idea of God helps to give a healthier perspective on many issues. It may not be so exciting to some theologians, but it surely does greater justice to the many parts of the Synoptic tradition. It is on the basis of our attempt to balance eschatology with theology that we can take seriously the proverbial wisdom material.

3. *Jesus and the Wisdom of the Kingdom*

Many of the sayings attributed to Jesus within the Synoptics are simply uncontroversial. They show Jesus as standing within a tradition of wisdom piety, which few of his contemporaries would have found objectionable. Of course, there are several themes of traditional wisdom absent from Jesus' teaching,[41] but the degree of similarity should not be underestimated.[42] It needs saying again and again that Jesus is presented as standing in continuity with many religious ideas current in the different forms of Judaism in first-century Palestine. He shared a concern for the Jewish people, a respect for their traditions, a belief in the same God, and many ideas about character, personal behaviour, and the activity of God. There seems no reason to suppose that this aspect of the Synoptic portraits of Jesus does not include a good deal that is historically accurate.

In a general way we could say that the significance of the proverbial material is that it shows Jesus' proclamation of the Kingdom to have been concerned with the old as well as the new. Jesus drew on the wisdom of the past: his innovation was probably most apparent in a change of emphasis, particularly in his practice, which was the source of much conflict (especially his fellowship with the marginalized[43] and his 'attack' on the Temple).[44]

The content of Jesus wisdom includes several traditional themes such as the handling of wealth (Mt. 6.19-21, 24; 19.24; Mk 10.25; Lk. 12.15, 23, 34; 16.13; 18.25; also Mt. 11.8; Lk. 7.25), good character, expressed in various ways (Mt. 6.22-23; 7.2, 16-20; 12.33-37; 15.11; Mk 4.24; 7.15, 20; Lk. 6.38, 43-45; 11.33-36), status, with humility as the wise course (Mt. 18.3; 19.30; 20.26, 27; 23.11, 12; Mk 9.35; 10.15, 31, 43-44; Lk. 9.48; 14.11; 18.14, 17. Also Mt. 10.24-25; Lk. 6.40; 17.33, Mk 8.35). As we have noted, these sayings (and others) can be seen as filling out Jesus' idea of God, and developing the implications of that idea in the area of human responsibilities. Some sayings have the force of challenging to a particular course of action (cf. Chapter 5), while others affirm, or serve to support and explain Jesus' actions, whether explicitly (e.g. Mt. 9.12 and parallels) or implicitly (e.g. Mt. 23.11-12).

Whatever else Jesus' concern with the Kingdom of God may have meant, it certainly included emphasizing the fact that, for him, God is closely involved in human affairs. Jesus' wisdom describes God's actions and involvement, and suggests the way of the wise person who wishes to live faithfully before God, and receive his blessing (now, in the future, at death, at the judgment, at the eschaton?). Sometimes this is placed in the context of crisis, and this may be in national or political terms, in terms of individual destiny (i.e. death or judgment), or in terms of an eschaton; at other points the element of crisis is not present. To elevate the element of eschatological crisis above the other aspects would certainly produce a more consistent Jesus, but there is little evidence that such a Jesus ever lived, and he is only to be found by reading between the lines of the three Synoptic Gospels.

NOTES

Notes to Chapter 1

1. G.T. Sheppard, *Wisdom as a Hermeneutical Construct: A Study in the Sapientializing of the Old Testament* (Berlin: de Gruyter, 1980), p. 2.

2. J. Fichtner, 'Jesaja unter den Weisen', *ThLZ* 74 (1949), ET 'Isaiah among the Wise', *Studies in Ancient Israelite Wisdom*, ed. J.L. Crenshaw (New York: Ktav, 1976), pp. 429-38.

3. G. von Rad, 'The Joseph Narrative and Ancient Wisdom', *The Problem of the Hexateuch and Other Essays* (London: Oliver E. Boyd, 1965), pp. 281-300.

4. See for example, L. Alonso Schökel, 'Motivos sapienciales y de alianza en Gen 2-3', *Bib* 43 (1962), pp. 295-316, ET 'Sapiential and Covenant Themes in Genesis 2-3', in J.L. Crenshaw (1976), pp. 468-80; M. Weinfeld, 'The Origin of Humanism in Deuteronomy', *JBL* 80 (1961), pp. 241-47; R.N. Whybray, *The Succession Narrative* (1968); S. Talmon, 'Wisdom in the Book of Esther', *VT* 13 (1963), pp. 419-55; R.E. Murphy, 'A Consideration of the Classification Wisdom Psalms', *VT Supp* 9 (1962), pp. 156-67; J. Lindblom, 'Wisdom in the Old Testament Prophets', *VT Supp* 3 (1960), pp. 192-204; J.W. Whedbee, *Isaiah and Wisdom* (Nashville: Abingdon, 1971); S. Terrien, 'Amos and Wisdom', *Israel's Prophetic Heritage*, ed. B.W. Anderson and W. Harrelson (1962), pp. 108-15; J.L. Crenshaw, 'The Influence of the Wise upon Amos', *ZAW* 79 (1967), pp. 42-52.

5. McKane (*Prophets and Wise Men* [London: SCM, 1965]) defines wisdom in its earlier manifestations 'as primarily a disciplined empiricism engaged with the problems of government and administration' (p. 53). G.T. Sheppard comments 'few scholars have been convinced that the term can be limited in this manner' (p. 3). Crenshaw, on the other hand, offers such a broad definition of Wisdom as to make it applicable to almost any body of literature: 'Wisdom. . . . may be defined as the quest for self-understanding in terms of relationships with things, people and the Creator' (p. 132) ('Method in Determining Wisdom Influence upon Historical Literature', *JBL* 88 [1969] pp. 129-42). Cf. also Crenshaw (1976), 'Prolegomenon', especially pp. 9-13.

6. D.F. Morgan, *Wisdom in the Old Testament Traditions* (Oxford: Blackwell, 1981): 'The wisdom tradition is responsible for the wisdom literature found in the Old Testament... Therefore literary forms and the social and theological perspectives which have their provenance and occur primarily in this literature should form the foundation for any discussion of the nature, scope, and particular perspectives of the wisdom tradition, (p. 25).

7. R.N. Whybray, *The Intellectual Tradition in the Old Testament* (Berlin: de Gruyter, 1974), p. 155.

8. These are texts which represent the tradition, i.e. derive from it—Job, Proverbs etc., rather than commenting on it, or describing it in a more detached way. We have very little knowledge of the 'wisdom tradition' from other sources.

9. This is not to say that we posit a direct literary relationship between texts, but even if we conceive of a 'tradition' influencing a writer, our knowledge of that 'tradition' is largely gained only from certain representative texts: thus talk of 'influence', when reduced to tangible evidence, remains on the level of a literary claim.

10. Q. Skinner, *Philosophy* 41 (1966), pp. 199-215, quotation from p. 212.

11. J.M. Robinson and H. Koester, *Trajectories through Early Christianity* (Philadelphia: Fortress, 1971), p. 12.

12. Thus the debate about the derivation of 'apocalyptic' from 'wisdom' or 'prophecy' continues, but it is hard to imagine what would constitute a satisfying answer: the categories in which the question is conceived require re-assessing. M. Hengel in *The Charismatic Leader and his Followers* (Edinburgh: T&T Clark, 1981) offers a historical criticism of the use of these categories in the Hellenistic age: 'The entire controversy about the derivation of apocalyptic from prophecy or wisdom is basically an idle one, because—in their opposition to the spirit of the Hellenistic age—both had become inseparably bound up with each other' (p. 48). This is an issue to which we will return in the course of our study.

13. Thus the designation of Jesus as a wise-man requires evidence about the social institution in first-century Palestine, other than the fact that material attributed to him within the Synoptic tradition has affinities with wisdom. Unfortunately, there is little evidence about the social setting of wisdom from outside the tradition itself. Thus D.F. Morgan (1981) concludes his work: 'Throughout this study we have continually noted that the evidence provided by non-wisdom literature which would lead to a clearer picture of the social setting of the wisdom tradition itself has not been present' (p. 141).

14. In a review of Whedbee's 'Isaiah and Wisdom', *Int* 26 (1972), pp. 74-76, Crenshaw comments, 'I am convinced that the task attempted is an impossible one. The assumption of specific wisdom influence upon a prophet

rests on the premise that one knows precisely what makes up both wisdom and prophecy and that each existed in isolation. . . . Given the interplay of disparate traditions in the period of the clan, one should expect to find areas of common concern and vocabulary in prophet, priest and sage (p. 75).

15. W. Brueggemann, *In Man We Trust: The Neglected Side of Biblical Faith* (Richmond: John Knox, 1972), p. 121.

16. J.L. McKenzie, 'Reflections on Wisdom', *JBL* 86 (1967), p. 3.

17. At an earlier period in the history of research Gnostic and Hellenistic backgrounds were argued.

18. Other texts include: *4 Ezra* 5.9; *2 Bar*. 48.36; 11 QPs[a] 18 (David's Compositions).

19. See H. Ringgren, *Word and Wisdom: Studies in the Hypostatization of Divine Qualities and Functions in the Ancient Near East* (Lund: Ohlssons, 1947); R.N. Whybray, *Wisdom in Proverbs* (London: SCM, 1965); B.L. Mack, *Logos und Sophia: Untersuchungen zur Weisheitstheologie im hellenistischen Judentum* (Göttingen: Vandenhoeck and Ruprecht, 1973). Debate often revolves around the origin of the figure of Wisdom, and its relation to similar figures (goddesses, myths) in other cultures. Also the question of the function of the language used of Wisdom is important: is it poetic or mythological, should we speak of a hypostasis, a personification of a divine attribute, or a 'real' figure? For a recent treatment of the subject including a history of interpretation, see C.V. Camp, *Wisdom and the Feminine in the Book of Proverbs* (Sheffield: Almond, 1985).

In New Testament studies see for example F. Christ, *Jesus Sophia: die Sophia-Christologie bei den Synoptikern* (Zürich: Zwingli, 1970), and P. Bonnard, *La Sagesse en personne annoncée et venue: Jésus Christ* (Paris: Les éditions du Cerf, 1966).

20. J.D.G. Dunn, *Christology in the Making: an inquiry into the origins of the doctrine of the incarnation* (London: SCM, 1980), p. 168. Dunn's order is Job, Proverbs, Ben Sira, Wisdom of Solomon, and Philo.

21. H. Gese, 'Wisdom, Son of Man, and the Origins of Christology: The Consistent Development of Biblical Theology', *HBT* 3 (1981), pp. 23-57.

22. Dunn, p. 168. It is unfortunate that Dunn's strong words against the History of Religions approach to the Wisdom figure in the Old Testament do not appear to have informed his treatment of the 'Wisdom Christology' passages in the New Testament. Thus, 'we cannot simply abstract statements and words out of the contexts of for example, an Isis hymn on the one hand and ben Sira on the other, and interpret them as equivalents—one of the mistakes too often made by the History of Religions school. In order to understand what meaning such words and statements had for those who used them, we must interpret them within the context in which they were used' (p. 170).

23. M. Hengel, 'Jesus als Messianischer Lehrer der Weisheit und die Anfänge der Christologie', *Sagesse et Religion: Colloque de Strasbourg, 1976*,

ed. E. Jacob (Paris: Presses Universitaires de France, 1979).

24. Wisdom and Messiah were associated in Jewish literature and would appear to have been a most appropriate way of describing Jesus. However, Hengel argues that in the classic text uniting Messiahship and Wisdom, Isaiah 11.1f, the ideas of judgment and strength are associated, and this tradition has influenced other Messianic texts. These have been suppressed as a source of Messianic teaching relating to Jesus (p. 170), because Wisdom is here overshadowed by a warlike and judicial demonstration of power, which was deemed inappropriate to Jesus whose Messiahship focused rather on texts like Isa. 61.1-3, in which the servant tradition was primary.

25. Hengel is particularly dismissive of the 'History of Religions' approach, represented by Bultmann's idea of a pre-Christian Gnostic Sophia myth: 'Wir wollen im folgenden keine weiteren Früchte vom Baume einer allumfassenden, rein hypothetischen vorchristlichen 'Gnosis' pflücken, zumal diese Früchte der Forschung schlecht bekommen sind, wir werden uns vielmehr auf einige Texte der Evangelien konzentrieren' (p. 149).

26. 'Wisdom Mythology and the Christological Hymns of the New Testament', *Aspects of Wisdom in Judaism and Early Christianity*, ed. R.L. Wilken (Notre Dame: University of Notre Dame Press, 1975), pp. 17-42. For an appropriation of her insights to the issue of Wisdom Christology in 'Q', see J.S. Kloppenborg, 'Wisdom Christology in Q', *Laval Théologique et Philosophique* 34 (1978), pp. 129-47.

The methodological distinction, which Fiorenza exploits, between 'myth' and 'reflective mythology', may be traced back to an essay by H. Conzelmann, 'The Mother of Wisdom', *The Future of our Religious Past*, ed. J.M. Robinson (London: SCM, 1971) and also the work of B.L. Mack (1967) and 'Wisdom Myth and Myth-ology: An Essay in Understanding a Theological Tradition', *Int* 24 (1970), pp. 46-90. Mack wants to move on from the traditional concern with showing parallels between Israel's figure of Wisdom and foreign mythic language, to the question of how and why Israel came to speak of Wisdom in this way. Thus in considering Prov. 1–9 he notes the parallels with Maat and Isis, but concentrates on the points of divergence so as to explore the theological problem(s) at the basis of this material. Mack suggests that at the centre of Prov. 1–9 we find the problem of the exile: the wisdom sermon takes the form of a theodicy, in which the refusal of Israel to listen has become the 'reason' for the exile (1970, p. 57). Mack summarizes the conclusions of his study showing the differences between his concerns and those of the older History of Religions approach in regard to the relationship between Prov. 1–9 and any older mythical material: 'The occasion for these borrowings from this living mythos appears, however, not to have been what ordinarily is understood by the word 'influence', but to have been the existential and reflective needs of the postexilic wisdom schools to bring to expression the new insights and make clear the new affirmations which the burning question of theodicy required of those who wished to understand and confess their religious heritage as the children of Israel in the new situation' (p. 59).

27. Fiorenza's notion of 'reflective mythology' corresponds to Mack's 'myth-ology'.

28. *Ibid.*, p. 18.

29. *Ibid.*, p. 38.

30. *Ibid.*, pp. 27, 28.

31. *Ibid.*, p. 27.

32. In relation to our theme, W.G. Thompson offers a telling comment on Suggs' work along these lines: 'I would wish, however, that S. had balanced his exposition of this background material (i.e. parallels from Jewish Wisdom speculation) with a more careful study of the Matthean sayings in their present context and in relation to the Gospel as a whole' [review of M.J. Suggs, *Wisdom, Christology and Law in Matthew's Gospel* (Cambridge, Mass: Harvard University Press, 1970), in *CBQ* 33 (1971), pp. 145-46].

33. Lk. 7.31-35/Mt. 11.16-19; Lk. 10.21-22/Mt. 11.25-27; Mt. 11.28-30; Lk. 11.49-51/Mt. 23.34-36; Lk. 13.34-35/Mt. 23.37-39; Lk. 11.31/Mt. 12.42; some also include Lk. 9.58/Mt. 8.20; Lk. 14.16-24/Mt. 22.1-14, see especially W. Grundmann, 'Weisheit im Horizont des Reiches Gottes. Eine Studie zur Verkündigung Jesu nach der Spruchüberlieferung Q', *Die Kirche des Anfangs: Festschrift für H. Schürmann*, ed. R. Schnackenburg, J. Ernst & J. Wanke (Leipzig: St-Benno Verlag, 1978), pp. 175-99.

34. Dunn, p. 210. For Suggs, Q is moving in the direction of a Wisdom Christology. Jesus is identified as Wisdom's envoy, but it is not so advanced that Sophia and envoy are identified. S. Schulz (1972) reaches a similar conclusion: 'Der Täufer und der Endzeitprophet Jesus sind die letzten Propheten, die die Sophia in der Geschichte Israels inspiriert und ausgerüstet hat' (p. 386). Also Kloppenborg: 'The appropriation of the mythic language of Wisdom—perhaps suggested by the sapiential motifs of 11.25f and other Q passages—did not as such constitute an identification of Jesus with Sophia, but it allowed the development of an authentic Sophia Christology in later Christian tradition (e.g. John 1.1-18, Col. 1.15)' (p. 147). J.M. Robinson ('Jesus as Sophos and Sophia: Wisdom Tradition and the Gospels', in R.L. Wilken [1975] pp. 1-16): 'Hence Q displays in its wisdom sections a tendency to relativize the uniqueness of Jesus by embedding his pre-eminent message within a long chain of wisdom's spokesmen throughout the Old Testament, and though culminating in John and Jesus, continuing in the Church'.

35. Suggs' thesis is that: 'Wisdom speculation was a major current in Matthew's Christian environment and that Matthew was a lively participant in the current... Matthew used the Wisdom themes in his own way ... Matthew daringly identified Jesus with Wisdom' (p. 130). In his article on this question, which is largely a review of Suggs' thesis, M.D. Johnson offers an alternative exegesis of certain of the key Matthean texts, and interestingly argues that the evidence points to the motif being already

present in Q (Lk. 7.35; 11.49) rather than being a feature of Matthew's concern. However, Johnson is reluctant to speak of an actual 'Wisdom Christology' in Q; the few references could not bear such significance. See M.D. Johnson, 'Reflections on a Wisdom Approach to Matthew's Christology', *CBQ* 36 (1974), pp. 44-64.

36. W.D. Davies, *Paul and Rabbinic Judaism* (London: SPCK, 1979): 'While it is clear that the early Church regarded Jesus as the personified Wisdom of God and that Jesus himself may have regarded himself as speaking in the name of the Holy Wisdom of God, nevertheless, the evidence does not warrant the view that Jesus himself had entertained a Wisdom Christology' (p. 158). See also Dunn, p. 210.

37. In chapter 5, on the rhetoric of the proverb we will offer an account of this passage which does not rely on any possible allusion to other 'Wisdom' texts.

38. Robinson posits an important appropriation of Wisdom speculation in the development of the Son of Man Christology. In Mt. 11.27, there is a combining of Wisdom and Son of Man traditions, whereby the exclusive place of Wisdom is applied to the Son. He quotes with approval S. Schulz, *Die Spruchquelle der Evangelisten* (Zürich: Theologischer Verlag, 1972), pp. 224-25. Up till now Jesus had been seen in Q merely as the most important spokesman of Sophia—but in the last stage the exclusivity of Sophia is attributed to the Son.

39. G. Stanton, 'Matthew 11.28-30, Comfortable Words?' *ET* 94 (1982), p. 6.

40. See the review of the interpretation of this text in H.D. Betz, 'The Logion of the Easy Yoke and of Rest (Matt. 11.28-30)', *JBL* 86 (1967), pp. 10-24. Betz describes the original work of Norden, and its refinements in Weiss, Arvedson, and Bultmann.

41. However, the situation may be more complicated since we have to take account of the context of these verses in Matthew which makes a fairly 'exalted' claim for the speaker (v. 27).

42. R.H. Fuller, 'The Double Commandment of Love: A Test Case for the Criteria of Authenticity', *Essays on the Love Commandment*, ed. L. Schottroff, C. Burchard, M.J. Suggs & R.H. Fuller (Philadelphia: Fortress, 1979), p. 56 n. 23.

43. R.E. Brown, *The Gospel according to John I-XII* (New York: Doubleday, 1966), p. cxxii.

44. C.K. Barrett, *The Gospel according to St John* (London: SPCK, 1978), pp. 153f.; R. Bultmann, 'Der religionsgeschichtliche Hintergrund des Prologs zum Johannes-Evangelium', *Exegetica: Aufsätze zur Erforschung des Neuen Testaments* (Tübingen: Mohr, 1967), pp. 10-35. C. Spicq, 'Le Siriacide et la structure littéraire du Prologue de saint Jean', *Memorial Lagrange* (Paris: Gabalda, 1940), pp. 183-95.

45. P. cxxii. Cf. Prov. 1.20-21; 8.1-4; Wis. 6.16; Jn 1.36-38, 43; 5.14; 9.35;

7.28, 37; 12.44 for Wisdom roaming the streets seeking men and crying out to them. Also in the gathering and teaching of disciples. Some men reject Wisdom—Prov. 1.24-25; Bar. 3.12; *Enoch* 42.2; cf. Jn 8.46; 10.25.

The coming of Wisdom provokes a division: some seek and find (Prov. 8.17; Sira 6.27; Wis. 6.12); others do not seek and when they change their minds, it will be too late (Prov. 1.28). John describes Jesus' effect on men in a similar way (7.34; 8.21; 13.33).

46. P. cxxv. The words of Jesus in Mt. 11.28-30 are often seen to cohere with the Johannine picture of Jesus and Wisdom, hence Feuillet speaks of 'le logion johannique', see A. Feuillet, 'Jésus et la Sagesse divine d'après les évangiles synoptiques', *RB* 62 (1955), pp. 161-96.

47. 1 Cor. 1 and 2; Eph. 2.14-16; Phil. 2.6-11; Col. 1.15-20; 1 Tim. 3.16; also Rom. 10.6, 7; 1 Cor. 10.1-4; 1 Pet. 1.20: 3.18, 22; Heb. 1.1-4. See W.D. Davies, 'The Old and the New Torah: Christ and the Wisdom of God', *Paul and Rabbinic Judaism* (London: SPCK, 1979), pp. 147-76; also M. Hengel (1979); A. Van Roon, 'The Relation between Christ and the Wisdom of God according to St. Paul', *NT* 16 (1974), pp. 207-39.

48. S.L. Davies, *The Gospel of Thomas and Christian Wisdom* (New York: Seabury, 1983), esp. pp. 36-61; G.W. MacRae, 'The Jewish Background of the Gnostic Sophia Myth', *NT* 12 (1970), pp. 86-101.

49. R. Bultmann, *The History of the Synoptic Tradition* (Oxford: Blackwell, 1972), pp. 69f.

50. J.L. McKenzie (1967), p. 2.

51. The New Testament itself provides a large part of our evidence for the social make-up of first century Judaism. The problems associated with using Josephus as evidence will be seen in our consideration of *Ant.* 18.63 and related passages.

52. Evidence is often drawn from later Rabbinic literature, or from the earlier intertestamental literature such as Ben Sira. The use of such material to inform our understanding of the social institutions of first century Palestine is not to be completely rejected, but must proceed cautiously, taking due account of the large periods of time which separate the literature, and also the significant changes in society during this period. It is not always easy to tell how far the literary portrayal of a social type bears much relation to the actual historical and sociological reality.

53. Part of the problem is that we have little comparative literature including narrative accounts of 'teaching', so that it is difficult to make a judgment about the significance of the proverbial material. Should it lead us to assign Jesus a specific social role, or would Jesus have simply been considered 'wise' in a non-technical sense? The Mishnah offers interesting comparative sayings material, often of a proverbial kind (*Pirke Aboth*). It is attributed to individual rabbis, and often makes reference to the sages החכמים. From the perspective of the Mishnah Jesus might have qualified as a rabbi or a sage, but this does not really help us in understanding his social

identity in first century Palestine.

54. Cf. W. McKane (1965); R.N. Whybray (1974), especially pp. 33f.; D.F. Morgan (1981).

55. Cf. the optimistic approach of R. Gordis, 'The Social Background of Wisdom Literature', *Poets, Prophets and Sages: Essays in Biblical Interpretation* (Bloomington: Indiana University Press, 1971), pp. 160-97. Gordis posits two schools of wisdom, pragmatic and speculative, based on the two distinct kinds of wisdom literature: Proverbs and Ben Sira: and Job, Ecclesiastes and perhaps Agur ben Yakeh (Prov. 30)—see esp. pp. 161, 162.

56. M. Hengel (*Judaism and Hellenism* [London: SCM, 1974]) sees Ben Sira as an institutional 'wisdom teacher' (p. 132), i.e. giving regular instruction at a school. This is based on 51.23f., which forms part of the hymnic material, a problematic source of evidence for Ben Sira's social identity. However, Hengel does present Ben Sira in an interesting way as a 'quite unique mixture of wisdom and prophecy' (p. 134). The complementarity of these two 'traditions' (often presented as opposites) in Ben Sira provides a suggestive parallel to the message of Jesus (on this see the first section of our Chapter 6). Ben Sira does not offer much help regarding the social identity of Jesus in first-century Palestine, but he offers an example of a trajectory in which wisdom and prophetic concerns are joined in a way that has some affinity with the Synoptic presentation of Jesus (see e.g. 36.1-17 for Ben Sira's vision of a future state for the righteous vindicated by God, which is presented in the form of a prayer). For a fuller treatment of the confluence of wisdom and prophetic motifs in Ben Sira's presentation of the wisdom of the scribe (38.24–39.11) see D.E. Orton, *The Understanding Scribe: Matthew and the Apocalyptic Ideal* (Sheffield: JSOT, 1989).

57. Judas the Galilean—*Ant.* 18.4f., 23f.; *Bell.* 2.118. The Egyptian prophet—*Ant.* 20.169f.; *Bell.* 2.261. John the Baptist—*Ant.* 18.116f. He notes the working of miracles and signs, the wilderness motif, the gathering of the people on the Mount of Olives, and the eschatological rite of baptism.

58. Wisdom terminology in the ancient sources, and in the modern discussion can be misleading. Our interest in Jesus as a 'wise man' derives from the large number of proverbial sayings attributed to him, and hence the apparent continuity, in some respects, between his teaching and piety and that represented in the wisdom literature (Proverbs, Ecclesiastes, Job, Ben Sira, and the Wisdom of Solomon). However, the terms 'wisdom' and 'wise man' are often used in discussion of first century Judaism in ways that have no connection with our interests. For example, the discussion concerning the *theios anēr* in Greek and Jewish literature of the period and its relation to New Testament Christology often focuses on the issue of wisdom, cf. D.L. Tiede, *The Charismatic Figure as Miracle Worker* (Missoula: Scholars Press, 1972) and C.R. Holladay, *Theios Aner in Hellenistic Judaism: A Critique of the use of this category in New Testament Christology* (Missoula: Scholars Press, 1977). However, in this connection, the wisdom of Israel's heroes, for

example, is to be understood in terms of the Stoic idea of virtue ἀρετη (cf. Holladay, pp. 67f.) rather than in the sense of 'wise man' with which we are concerned.

59. M. Hengel (Edinburgh: T&T Clark, 1981), pp. 42ff.

60. E. Käsemann, *Essays on New Testament Themes* (London: SCM, 1964), p. 41. He also speaks of 'the remarkable importance which the writers attach to representing him (Jesus) as a teacher of wisdom' (pp. 40, 41).

61. 11QPs[a] 18.

62. *Ibid.*, p. 48. In a different way, wisdom and prophetic concerns are combined in the figure of Daniel (esp. 2.19-23) who serves as a reminder that some aspects of the wisdom tradition and the apocalyptic outlook are not to be considered antithetical, cf. H. Koester, *History, Culture, and Religion of the Hellenistic Age* (Philadelphia: Fortress, 1982), p. 246. Also C. Rowland, *The Open Heaven* (London: SPCK, 1982): in moving away from a stress on equating apocalyptic with eschatology, Rowland is able to give more room for a connection between some forms of wisdom and prophetic/apocalyptic concerns (pp. 203f.).

63. *Ibid.*, pp. 44, 68.

64. Cf. also the list of designations for Jesus in D.J. Harrington, 'The Jewishness of Jesus: Facing Some Problems', *CBQ* 49 (1987), pp. 1-13, esp. pp. 7, 8.

65. Brueggemann speaks of Jesus as a wise man, not simply in the sense of one who teaches wisdom, but as the embodiment of the ideal figure envisaged in wisdom literature. Jesus embodies the ideal man that wisdom anticipates, and summons others to fulfilment by following the way of wisdom (p. 123). Jesus is the manifestation in a human life of the kind of style the wise urged upon people: he also enables people to attain that style.

The Wisdom of Solomon presents an interesting ideal figure (see 2.10-20; 4.16-19), who combines righteousness and wisdom with innocent suffering in a way reminiscent of the servant in Deutero-Isaiah, especially ch. 53. This represents part of the rich stock of idealized figures in Early Judaism which may have served to illuminate the understanding of Jesus, possibly influencing the New Testament presentations of Jesus.

66. N. Perrin and D.C. Duling (*The New Testament: an Introduction* [New York: Harcourt, Brace, Jovanovich, 1982], pp. 26, 27) speak of the parable as a characteristic form of the wisdom movement. In 2 Sam. 14.1-21 we find a parable on the lips of the wise woman of Tekoa, and in Sira 39.3 the wise scribe is to be concerned with parables. It is interesting that in both these examples the connection of the parable with wisdom also involves a prophetic element. The woman's words read like a prophetic denunciation of the King, and as we noted earlier, the wise scribe of Ben Sira has a prophetic charismatic/function as well. In 2 Sam. 12.1-15, Nathan utters a parable in a prophetic rebuke of David.

See also P. Perkins, *Hearing the Parables of Jesus* (New York: Paulist Press, 1981) on the wisdom background of the parables of Jesus.

67. Thus the classic studies of C.H. Dodd, *The Parables of the Kingdom* (London: Nisbet, 1935), and J. Jeremias, *The Parables of Jesus* (New York: Charles Scribner, 1972).

68. See R.A. Edwards, *A Theology of Q: Eschatology, Prophecy, and Wisdom* (Philadelphia: Fortress, 1976), p. 61.

69. Use of φρόνιμος in Mt. 24.45f.; 25.2f.; Lk. 12.42.

70. Use of σοφία at Lk. 2.40, 52; Mt. 13.54; Mk 6.2.

71. σοφία Lk. 21.15; φρόνιμος Mt. 10.16; Lk. 16.8. The question of the disciples' role as scribes or wise men is picked up by several writers; see M.J. Suggs, pp. 120-27, D.E. Orton (1989), especially chapter 6, and F.W. Burnett, *The Testament of Jesus Sophia* (Washington: University Press of America, 1979) on Mt. 23.34. In an interesting essay, 'Salt as a Metaphor in Instructions for Discipleship', *Studia Theologica* 6 (1952), pp. 165-78, W. Nauck sees the salt metaphor in Mt. 5. as rooted in Rabbinic instructions to disciples in which 'to be salted' means 'to be wise'. Thus Nauck understands Mt. 5.13-15 to mean 'Jesus calls his disciples the real teachers, the true wise men in opposition to the Jewish wise men' (p. 177).

72. J. Jeremias (1972), p. 194: 'The φρόνιμος, i.e. the man who has recognized the eschatological situation'.

73. Cf. 1.22-25. See R.P. Halson, 'The Epistle of James: "Christian Wisdom"?' in *Studia Evangelica* IV (Berlin: Akademie Verlag, 1968), pp. 308-14, and M.H. Shepherd, 'The Epistle of James and the Gospel of Matthew', *JBL* 75 (1956), pp. 40-51. Shepherd notes the affinity between various discourses in James centred on one gnomic saying, and sayings from Matthew's Gospel. Halson develops the notion of James' teaching as wisdom emanating from a 'school' of catechists: 'The material preserved and used by this school has been cast in the mould of the Wisdom tradition as a conscious attempt to use a teaching form with Jewish antecedents yet with an 'international flavour' suitable for use in the Hellenistic world' (p. 313). Other commentators stress the continuity between the idea of Wisdom in James and the Holy Spirit; thus P.H. Davids, *The Epistle of James: A Commentary on the Greek Text* (Grand Rapids: Eerdmans, 1982), while rejecting the suggestion of affinity between James and wisdom literature (pp. 23, 24), speaks of a wisdom pneumatology in James (pp. 55, 56). Cf. also J.A. Kirk, 'The Meaning of Wisdom in James: Examination of a Hypothesis', *NTS* 16 (1969), pp. 24-38.

74. J.L. McKenzie (1967), p. 2.

75. J.M. Robinson, 'Logoi Sophon—On the Gattung of Q', in Robinson and Koester (1971), pp. 71-113.

76. Cf. also Acts 20.35; 'Remember the logoi of the Lord, for he said...'

77. Thus in seven of the *Testaments of the Twelve Patriarchs* there is a

reference to *logoi* in the incipit. See F.W. Burnett (1979) for the development of this theme with reference to Matthew's Eschatological Discourse.

78. See 'Thomas the Contender' and 'Pistis Sophia' as the later stages in this development.

79. Robinson, *op. cit.*, p. 104.

80. R.L. Wilken (1975), pp. 1-16.

81. It is an interesting thesis built on a number of tentative hypotheses, not least of which is the claim that the 'Q' tradition was once a fixed literary work. Even if Robinson's thesis were to be supported, it would only tell us about one moment in the history of the tradition, namely, the point of literary fixation of 'Q': further questions about the origins and significance of the proverbial material would still remain. For a recent development of Robinson's thesis with regard to 'Q', see J.S. Kloppenborg, *The Formation of Q. Trajectories in ancient Wisdom Collections* (Philadelphia: Fortress, 1987).

82. For example see R. Bultmann (1972), pp. 69-108.

83. D. Zeller, *Die weisheitlichen Mahnsprüche bei den Synoptikern* (Würzburg: Echter Verlag, 1977).

84. E.g. Mt. 20.27; 23.11; Mk 10.44; 9.35. In these cases the future indicative of 'to be' is taken by many as an imperative: cf. Blass, Debrunner, Funk, *A Greek Grammar of the New Testament*, p. 183. Also N. Turner, *Grammar of New Testament Greek, Volume III, Syntax*, p. 86.

85. Cf. U. Wilckens, 'σοφία—Wisdom', *TDNT* VIII, pp. 465-526.

86. See H-P. Müller, 'Mantische Weisheit und Apokalyptik', *VT Supp* 22 (Leiden: Brill, 1972), pp. 268-93. This is a useful introduction to the phenomenon of mantic wisdom, regardless of whether one accepts Müller's views on the origin of apocalyptic.

Notes to Chapter 2

1. It is possible to explain the wisdom admonitions in the Synoptics as representing instruction which can simply be drawn into a discussion of the ethical teaching of Jesus. However, the descriptive wisdom sayings have a more ambiguous place with respect to the usual characterization of Jesus' message and work. We will explore, in the next chapter, the ways in which New Testament interpretation has tried to understand this ambiguity. Cf. W. Beardslee, 'Plutarch's Use of Proverbial Sayings', *Semeia* 17 (1980), p. 106.

2. W. McKane's commentary, *Proverbs: A New Approach* (London: SCM, 1970), offers a good survey of the field. See also J.M. Thompson, *The Form and Function of Proverbs in Ancient Israel* (The Hague: Mouton, 1974); H.J. Hermisson, *Studien zur israelitischen Spruchweisheit* (Neukirchen-Vluyn: Neukirchener Verlag, 1968); C.R. Fontaine, *Traditional Sayings in the Old Testament* (Sheffield: Almond, 1982).

3. A number of writers focus on the poetic features of the sayings of Jesus, principally C.F. Burney, *The Poetry of Our Lord* (Oxford: Clarendon, 1925); see also T.W. Manson, *The Teaching of Jesus* (Cambridge: CUP, 1967), esp, pp. 50-56; J. Jeremias, *New Testament Theology* (London: SCM, 1971), pp. 14-29; R.C. Tannehill, *The Sword of his Mouth* (Philadelphia: Fortress, 1975). The work of R. Bultmann, *The History of the Synoptic Tradition* (Oxford: Blackwell, 1972) is probably the most helpful introduction to the material in the Gospels; we will consider this work in some detail in the next chapter.

4. A. Jolles, *Einfache Formen* (Tübingen: Max Niemeyer, 1930), p. 153. This position is taken up by Hermisson, who argues against 'Volkssprichwörter'.

5. Compare J.D. Crossan, *In Fragments. The Aphorisms of Jesus* (New York: Harper & Row, 1983). Crossan uses 'aphorism' very loosely to apply simply to short sayings. Thus, he records 133 in the Synoptic tradition, including Mk 1.15 'The time is fulfilled, and the Kingdom of God is at hand; repent and believe in the gospel', and Mt. 19.28 'Truly, I say to you, in the new world, when the Son of man shall sit on his glorious throne, you who have followed me will also sit on twelve thrones, judging the twelve tribes of Israel'. Crossan's use of the designation 'aphorism' is not unreflective, but appears to focus on the creative and individual nature of the aphorism, over against the traditional and community based proverb, for 'proverb gives no reason since none is necessary; it is the summation of the wisdom of the past. Aphorism, on the other hand, gives no reason because none is possible; it is the formulation of the wisdom of the future. Proverb is the last word, aphorism is the first word. . . . whether in form alone or content alone or in form and content together, the aphorism appears as a voice from Eden, a dictum of dawn' (p. 25). Again, we will explore further, in the following chapter, Crossan's focus on the heuristic function of the 'aphorisms' of Jesus.

6. There are many works which seek to show parallels to the proverbial wisdom of Jesus. It is our view that precedents or parallels can be found for the majority of Jesus' proverbial sayings, and we should not overemphasize the importance of sayings for which no precedent exists in the literature available to us. Should a particular saying of Jesus actually be a new creation or aphorism its function will, in any case, be very similar to the traditional proverbial sayings. For comparative studies see R.F. Horton, 'Christ's Use of the book of Proverbs', *The Expositor* 3rd series, 7 (1888), pp. 105-23; D. Smith, 'Our Lord's Use of Common Proverbs', *The Expositor* 6th series, 6 (1902), pp. 441-54; G. Dalman, *Jesus Jeshua* (London: SPCK, 1929); C.E. Carlston, 'Proverbs, Maxims, and the Historical Jesus', *JBL* 99 (1980), pp. 87-105; also the standard reference works, such as Strack-Billerbeck.

7. A. Taylor, *The Proverb and an Index to the Proverb* (Pennsylvania: Rosenkilde & Baggers, 1962), p. 3.

8. D. Zeller, *Die weisheitlichen Mahnsprüche bei den Synoptikern* (Würzburg: Echter Verlag, 1977).
9. *Ibid.*, p. 17.
10. *Ibid.*, p. 18.
11. *Ibid.*, p. 17.
12. Crossan, pp. 20, 21.
13. Zeller, p. 18.
14. *Ibid.*, p. 19.
15. Quoted in Zeller, p. 20.
16. Burney gave a detailed treatment of the material along these lines demonstrating the poetic form, and attempting to find an Aramaic original behind many of the sayings.
17. Zeller, p. 18.
18. Cf. n. 3.
19. In terms of paroemiology, our distinction between 'historical' and 'contextual' studies may be a little misleading. Older proverb studies involved collecting proverbial sayings and pursuing largely historical questions about the origins and earlier forms of the sayings. Contextual studies are, of course, interested in historical questions, but have moved on to different interests, from origins, to the contexts of proverb performance. This is reflected in the way that proverbs are now collected with contextual information.
20. A. Dundes, 'On the Structure of the Proverb', *Analytic Essays in Folklore*, ed. Dundes (The Hague: Mouton, 1975), pp. 103-18, also reprinted as 'The Structure of the Proverb', *The Wisdom of Many, Essays on the Proverb*, ed. A. Dundes and W. Mieder (London; Garland, 1981), pp. 43-64.
21. Beardslee's treatment of the proverbial saying, although not primarily concerned with classification, does involve classifying material according to function, and it is clear, for example, that the function of 'disorientation' which he applies to "Jesus'" use of paradoxical proverbs is also used to describe many parables.
22. M. Kimmerle, 'A Method of Collecting and Classifying Folk Sayings', *WF* 6 (1947), pp. 351-66.
23. This is part of a broader interest, on the part of Dundes, in the structural study of folklore. He is interested in the proverb as the shortest and simplest folklore genre, as a test case for further study. An obvious advantage of a method of analysis which is not too closely tied to linguistic and syntactic features, is that it opens up the possibility of cross-cultural comparison, and this proves helpful in Dundes' general interest in the phenomena of folklore in various cultures. It may also be helpful in a study of the Gospels, in which a comparison of Greek, Hebrew and Aramaic sources may at times be necessary.
24. M. Kuusi, 'Towards an International Type-System of Proverbs', *FFC*

211 (1972), pp. 5-41, quotation from p. 41.

25. Dundes' interest in the structure of the proverb may be compared to the work of other folkorists, e.g. G.L. Permyakov, *From Proverb to Folk-tale* (Moscow: Nauka, 1979): R.D. Abrahams, 'Proverbs and Proverbial Expressions', in R.M. Dorson, ed., *Folklore and Folklife* (Chicago: Chicago University Press, 1972), pp. 117-27.

26. A. Dundes and R.A. George, 'Toward a Structural Definition of the Riddle', *JAF* 76 (1963), pp. 111-18.

27. *Ibid*., p. 113.

28. *Ibid*., p. 116.

29. We avoid using the ambiguous term 'parallelism', in favour of the more accurate 'doubling' or 'seconding'.

30. In context, this saying forms half of a longer saying, 'With men this is impossible, but with God all things are possible'. Compare Lk. 18.27, and 1.37. There is opposition and contrast created in this fuller form of the saying, but the introduction of the specific referent 'this', in the first line, makes it a major transformation of the proverbial saying.

31. 'It will be fair, for the sky is red'. 'There will be a storm today, for the sky is red and threatening'. These are traditional wise sayings, reported to have been quoted by Jesus (the form is somewhat different in Lk. 12.54, 55). They are identificational, being a transformation of A > B, which might be written 'A on account of B'.

There is a possibility that contrast is implied in the juxtaposition of the two sayings: noting that the sky is red leads to two different/contradictory conclusions. This would be an ironic juxtaposition of contrasting proverbs, which is not unusual in proverb collections, and usage (cf. Lk. 9.50; 11.23).

32. 'Whoever does the will of God, he is my brother and sister and mother'. The structure is identificational, 'whoever is A, is B'. We might say that the form is proverbial, but the use of the personal pronoun prevents the generalizing nature that characterizes the proverbial saying. In this regard, compare Mt. 10.38 and Lk. 14.27.

33. Matthew has σου, Luke ὑμῶν.

34. Luke has ὑγιαίνοντες for ἰσχύοντες.

35. The contrastive relationship of 'teacher'-'disciple', in this saying and in the fuller form in Mt. 10.24, becomes an identification in the context of both passages. In the Matthean form, this is achieved by juxtaposing beside the contrastive saying what might be considered an identificational proverbial saying.

36. This saying could alternatively be grouped with those with primarily identificational features.

37. There are a number of other sayings in the Synoptic material which have not been covered in our analysis thus far:

(a) sayings with a proverbial form, but with some specific referent that ties them to a particular context: Mt. 5.19; 6.14, 15; 10.32, 33; 15.13; 18.4-6; 18.18; 19.29; 21.44; 25.40, 45; Mk 7.8; 8.38; 9.37; Lk. 6.5; 7.28b; 9.26; 48; 10.16; 12.8, 9, 21; 14.33; 18.29, 30;

(b) sayings on the lips of people other than Jesus: Mt. 3.10b; 15.27; Lk. 1.37; 2.34-35; 3.9.

(c) longer wisdom sayings and clusters of sayings: Mt. 5.15; 9.15-17, 10.37-42; 23.18-22; Mk 2.21-22; 3.23-27; 9.39, 41, 42; 10.29, 30; Lk. 5.33-39; 6.32-34; 8.16-18; 11.33-36.

38. As a more modern example, the kind of treatment undertaken by writers such as J.G. Williams and W. Beardslee is also inadequate for an analytic description of the material. Their terminology of 'disorientation' and 'reorientation' offers a description at the level of function, which is, in many cases, very questionable.

39. Burney, p. 67.

40. *Ibid*., p. 76.

41. Crossan, p. vii.

42. *Ibid*., p. 37f.

43. Thus K.E. Dewey is perhaps wrong to claim that the frequent use of an either/or contrast in the proverbial material of the fourth Gospel is 'characteristic of johannine dualism'. Such contrast is a common structural feature of proverbs in general. What is, perhaps, peculiar to John is the close relationship between the structural oppositions in the proverbial material and in other discourse or narrative material in the Gospel. See K.E. Dewey, '*Paroimiai* in the Gospel of John', *Semeia* 17 (1980), pp. 81-99.

44. Such oppositions are a common feature of most proverbial wisdom, cf. the book of Proverbs for the issue of positive and negative status: wise—foolish, righteous—wicked, rich—poor.

45. In an interesting essay 'Proverbs and Practical Reasoning: A Study in Socio-Logic', *The Wisdom of Many*, ed. A. Dundes and W. Mieder (London: Garland, 1981), pp. 140-60, P.A. Goodwin and J.W. Wenzel study the proverb in terms of conventional patterns of argument or reasoning. Several of their conventional categories of argument are reflected in the proverbial sayings of Jesus. Thus, they draw attention to the fact that most reasoning and argument begins with some perception of the outward appearances of phenomena. Reasoning from sign occurs when someone takes such perceptions as signs of something else, and draws conclusions accordingly. Dozens of proverbs embody the principle of reasoning from sign: 'A man is known by the company he keeps', or 'The empty vessel makes most noise'. The largest number of proverbs in this group have to do with potential fallacies, warning that appearances may be deceptive. The same structural oppositions that we have noted are reflected in the examples used by Goodwin and Wenzel: 'Through all of the examples cited so far run certain underlying contrasts: appearance v. essence, outward show v. inner reality etc. ... Certain proverbs teach by example that a shrewd attention to

contrasting concepts (e.g. general—particular, symbol—thing, appearance—reality) may save the reasoner from faulty inferences based on merely accidental connections. The same contrasting pairs have a role in those proverbs which suggest how one may go about reasoning from signs more reliably. The appearance—reality pair predominates ... "Do not look upon the vessel, but upon that which it contains"' (pp. 146, 147). There are several Synoptic examples of sign reasoning in proverbs, and also in other forms of speech (e.g. Lk. 6.46-49, word—deed). Other logical principles which form part of proverbial wisdom include cause and effect and analogy. Structural classification of proverbial sayings can help to show up the conventional patterns of reasoning which Synoptic sayings share with other traditional proverbial sayings, and, indeed, other speech forms.

46. Cf. P. Berger and T. Luckmann, *The Social Construction of Reality* (Harmondsworth: Penguin, 1966), see esp. pp. 110f. In a section on the Proverb in an African culture in M.J. and F.S. Herskovits, *Dahomean Narrative* (Evanston: Northwestern University Press, 1958) we find a significant role given to the proverb: 'we gain from it insight into behaviour, derive from it a commentary on happenings that reveal the system of values under which the culture functions. Indeed, in this last sense it makes one of its greatest humanistic contributions, for the total corpus of the Proverbs of Africans, as with proverb-users in other societies, is in a very real sense their grammar of values' (p. 57). Also E.E. Evans-Pritchard has called the proverb 'the collective expression of a people' (in 'Zandu Proverbs: Final Selection and Comments', *Man* 64 [1964], pp. 1-5). Okogbule Nwanodi claims that proverbs 'reveal the cultural attitudes and system of values of the society in which they exist', in 'Ibo Proverbs', *Nigeria Magazine* 80 (1964), p. 61.

47. G. Theissen, 'Itinerant Radicalism; The Tradition of Jesus' Sayings from the Perspective of the Sociology of Literature', *RR* 2 (1975), pp. 84-93; also his *Sociology of Early Palestinian Christianity* (Philadelphia: Fortress, 1978).

48. W. Stegemann, 'Vagabond Radicalism in Early Christianity?: A Historical and Theological Discussion of a Thesis Proposed by Gerd Theissen', in W. Schottroff and W. Stegemann, *God of the Lowly: Socio-Historical Interpretations of the Bible* (Maryknoll: Orbis, 1984), pp. 148-68.

49. J.G. Gager, Review of R.M. Grant, A.J. Malherbe, & G. Theissen, *RSR* 5 (1979), pp. 174-80, quotation from p. 176.

50. There are a great many introductory articles and books on the subject of sociological approaches to the New Testament, all covering a very small number of contributions to the subject, and with a very narrow sociological base. See for example R. Scroggs, 'The Sociological Interpretation of the New Testament: The Present State of Research', *NTS* 26 (1980), pp. 164-79; J.Z. Smith, 'The Social Description of Early Christianity', *RSR* 1 (1975), pp. 19-25; S.R. Isenberg, 'Some Uses and Limitations of Social Scientific Methodology in the Study of Early Christianity', *SBL Seminar Papers 1980*,

pp. 29-49, P.W. Hollenbach, 'Recent Historical Jesus Studies and the Social Sciences', *SBL Seminar Papers 1983*, pp. 61-78; J.G. Gager, 'Shall We Marry Our Enemies? Sociology and the New Testament', *Int* 36 (1982), pp. 256-65, O.C. Edwards, 'Sociology as a Tool for Interpreting the New Testament', *ATR* 65 (1983), pp. 431-48; T.F. Best, 'The Sociological Study of the New Testament: Promise and Peril of a New Discipline', *SJT 36* (1983), pp. 181-94; P.J. Richter, 'Recent Sociological Approaches to the Study of the New Testament', *Religion* 14 (1984), pp. 77-90. For a more broadly based analysis of the role of the sociology of knowledge in New Testament study see the article by R.L. Rohrbaugh, '"Social Location of Thought" as a Heuristic Construct in New Testament Study', *JSNT* 30 (1987), pp. 103-19.

51. For a good introduction to some of the important issues see L. Goldmann, 'The Sociology of Literature: Status and Problems of Method', *The Sociology of Art and Literature: A Reader*, ed. M.C. Albrecht, J.H. Barnett, & M. Griff (London: Duckworth, 1970), pp. 582-609. Goldmann's essay argues for the 'genetic structuralist' approach, which is a sociological development of structuralism. This argues for a close relation between the structure of the consciousness of a group and the universe of a work of literature. This remains the case even with a work of fiction, thus: 'An imaginary universe, apparently completely removed from any specific experience—that of a fairy tale, for instance—may, in its structure, be strictly homologous with the experience of a particular social group or, at the very least, linked, in a significant manner, with that experience' (p. 585). It remains a major problem knowing how to construe the relationship between the structure of the text's universe and that of the actual social group to which the text is related. Much New Testament criticism, like Goldmann, works in terms of a 'strictly homologous' relationship, but this is a difficult assumption to defend. If there are to be any significant advances New Testament sociology needs to give more attention to the strictly textual nature of the evidence, and draw more on the branches of literary theory concerned with the relationship between texts and social reality.

52. We will see how the issue of the rhetorical function of 'Jesus' proverbial wisdom has been an important one in the history of the interpretation of the material. At this stage, we might distinguish two kinds of 'function'. The 'function' associated with rhetorical interests concerns the 'once off' situation of proverb performance and the effects which will not necessarily be the same a second time; particularly if the function is to disorient. This may be true in the realm of hearing or reading. In our fifth chapter on the literary function of proverbial wisdom we hope to give a more satisfactory account of the rhetoric of the proverb than has thus far been suggested. 'Function' is also of interest to sociologists, like Berger and Luckmann, in a much broader sense, and has to do with the social world of a community, its building, maintenance, and legitimation.

Notes to Chapter 3

1. R. Bultmann, *The History of the Synoptic Tradition* (Oxford: Blackwell, 1972), pp. 69-108.

2. For detailed studies of tendencies of tradition see E.P. Sanders, *The Tendencies of the Synoptic Tradition* (Cambridge: CUP, 1969); W. Kelber, *The Oral and the Written Gospel* (Philadelphia: Fortress, 1983); A.B. Lord, 'The Gospels as Oral Traditional Literature', in W.O. Walker Jr, ed., *The Relationships among the Gospels* (San Antonio: Trinity University Press, 1978); E. Güttgemanns, *Candid Questions Concerning Gospel Form Criticism* (Pittsburgh: Pickwick, 1979).

3. Bultmann, pp. 88-89.

4. See W.R. Farmer, *The Synoptic Problem. A Critical Analysis* (Dillsboro: Western North Carolina Press, 1976).

5. For a discussion of the idea of 'Original Form', see Kelber, pp. 30f.

6. 'The new approach to the Synoptic Problem', in *Existence and Faith* (London: Collins, 1964), pp. 39-62, quotation from pp. 45, 46.

7. 'History', p. 88.

8. Kelber, p. 14. Cf. also E.L. Abel, 'The Psychology of Memory and Rumour Transmission and their bearing on theories of Oral Transmission in Early Christianity', *JR* 51 (1971), pp. 270-81: 'there is no reason to assume that the changes which occur in the written tradition also occurred in the oral phases of transmission. Here biblical scholars must be willing to consult the findings of other disciplines if they wish to make inferences about changes which occur in periods prior to the evidence of written testimony' (p. 275).

9. 'New Approach', p. 57.

10. *JTC* 4 (1967), pp. 153-62.

11. Cf. W.A. Beardslee, *A House for Hope: A Study in Process and Biblical Thought* (Philadelphia: Westminster, 1972).

12. Beardslee explores how to relate a Christian perspective of faith as something concrete and historical, to other perspectives from which people find meaning and express their deepest convictions. Obviously, the wisdom tradition is important in this respect, and Beardslee focuses on the practical wisdom of the proverb. He offers some interesting comments about the use of the proverbial form tending toward a hermeneutic based on a common human nature. This could lead to a theology in which christological terms need not be central, and the recognition that: 'a significant response to the substance of the message of faith can be made without the expression or response to any explicitly christological affirmations' (*Int* 24 [1970], p. 72). Such a theology would indeed be taking seriously the wisdom elements in the Synoptic picture of Jesus' message.

13. Such as the work of A. Jülicher on the parables (*Die Gleichnisreden Jesu* [2 vols.; Tübingen: Mohr, 1899]); W.W. Fenn, *The Theological Method*

of Jesus (Boston: Beacon, 1938); A. Harnack, *What is Christianity?* (London: Williams & Norgate, 1901).

14. W.A. Beardslee, *Literary Criticism of the New Testament* (Philadelphia: Fortress, 1970). An earlier article, 'The Wisdom Tradition and the Synoptic Gospels', *JAAR* 35 (1967), pp. 231-40, introduced similar ideas in briefer form, and in the context of a broader treatment of wisdom and the Gospels, thus looking also at the speculative strand of wisdom and its relation to Christology.

15. P. 32. Cf. *Int* 24 (1970), p. 65, where Beardslee again mentions the narrative aspects of the proverb. The relation of the proverb to narrative is illustrated with motifs from Old Testament proverbs paralleled in some of Jesus' parables.

16. The work of Crossan appears to miss the subtlety of Beardslee's position, as we shall see later.

17. P. 41. This is a phrase which occurs time and again in the work of Beardslee, and those who value his insights.

18. W.A. Beardslee, 'Uses of the Proverb in the Synoptic Gospels', *Int* 24 (1970), pp. 61-73.

19. It may be useful to introduce the terminology of Speech Act theory (a branch of the philosophy of language), which will help to clarify some important distinctions at this point. Although speech act theory was developed with oral performance in mind it would seem feasible to apply its insights to the literary record of speech.

In regard to Bultmann's work, we noted earlier a distinction between the grammar of a saying and its function. A case in point is Mt. 6.24, 'No one can serve two masters; for either he will hate the one and love the other, or he will hold to one and despise the other. You cannot serve God and mammon'. The grammar of this saying is indicative (as opposed to imperative), but Bultmann notes its character of 'address', for it issues a challenge. Bultmann uses the somewhat ambiguous, theologically loaded term 'address'; however, this distinction, between the indicative grammar and the function can be made at the level of language functions. Among other things, speech act theory distinguishes the syntax or grammar of a sentence from its 'illocutionary' force. The possible illocutionary force could be: stating, describing, warning, commanding, requesting, approving, promising, or criticizing [J.L. Austin argued that there are over one thousand such expressions in English which could characterize illocutionary force, *How to Do Things with Words* (Oxford: OUP, 1978) p. 150]. The illocutionary force cannot be read off simply from the grammar of the sentence, but other factors in its performance will affect the force, i.e. context, intention, addressee, intonation etc. A good example from our material would be the saying: 'The first will be last and the last first'. The grammar of the sentence is indicative, but the function of the saying is usually seen as challenge. However, depending on the context and audience the illocutionary force could be 'warning' to those who identify with the 'first', or 'approving/affirming/promising' to those who identify with the 'last'. With proverbial speech the question of illocutionary force is extremely important, for the presence of doubling in many of the sayings attributed to Jesus means that the force may vary according to the audience. Also different (literary or oral) performances of the same saying may have different illocutionary forces. We will develop these ideas further in our fifth chapter in a more comprehensive treatment of speech act theory and pragmatics.

20. W.A. Beardslee, 'Proverbs in the Gospel of Thomas', in *Studies in New Testament and Early Christian Literature: Essays for A.P. Wikgren*, ed. D.E. Aune, Novum Testamentum Supplement 33 (Leiden: Brill, 1972), pp. 92-103.

21. W.A. Beardslee, 'Plutarch's Use of Proverbial Speech', *Semeia* 17 (1980), pp. 101-12.

22. W.A. Beardslee, 'Saving One's Life by Losing it', *JAAR* 47 (1977), pp. 57-72.

23. W.A. Beardslee, 'Parable, Proverb and Koan', *Semeia* 12 (1978), pp. 151-77.

24. J.D. Crossan, *Raid on the Articulate: Comic Eschatology in Jesus and Borges* (New York: Harper & Row, 1976).

25. J.D. Crossan, *The Dark Interval: Towards a Theology of Story* (Illinois: Argus Communications, 1975).

26. A.N. Wilder, *Theopoetic: Theology and the Religious Imagination* (Philadelphia: Fortress, 1976).

27. Again (cf. n. 19) Crossan has a restricted view of the illocutionary force of Jesus' language, which does not seem to take into account the many other factors in performance which may affect the force of an utterance.

28. J.B. Cobb, 'A Theology of Story: Crossan and Beardslee', in R.A. Spencer (ed.) *Orientation by Disorientation. Studies in Literary Criticism and Biblical Literary Criticism, presented in honour of William A. Beardslee* (Pittsburgh: Pickwick, 1980), pp. 151-64.

29. In reading Crossan's work one is struck both by the vagueness in his use of the term 'world', and its apparent similarity to the concept of a 'socially constructed world' in the field of the sociology of knowledge. Although Crossan does not acknowledge any dependence on this discipline, it is instructive to compare his work with the early work of the sociologist Peter Berger. In his *The Precarious Vision* (Garden City: Doubleday, 1961), Berger is attempting to synthesize his sociological and theological interests, having already begun to develop his ideas on the social origin of all knowledge. In a helpful review article 'Religious Faith and the Sociology of Knowledge: The Unburdening of Peter Berger', *RSR* 5 (1979), pp. 1-10, Van A. Harvey explores Berger's dependence on existentialist thinkers such as Heidegger and Sartre: 'The socially constructed worlds are basically "fictions" and constitute a massive temptation to "bad faith" (Sartre) and

"inauthenticity" (Heidegger) because these fictions obscure the precariousness of existence' (p. 3). Religion is dangerous because it tends to serve as a large fiction, to sanctify and endorse the smaller ones. Liberation involves 'seeing through' the fiction of society, and this requires what Berger calls 'ecstasy'. This can be a kind of religious experience, which 'strips human beings of their social roles and gives them one brief glimpse of a mystery of "such magnitude of splendour that this one glimpse is all we need to light our path for the remainder of our days" (1961, 165)' (p. 3). This interpretation of Christian faith shares Crossan's iconoclastic emphasis, both with regard to theology whereby all that is socially constructed is inauthentic; and politically, in seeing through the fictitiousness of all social orders.

Berger's work shares similar problems to that of Crossan; chiefly, how can he sustain the primacy of his interpretation of Christian faith without that too being seen as socially constructed and thereby inauthentic. We cannot pursue the way in which Berger's work has been adapted over the years, as he became aware of some of the difficulties in his position. A fuller treatment of Crossan's work would need to explore this relationship between the 'story world' and the socially constructed world.

30. See for example the treatment of Judg. 8.2, 21; 1 Sam. 16.7; 24.14; 1 Kgs 20.11 in C.R. Fontaine, *Traditional Sayings in the Old Testament* (Sheffield: Almond, 1982).

31. Cf. B. Kirshenblatt-Gimblett, 'Towards a Theory of Proverb Meaning', *The Wisdom of Many*, ed. W. Mieder and A. Dundes (New York: Garland, 1981), pp. 111-21. The truths which proverbs proclaim feel absolute, but K-G argues that proverbs do not state absolute or general truths, 'When examined in terms of their actual use in specific situations, we see that a proverb can be made to express more than one meaning, that sometimes these meanings are contradictory, and that a proverb's meaning, rather than being autonomous of the proverb's use as we are led to believe by proverb collections, is indeed contextually specified' (p. 112). K-G wants to explore the sources of the proverb's multiple meanings and thus to demonstrate that it expresses relative rather than absolute truths. She concludes: 'In everyday life proverbs only exist as socially situated meanings in contrast with proverb compilations in which proverbs are "unsituated" and appear to express absolute truths' (p. 120). There is a danger of stressing the importance of oral performance above literary use in a collection, which seems to depend on a value judgment concerning the priority of the oral over the written. Rather than presenting oral performance as the privileged use of the genre, we should merely speak of two distinct uses. Comparison would show the differing importance and effects of contextual factors in these distinct spheres of use.

32. See J.C. Messenger, 'The Role of Proverbs in a Nigerian Judicial System', in A. Dundes (ed.), *The Study of Folklore* (Englewood Cliffs: Prentice-Hall, 1965), pp. 299-307.

33. G. von Rad, *Old Testament Theology*, I (London: SCM, 1975), p. 420.

34. J.W. Rogerson, *Anthropology of the Old Testament* (Oxford: Blackwell, 1978).

35. *Ibid*., p. 118. From J. Goody, *The Domestication of the Savage Mind* (Cambridge: CUP, 1977), pp. 125-26. We would not necessarily agree that with literacy proverbs 'are now tested for a universal truth claim', but the literary setting merely reinforces in a stark way the restricted nature of their claim to truth.

36. From B. Lindfors, 'The Palm-Oil with which Achebe's Words are Eaten', in *Critical Perspectives on Chinua Achebe*, ed. C.L. Innes and B. Lindfors (London: Heinemann, 1979), pp. 47-66.

37. See J.G. Williams, *Those who Ponder Proverbs* (Sheffield: Almond, 1981), p. 25. Also S. Amsler, 'La Sagesse de la Femme', in M. Gilbert (ed.), *La Sagesse de l'Ancien Testament* (Gembloux: Leuven University Press, 1979), pp. 112-16.

38. N.K. Gottwald, *The Hebrew Bible. A Socio-Literary Introduction* (Philadelphia: Fortress, 1985). Gottwald, for example, stresses the 'dissonance in emphasis and explanatory frameworks' within the book of Proverbs (p. 573), and argues that the coherence of the work and its ideology should not be too easily assumed: 'The attitudes and directives, for example, with respect to production, distribution, exchange, and consumption of goods illustrate a variety of viewpoints, which may at times represent side-by-side competing outlooks and at other times the changing emphases of differing historical settings' (p. 573).

39. The work of J.G. Williams (1981) on the biblical aphorism, with special reference to Qoheleth and Jesus, focuses on the idea of order as defining wisdom. 'There is now consensus in biblical studies that a concept of order is at the very center of wisdom thinking' (p. 17). Some recent studies have, however, begun to question this definition of wisdom in terms of order. In a review of Williams' work (*JBL* 102 [1983]), G.T. Sheppard comments: 'I do not agree that a consensus on "order" behind wisdom has been achieved. Von Rad's reservations in *Wisdom in Israel*, and his careful proposal of the "act consequence" relationship still stand as a challenge. The absence of a technical term for "order" in the wisdom literature itself is a further caution. In this respect, Williams's heavy dependence on and lack of clear definition for "order" becomes increasingly a problem when it is used as a pivotal term' (p. 320). Criticism of the concept of order also comes in two essays by R.E. Murphy, 'Wisdom and Yahwism', *No Famine in the Land: Studies in honour of J.L. McKenzie*, ed. J. W. Flanagan and A.N. Robinson (Missoula: Scholars Press, 1975), pp. 117-26; 'Wisdom—Theses and Hypotheses', *Israelite Wisdom: Theological and Literary Essays in Honour of Samuel Terrien*, ed. J.G. Gammie, W.A. Brueggemann, W.L. Humphreys & J.M. Ward (Missoula: Scholars Press, 1978), pp. 35-42.

40. *JBL* 99 (1980), pp. 87-105.

41. N. Perrin, *Rediscovering the Teaching of Jesus* (London: SCM, 1967), p. 145.

42. Cf. D. Zeller's warning against ignoring the long chain of precedents to Lk. 14.11 which recognize the surprising reversals in God's world order (p. 182).

43. J.D. Crossan, *In Fragments. The Aphorisms of Jesus* (New York: Harper & Row, 1983).

44. R.H. Stephenson, *Modern Language Review* 75 (1980), pp. 1-17.

45. Cf. N.R. Norrick, *How Proverbs Mean. Semantic Studies in English Proverbs* (Berlin: Mouton, 1985) especially ch. 2, and C.R. Fontaine, *Traditional Sayings in the Old Testament* (Sheffield: Almond, 1982), pp. 51f. A similar distinction in function is discussed in C.S. Lewis' essay on metaphor, in which he develops a distinction between pupil and master metaphors: 'Bluspels and Flalansferes', *The Importance of Language*, ed. M. Black (Englewood Cliffs: Prentice-Hall, 1962), pp. 36-50.

46. W.H. Kelber, review of Crossan in *JBL* 104 (1985), pp. 716-19.

47. R.A. Edwards, *A Theology of Q: Eschatology, Prophecy and Wisdom* (Philadelphia: Fortress, 1976). Edwards stresses the importance of understanding wisdom in the light of eschatology: 'Wisdom instruction emphasizes the practical. The disciple is taught (instructed) by reference to the way of things in the world. But it is a world in which experience must be modified by the new understanding, that is, that the Kingdom is at hand. Thus, a basically prophetic statement is developed in a wisdom context. Knowing that the end is imminent allows or even demands a fuller comprehension of the lessons of experience' (p. 78). Edwards seems to argue for a form of interim ethics (p. 147). However, he also suggests that wisdom and prophecy are not so distinct as has often been assumed (e.g. wisdom forms in prophetic literature). We will consider this idea further in our final chapter.

M. Küchler, *Frühjüdische Weisheitstraditionen: zum Fortgang weisheitlichen Denkens im Bereich des frühjüdischen Jahweglaubens* (Göttingen: Vandenhoeck & Ruprecht, 1979). Küchler also interprets Jesus' wisdom in the context of the eschatological Kingdom: thus, wisdom is worldly in the sense of a world rapidly coming to an end. Küchler's 1972 Fribourg dissertation *Die weisheitlichen Logien Jesu nach den Synoptikern* was, unfortunately, not available for consultation.

P. Minear, 'Become Last of All', *Commands of Christ* (Nashville: Abingdon, 1972), pp. 83-97. This traces the history of the humble—exalt, first—last sayings from the earliest and original eschatological use by Jesus, through the various ways in which the sayings are contextualized to address the needs of the early Christian communities (in all, eight stages are posited).

J.G. Williams, 'The Power of Form: A Study of Biblical Proverbs', *Semeia* 17 (1980), pp. 35-58, and *Those who Ponder Proverbs: Aphoristic Thinking and Biblical Literature* (Sheffield: Almond, 1981). The earlier essay sought to save the book of Proverbs from the frequent judgment that it is uninteresting and stereotyped. This serves as an introduction to his more comprehensive work which seeks to argue the thesis that the aphorism is both literary and conceptual, poetic and philosophical. This work proceeds through a treatment of proverbial wisdom in terms of the opposition between order and counter-order, with traditional wisdom being contrasted with the aphoristic wisdom of Jesus and Qoheleth. Williams' treatment is one of the more subtle attempts to discuss biblical aphorism. However, it does rely on positing the primacy of eschatology for understanding Jesus' language: 'He (Jesus) envisions a new divine order arriving in the world, and this new reality imposes a demand that one commit oneself to it rather than preserving an old one. The aphoristic sayings of Jesus actually function as mediating insights between the old order and the new order' (p. 31). Williams talks of 'a dynamic tension of continuity and discontinuity' (p. 55), and this leads him to be critical of Bultmann's work and the criterion of dissimilarity. He is also concerned, in the context of a critique of Crossan's view of paradox, to see both disorientation and the construction of a new life in Jesus' message (p. 63). However, as in Beardslee's work, this aspect of the material is not developed, for Williams is more keen to show Jesus' (and Qoheleth's) use of aphorism as a critique of traditional wisdom.

D. Zeller, *Die weisheitlichen Mahnsprüche bei den Synoptikern* (Würzburg: Echter Verlag, 1977). Much of Zeller's study is taken up with a detailed examination of the formal characteristics of the *Mahnspruch* in Jewish literature, and an exegesis of each of the relevant sayings in the Synoptics. He is concerned with the question of Jesus' ethic, and how to relate the imperitival wisdom sayings to the Kingdom preaching. Zeller draws a distinction between the Kingdom material and the *Mahnsprüche*: the former is *kerygma*, the latter *didache*; the former prophetic message is addressed to all the Jews, the latter concerns the individual 'disciple' who has already responded to the Kingdom proclamation. There is certainly some continuity between traditional Jewish wisdom and Jesus' *Mahnsprüche*, but Jesus' speech undergoes an 'intensification' because of the nearness of the Kingdom—the newness and radicalism of Jesus' wisdom teaching to the disciples derives from his perception of the imminent crisis of the Kingdom. Here, Zeller is explicitly dependent on Beardslee (p. 151). In contrast to our approach (argued in Chapter 6), Zeller maintains a traditional view of the Kingdom, not really allowing the wisdom material to inform this view. See also: 'Weisheitliche Überlieferung in der Predigt Jesu', in *Religiöse Grunderfahrungen Quellen und Gestalten*, ed. W. Strolz (Freiburg: Herder, 1978)

T.W. Manson, *The Teaching of Jesus: studies in its form and content* (Cambridge: Cambridge University Press, 1943). Manson treats our material under the heading 'Formal Characteristics of the Teaching', and is concerned mainly with the poetic features of Jesus' language, and how this aspect might be used in the work of historical reconstruction (p. 53).

W. Grundmann, 'Weisheit im Horizont des Reiches Gottes. Eine Studie zur Verkündigung Jesu nach der Spruchüberlieferung Q', in *Die Kirche des Anfangs: Festschrift für H. Schürmann*, ed. R. Schnackenburg, J. Ernst & J. Wanke (Leipzig: St-Benno Verlag 1978), pp. 175-99. Grundmann is concerned with the coming together of wisdom and prophecy in Jesus' message, he therefore sees him as both teacher and prophet, and compares his outlook to that represented in other early Jewish literature: 'Der Inhalt der Lehre dieses Lehrers ist Weisheit .... Er ist also prophetischer Weisheitslehrer und vertritt einen Typus, zu dem sich in der späteren nachexilischen Zeit, etwa vom dritten vorchristlichen Jahrhundert ab die Durchdringung von Prophetie und Weisheit entwickelt hat' (pp. 175, 176). Grundmann is also concerned to show the transformations in Jewish wisdom in the Hellenistic period, particularly how the great human themes of wisdom are translated in the context of apocalyptic wisdom to the realm of the new age. The question remains whether the proverbial wisdom in the Synoptics is in continuity with the sort of apocalyptic wisdom that Grundmann describes.

M. Hengel, 'Jesus als Messianischer Lehrer der Weisheit und die Anfänge der Christologie', in *Sagesse et Religion: Colloque de Strasbourg, 1976*, ed. E. Jacob (Paris: Presses Universitaires de France, 1979). Hengel explores the relationship between Jesus as a teacher of experiential wisdom and speculation about a wisdom Christology (cf. our first chapter).

J.M. Robinson, *Trajectories through Early Christianity* (Philadelphia: Fortress, 1971) ed. with H. Koester; also, 'Jesus as Sophos and Sophia: Wisdom Tradition and the Gospels', in R.L. Wilken (ed.), *Aspects of Wisdom in Judaism and Early Christianity* (Notre Dame: Notre Dame University Press, 1975), pp. 1-16 (cf. our first chapter); also 'The Formal Structure of Jesus' Message', in W. Klassen and G. Snyder (eds.), *Current Issues in New Testament Interpretation* (London: SCM, 1962), pp. 91-110. In this essay, Robinson's emphasis is on eschatology as the centre of Jesus' message, and hence the interpretive key to understanding the wisdom materials. This is argued in the language of the New Quest (cf. Chapter 4).

C.E. Carlston, 'Wisdom and Eschatology in Q', *Logia. Les Paroles de Jésus*, ed. J. Delobel (Leuven: Leuven University Press, 1982), pp. 101-19. Carlston maintains that 'in general.... it may be said that wisdom materials are shaped in an eschatological direction' (p. 113). However, like Edwards and others, he is keen to explore aspects of the compatibility of wisdom and eschatology/apocalyptic.

A.A.T. Ehrhardt, 'Greek Proverbs in the Gospels', in *The Framework of the New Testament* (Manchester: Manchester University Press, 1964), pp. 44-63.

D. Smith, 'Our Lord's Use of Common Proverbs', *The Expositor* 6

(1902), pp. 441-54.

48. For a fuller and more general discussion of Perrin's work see C.R. Mercer, *Norman Perrin's Interpretation of the New Testament: From 'Exegetical Method' to 'Hermeneutical Process'* (Macon: Mercer University Press, 1986). This includes a good description and analysis of Perrin's historical interests, but tends to exaggerate his significance as an early literary critic of the Gospels.

Notes to Chapter 4

1. C.E. Carlston, 'Wisdom and Eschatology in Q', in *Logia. Les Paroles de Jésus*, ed. J. Delobel (Leuven: Leuven University Press, 1982), p. 113. Carlston follows the somewhat confusing tendency of using 'apocalyptic' and 'eschatology' interchangeably; presumably he does not intend to differentiate the two.

2. See for example L.E. Keck, *A Future for the Historical Jesus* (London: SCM, 1972): 'He who studies only the Synoptics and ignores John understands neither' (p. 26). Also G.N. Stanton, *Jesus of Nazareth in New Testament Preaching* (Cambridge: CUP, 1974); J.A.T. Robinson, *The Priority of John* (London: SCM, 1985).

3. Keck (1972, p. 26): 'He who studies only the canonical Gospels does not understand them'. Also J.D. Crossan, *Four Other Gospels. Shadows on the Contours of Canon* (Minneapolis: Winston, 1985).

4. See for example the discussion in M.I. Finley, *Ancient History. Evidence and Models* (London: Chatto & Windus, 1985), ch. 2: 'The Ancient Historian and his Sources', p. 15: 'We have no good reason for taking the speeches of Thucydides and others to be anything but inventions by the historians, not only in their precise wording but also in their substance'. Finley also notes F.E. Adcock, *Thucydides and his History* (Cambridge: CUP, 1963), pp. 27-35. P.A. Stadter (ed.), *The Speeches of Thucydides* (Chapel Hill: University of North Carolina Press, 1973). F.W. Walbank, *Speeches in Greek Historians* (Oxford: Blackwell, 1965); R.G. Collingwood, *The Idea of History* (Oxford: OUP, 1961), pp. 30-31.

5. M. Kähler, *The So-called Historical Jesus and the Historic, Biblical Christ* (Philadelphia: Fortress, 1964), p. 47.

6. See for example R.A. Johnson, *The Origins of Demythologizing* (Leiden: Brill, 1974), and A.C. Thiselton, *The Two Horizons. New Testament Hermeneutics and Philosophical Description with special reference to Heidegger, Bultmann, Gadamer and Wittgenstein* (Exeter: Paternoster, 1980), pp. 205ff.

7. J. Weiss, *Die Predigt Jesu vom Reiche Gottes* (Göttingen: Vandenhoeck & Ruprecht, 1892), ET, *Jesus' Proclamation of the Kingdom of God* (Philadelphia: Fortress, 1971); also the revised and significantly enlarged edition of the German published in 1900.

8. E. Käsemann, 'The Problem of the Historical Jesus', in *Essays on New*

Testament Themes (London: SCM, 1964), pp. 15-47.

9. J.M. Robinson, *The New Quest of the Historical Jesus and Other Essays* (Philadelphia: Fortress, 1983), p. 66.

10. Robinson wants to trace his 'new view of history' to Dilthey: 'It was primarily Wilhelm Dilthey who introduced the modern period by posing for historiography the "question about the scientific knowledge of individual persons, the great forms of singular human existence"' [p. 67, from *Die Entstehung der Hermeneutik* (1900)]. This attempt to reduce 'modern historiography' to one view is not persuasive; cf. J. Barr, *Holy Scripture. Canon, Authority, Criticism* (Oxford: Clarendon, 1983) in which he is critical of the 'new idea' of historiography and its usefulness: 'In fact it is doubtful whether a single inch of progress was made: no more seems to be known about the historical Jesus than before the New Quest was launched' (p. 143).

11. R. Bultmann, *Jesus and the Word* (New York: Scribners, 1958).

12. The central issue of consistency, with respect to Jesus' message, will be dealt with at some length.

13. W.O. Walker explains the difference between the Old and the New Quest as follows: 'The essential differences between the new quest and the old are two. The first difference is that the new quest has no intention of creating a "biography" or a comprehensive picture of Jesus, for it recognizes full well that the New Testament materials in their final literary form are direct expressions only of the faith of the various authors, that they reflect indirectly the corporate life and developing faith of the first century Christian communities, and that they can be used, therefore, only with extreme caution as sources for the actual history of Jesus; rather, the new quest seeks to establish the probable authenticity of particular episodes, sayings, and motifs which are reported in the Gospels and, on the basis of these, to depict as accurately and comprehensively as possible the characteristic message and activity of Jesus. A second difference is that the new quest, unlike the old, is concerned to demonstrate the continuity, not the discontinuity, between the Jesus of history and the Christ of Christian faith' [pp. 40, 41, 'The Quest of the Historical Jesus: A Discussion of Methodology', *ATR* 51 (1969), pp. 38-56]. Thus we see a difference in emphasis, a more realistic view of the limitations of the sources, and hence a more modest goal. In practice, we do not see 'a new view of history' separating the two quests.

14. C. Rowland, *Christian Origins. An Account of the Setting and Character of the most Important Messianic Sect* (London: SPCK, 1985), p. 123.

15. *Op. cit.*, pp. 23-108; cf. E.P. Sanders, *Jesus and Judaism* (London: SCM, 1985), which draws on his earlier work, *Paul and Palestinian Judaism* (London: SCM, 1977).

16. In an interesting review of the development of the history of religions

movement, R.A. Oden explains: 'Because it is now deeply entrenched in our thoughts, it is easy to forget that the tendency to view all matters in terms of their histories may itself have had a history'. [From 'Hermeneutics and Historiography: Germany and America', *SBL Seminar Papers 1980,* p. 135]. Oden goes on to trace that history, and concludes that the present reaction to 'synchronic' interests in studies of biblical texts as being overly theoretical is a charge that could also be laid against 'diachronic' interests. Both are theoretical approaches brought to the study of literature: there can be nothing inherent in a text that demands it to be read as history.

17. H. Gunkel, 'The Religio-Historical Interpretation of the New Testament', *The Monist* 13 (1902/03), p. 404.

18. F.C. Grant seems to admit some connection between the History of Religions approach and the work of Weiss and Schweitzer; but he believes that a more rigorous application of the approach is called for: 'the study should be pursued more assiduously and by others than professional theologians, and with more attention to the immediate background to the New Testament than to "parallels" in somewhat remoter areas of religious history' [p. 438, 'The Idea of the Kingdom of God in the New Testament', in *Studies in the History of Religions IV. La Regalita Sacra. The Sacral Kingship* (Leiden: Brill, 1959)]. Grant seems to want to base his understanding of the term on the Old Testament background, and he traces the origins of the idea back several centuries in a way that he still considers helpful to an understanding of the New Testament usage: 'It is against the very earliest background of Israel's political history that the whole later political and religious development must be understood, including the very late idea of the Kingdom of God, in the form presupposed in the New Testament' (p. 439). Thus, Weiss and Schweitzer shared a similar approach to the one that Grant follows, but he considers that they chose the wrong History of Religions background. It might, however, be argued by some, that Schweitzer's use of Jewish apocalyptic as background to Jesus' conception does not represent a true History of Religions approach, for it lacks the emphasis on tracing historical development. We believe the categorization to be helpful, and use the expression (as others do) in a broader sense, accepting that there are important differences between Schweitzer and others like Gunkel.

19. I.G. Nicol, 'Schweitzer's Jesus: A Psychology of the Heroic Will', *ET* 86 (1974), p. 54.

20. A. Schweitzer, *The Quest of the Historical Jesus* (London: SCM, 1981), p. 366.

21. The idea of historical constraint is one taken up in an interesting way by A.E. Harvey in *Jesus and the Constraints of History* (London: Duckworth, 1982). Harvey asserts: 'No individual, if he wishes to influence others, is totally free to choose his own style of action and persuasion: he is subject to constraints imposed by the culture in which he finds himself. If

communication is to take place, there must be constraints which are recognised by both speaker and his listeners' (p. 6). This would seem to be a fairly obvious, and uncontentious point, although it is doubtful whether speakers or listeners are conscious of the constraints under which their communication takes place. However, Harvey wants to press this notion of constraints into the service of his interest in reconstruction: 'Much of the material which is discussed in the following chapters consists of evidence which is drawn from sources outside the New Testament and which helps us to give definition to the historical constraints within which Jesus must have lived, worked and died. These constraints, in turn, allow us to establish the options which were open to a person such as we believe Jesus to have been, and give objective content to those general statements about him which we regard as historically established. In this way we can begin to build up a profile of Jesus which is independent of Christian sources and which offers some kind of test by which the reliability of these sources can be checked' (pp. 7, 8). It is surely to claim too much to attempt a profile of Jesus through inference from the possibilities open to him in his religious and cultural environment.

In his section on 'Jesus and Time', Harvey explains that his method requires him to ask 'what options would have been open, in this matter of an attitude to time and history, to a man who lived and taught in first-century Palestine' (p. 67). Harvey tries to give sociological 'depth' to his argument at this point by invoking the ideas of K.L. Burridge and J. Gager on the rise of apocalyptic movements in response to situations where 'the old order is threatened by the impact of an alien colonial power' (p. 67). On the face of it, this would seem to describe the situation in first-century Palestine. However, as Harvey admits, this sort of argument does not have the force of a sociological law. The response to such a situation could involve a stricter enforcement of 'the law' as an attempt to define the religious group clearly in the face of a secular and foreign culture—cf. the Babylonian exile, or the rise of Rabbinic Judaism after 70 CE. Our knowledge of the historical context of Jesus' ministry, albeit limited, opens up a great variety of options and possibilities. For a fuller and more positive treatment of Harvey's work compare N.T. Wright's review article, '"Constraints" and the Jesus of History', *SJT* 39 (1986), pp. 189-210. See also the review articles in *JSNT* 17 (1983).

22. See for example B.B. Scott, *Jesus, Symbol-Maker for the Kingdom* (Philadelphia: Fortress, 1981), p. 11. In 'Schweitzer Revisited', *Explorations in Theology 1* (London: SCM, 1977), pp. 112-33, D. Nineham asserts: 'Since our sources contain no hint of Jesus' having explicitly redefined the eschatological terms he used, the assumption must be that he expected and meant them to be understood in the sense generally attached to them at the time.... any contention to the contrary.... is probably to be assigned largely to the natural desire for a Jesus less culturally conditioned, and more immediately acceptable by modern standards, than the figure who emerges

from the most natural interpretation of the data' (p. 126). It is hard to imagine what role Nineham would assign to the parables which begin 'The Kingdom of God is like. . . '. The notion of 'cultural conditioning' in Nineham's essay is overworked to the extent that it might make one wonder whether we really need the Gospels to know anything about Jesus: we could infer an adequate picture of him from the evidence of his religious and cultural environment which conditioned him.

23. In a recent essay, J.H. Charlesworth takes up the issue of the background to Jesus' Kingdom idea in early Jewish literature, 'The Historical Jesus in Light of Writings Contemporaneous with Him', *Aufstieg und Niedergang der römischen Welt*, ed. W. Haase, II 25.1 (Berlin: de Gruyter, 1982), pp. 451-76. Charlesworth criticizes writers such as Perrin and T. Walker who limit the comparative references in Jewish literature: 'Significant parallels to Jesus' teaching on the Kingdom of God can be found in earlier writings (viz Pss. 103.19, 145.11-13, Isa 52.7). In contrast to the claim that there are only two parallels to the term "Kingdom of God" in intertestamental writings, it is necessary to report that this term is found in the following early Jewish documents' (p. 464). Charlesworth then lists Dan. 3.54 (LXX), *Sib. Or*. 3.47, 767; Tobit 13.2(1), Wis. 6.4; 10.10; *T. Ben*. 9.1; *T. Abr*, 8.3; 1QM 6.6; 12.7. It is difficult to determine in what sense these are significant parallels other than the fact that they contain the lexical item 'Kingdom'. However, as Charlesworth goes on to introduce the most important parallel texts, namely *Psalms of Solomon*, *Testament of Moses*, and the *Qaddish*, he reveals in a footnote his interest in 'influence'. Thus, Charlesworth criticizes Perrin because: 'he did not share with us his thoughts on the way the Testament of Moses may have influenced Jesus, if it did' (p. 467, n. 68). As we noted in our first chapter, assertions concerning influence are notoriously problematic and the thesis that Jesus was influenced by the *Testament of Moses*, or any other text, would require a lot more evidence and argument. In any case, Charlesworth remains unclear about the form of significance he wants to claim for these texts in relation to Jesus' language about the Kingdom—he follows the usual practice of listing 'parallels' as though the connection were obvious.

24. T.F. Glasson, 'Schweitzer's Influence: Bane or Blessing?', in B.D. Chilton (ed.), *The Kingdom of God* (London: SPCK, 1984), pp. 107-20.

25. B.D. Chilton, *God in Strength, Jesus' Announcement of the Kingdom* (Freistadt: F. Plöchl, 1979; repr. Sheffield: JSOT, 1987). In this, and in subsequent works, Chilton argues for the Isaiah Targum as the appropriate background to understanding Jesus' use of Kingdom language.

In a recent work, *Königtum, Königsherrschaft und Reich Gottes in den frühjüdischen Schriften* (Freiburg: Orbis Biblicus and Orientalis, 1984), O. Camponovo offers a review of the term 'kingdom of God' in all the available early Jewish literature, i.e. Old Testament, Maccabean literature, *Psalms of*

Solomon, Qumran, *1 Enoch*, *Jubilees*, *Testaments of the Twelve Patriarchs*, LXX, Targums and others. In a review by G.I. Davies [*JTS* 37 (1986)] the conclusion is drawn from this survey that: 'not too much clarification of meaning should be expected from the Jewish writings available to us' (p. 505). However, Davies goes on: 'Nevertheless, it is clear from the texts that it had a prehistory in Judaism and it is a worthwhile, if rather hazardous, task to trace its development and potential in the contemporary literature' (p. 505). One wonders in what sense this continues to be a worthwhile task.

26. N. Perrin, *Rediscovering the Teaching of Jesus* (London: SCM, 1967), p. 55.

27. J.Z. Smith, 'Wisdom and Apocalyptic', *Visionaries and their Apocalypses*, ed. P.D. Hanson (London: SPCK, 1983), p. 115 'Apocalypticism is a learned rather than a popular religious phenomenon'.

28. C.E. Carlston, 'A Positive Criterion of Authenticity?', *BR* 7 (1962), pp. 33-44; N. Perrin, *Rediscovering the Teaching of Jesus* (London: SCM, 1967); F.G. Downing, *The Church and Jesus* (London: SCM, 1968); W.O. Walker, 'The Quest for the Historical Jesus: A Discussion of Methodology', *ATR* 51 (1969), pp. 38-56; M.D. Hooker, 'Christology and Methodology', *NTS* 17 (1970-71), pp. 480-87; and 'On Using the Wrong Tool', *Theology* 75 (1972), pp. 570-81; D.G.A. Calvert, 'An Examination of the Criteria for Distinguishing the Authentic Words of Jesus', *NTS* 18 (1971-72), pp. 209-19; R.S. Barbour, *Traditio-Historical Criticism of the Gospels* (London: SPCK, 1972); D.L. Mealand, 'The Dissimilarity Test', *SJT* 31 (1978), pp. 41-50; E.P. Sanders (1985).

29. Other criteria that are commonly invoked include: (1) The presence of Aramaisms in various forms. This does not help to authenticate material, but merely points to the possibility of an Aramaic source: the origin of the material remains unclear. (2) Multiple Attestation, either in sources or different forms of material. This is a relatively helpful principle, especially when an idea is present in a number of different forms. It then becomes essential to offer a persuasive explanation of the notable presence of such a motif within the tradition. For a fuller treatment of criteria see Calvert (1971/72).

30. Perrin (1967), pp. 39, 43.

31. R. Bultmann, *The History of the Synoptic Tradition* (Oxford: Blackwell, 1972), p. 205.

32. Cf. R.H. Fuller, *The New Testament in Current Study* (London: SCM, 1963), p. 33.

33. D.L. Mealand (1978), pp. 44, 45.

34. Perrin, p. 39: 'But if we are to seek that which is most characteristic of Jesus, it will be found not in the things which he shares with his contemporaries, but in the things wherein he differs from them'.

35. Cf. Hooker (1970/71).

36. *Op. cit.*, p. 116.

37. Also Mealand, p. 47: 'it is implausible that a controversial new religion owed its origin to someone utterly indistinguishable'. Many would argue, however, that the transition from Judaism to Christianity owes more to Paul than Jesus. In response, one might shift the question from asking how to account for the transition to Christianity, to seeking an explanation for the strong opposition to Jesus from various leading Jewish religious groups.

38. Barbour, p. 6.

39. Hooker (1970/71), p. 483.

40. Sanders (1985), p. 16.

41. E.g. Calvert and Hooker.

42. In an article which we shall consider later on 'Meaning and Understanding in the History of Ideas', *History and Theory* 8 (1969), pp. 3-53, Q. Skinner raises the important notion of development and seems to imply that it may have some explanatory force: 'The very suggestion . . .that the "contradictions and divergences" of a given writer may be "supposed to prove that his thought had changed" has been dismissed . . .as just another delusion of nineteenth-century scholarship' (p. 20). We may not be able to describe the exact course of development, or explain how and why it happened, but it may still be that the appeal to an idea of development offers a persuasive explanation of a difficult text.

43. E.D. Hirsch, *Validity in Interpretation* (New Haven: Yale University Press, 1967), p. 236.

44. S.H. Olsen, *The Structure of Literary Understanding* (Cambridge: CUP, 1978), p. 151.

45. W. Iser, *The Act of Reading* (London: Routledge & Kegan Paul, 1978), p. 15.

46. Cf. R. Alter, *The Art of Biblical Narrative* (London: George Allen & Unwin, 1981). A similar outlook motivates Alter's treatment of 'repetition': 'various commentators have attributed the repetitive features of biblical narrative to its oral origins, to the background of folklore from which it draws, and to the composite nature of the text that has been transmitted to us. The last of these three explanations is the least interesting and finally accounts for the smallest number of cases. There are occasional verses repeated out of scribal error, but under scrutiny most instances of repetition prove to be quite purposeful' (p. 89). And also J. Dewey, *Markan Public Debate* (Chico: Scholars Press, 1980).

47. M.E. Stone, *JBL* 102 (1983), pp. 229-43, esp. p. 242.

48. T. Eagleton, *Literary Theory: An Introduction* (Oxford: Blackwell, 1983), p. 138.

49. P. de Man, *Blindness and Insight. Essays in the Rhetoric of Contemporary Criticism* (London: Methuen, 1983), p. 28.

50. B. Johnson, 'The Critical Difference: Balzac's "Sarrasine" and Barthes's "S/Z"', *Untying the Text. A Post-Structuralist Reader*, ed. R.

Young (London: Routledge & Kegan Paul, 1981), p. 168.

51. For a feminist critique of the ideal of unified characterization see for example Toril Moi, *Sexual / Textual Politics* (London: Methuen, 1985), esp. pp. 7-18. She explores the sexual and political implications involved in the search for a unified meaning in literature.

52. Q. Skinner, 'Meaning and Understanding in the History of Ideas', *History and Theory* 8 (1969), pp. 3-53.

53. Skinner explains the tendency in the History of Ideas (as with the New Critical model in literary studies) to see contradictions as only apparent contradictions: 'The assumption .... is that the correct question to ask in such a doubtful situation is not whether the given writer was inconsistent, but rather "How are his contradictions (or apparent contradictions) to be accounted for?" The explanation dictated by the principle of Ockham's razor (that an apparent contradiction may simply *be* a contradiction) seems not to be considered' (p. 20).

54. See for example the work of Hans Frei, *The Eclipse of Biblical Narrative* (New Haven: Yale University Press, 1974) and *The Identity of Jesus Christ* (Philadelphia: Fortress, 1975).

55. Cf. W. D. Davies, 'A Quest to be Resumed in New Testament Studies', in *New Directions in Biblical Thought*, ed. M.E. Marty (New York: Association, 1960); T.W. Manson, 'The Quest of the Historical Jesus—Continued', in *Studies in the Gospels and Epistles*, ed. M. Black (Philadelphia: Westminster, 1962); J. Jeremias, 'The Present Position in the Controversy Concerning the Problem of the Historical Jesus', in *The Crucified Messiah* (Minneapolis: Augsburg, 1974), pp. 48-89.

56. Walker, 'The Quest of the Historical Jesus: A Discussion of Methodology', p. 54.

57. Cf. my comments in Chapter 3, particularly on the work of J.D. Crossan. Also in his critique of the extreme views of B.B. Scott (1981) and J. Breech, *The Silence of Jesus. The Authentic Voice of the Historical Man* (Philadelphia: Fortress, 1983), Sanders (1985) comments: 'Both of these are based on the assumption that the bedrock material about Jesus consists of a small core of sayings and parables .... The Jesus of these works, I think, could not have been an important historical figure.... A Jesus who was only a teacher, but as teacher did not even communicate striking ideas to his audience, surely was a person of little consequence' (p. 7).

58. Sanders (1985, p. 11) lists the following 'almost indisputable facts':

1. Jesus was baptized by John the Baptist.
2. Jesus was a Galilean who preached and healed.
3. Jesus called disciples and spoke of there being twelve.
4. Jesus confined his activity to Israel.
5. Jesus engaged in a controversy about the Temple.
6. Jesus was crucified outside Jerusalem by the Roman authorities.
7. After his death Jesus' followers continued as an identifiable

movement.

8. At least some Jews persecuted at least parts of the new movement (Gal. 1.13, 22; Phil. 3.6), and it appears that this persecution endured at least to a time near the end of Paul's career (2 Cor. 11.24; Gal. 5.11; 6.12; cf. Mt. 23.34; 10.17).

It is with the 'fact' of Jesus' controversy about the Temple that Sanders begins his study.

59. M. Hooker, Review of Sanders (1985), *Epworth Review* 13 (1986), p. 89.

Notes to Chapter 5

1. A. Dundes and E. Ojo Arewa, 'Proverbs and the Ethnography of Speaking Folklore', *Analytic Essays in Folklore*, ed. A. Dundes (The Hague: Mouton, 1975); R.D. Abrahams, 'Introductory Remarks to a Rhetorical Theory of Folkore', *JAF* 81 (1968), pp. 143-58; R.D. Abrahams and B. Babcock-Abrahams, 'A Sociolinguistic Approach to Proverbs', *MJLF* 1 (1975), pp. 60-64; B. Kirshenblatt-Gimblett, 'Towards a Theory of Proverb Meaning', *The Wisdom of Many*, ed. W. Mieder and A. Dundes (London: Garland, 1981), pp. 111-21; P. Seitel, 'Proverbs. A Social Use of Metaphor', *The Wisdom of Many*, pp. 122-39: 'The meaning of a proverb is made clear only when side by side with the translation is given a full account of the accompanying social situation—the reason for its use, its effect, and its significance in speech' (p. 123).

2. This is not intended as a dogmatically formalist position, but is at this stage a pragmatic point, since speculation about other contextual information not provided in the text is not a very firm basis for analysis.

3. Elsewhere in Matthew proverbial material occurs in similar contexts at 9.37; 12.25, 30; 13.57b; 15.11, 14; 16.25; 18.3; 20.26, 27; 26.41b, 52b. In Lk. 7.47c the saying is related to the behaviour of Jesus' host on this occasion, Simon the Pharisee. Cf. also in Lk. 9.48, 50; 10.2; 11.17, 23; 13.33b; 18.17. Other occurrences in Mark include 2.27; 3.24, 25; 6.4; 8.35, 9.35, 40; 10.43; 14.38b.

4. Mt. 19.30 (cf. Mk 10.31) includes reference to the event of the disciples having left all to follow Jesus, but the saying is more directly related to the implied events of their compensation. Lk. 9.24 is related to the predicted suffering of the Son of Man, while Lk. 12.15b is related to the request concerning the division of an inheritance. Lk. 17.37b is a somewhat enigmatic saying related to some event associated with the coming of the Son of Man.

5. Proverbial sayings occurring in extended discourse: Mt. 5.14b, 45b; 6.34b; 7.2a, b, 8, 13b, 14, 17, 18; 10.10c, 39; 11.8c, 19c; 12.33c, 34b, 35, 37; 23.11, 12; 24.28; Mk 7.15, 20; Lk. 6.38, 40; 7.25b, 35; 8.17, 18b; 10.7b; 11.10; 12.2, 23, 34; 17.33. Some could be considered proverb clusters: Mt. 10.24, 25,

26; Lk. 6.43-45; 11.33-36; Mk 4.21-25.

6. Proverbs summarizing narrative material occur at the end of parables: Lk. 12.48b; 15.7, 10; 16.8, 10, 13; 18.14; 19.26; Mt. 22.14; 25.29.

7. R. Bultmann, 'General Truths and Christian Proclamation', *JTC* 4 (1967).

8. G.N. Leech, *Principles of Pragmatics* (London: Longman, 1983), p. x.

9. The other main influence, usually discussed, would be J.P. Grice's work on meaning and conversational implicature; see for example J. Lyons' treatment of the issue in his section on 'Mood and Illocutionary Force', in *Semantics* Volume II (Cambridge: CUP, 1977), pp. 725f.

10. In her study of *Traditional Sayings in the Old Testament* (Sheffield: Almond, 1982) which includes a section on Proverb Performance, C.R. Fontaine notes the discrepancy at times between the grammar of a sentence and its rhetorical force. Her statement of the point betrays the same interests as pragmatic analysis: 'Whether cast as an interrogative, imperative or simple indicative statement, items tend to be manipulated in context in the same way, to further the same types of interactional ends' (p. 151). Fontaine's assessment of the goal of proverb performance in the texts she studied, as restoring peace in situations of conflict, would be similar to one aspect of the function of proverbs as nondiret speech acts which we will go on to demonstrate.

11. Although Leech's work is introductory he does wish to argue for a particular approach to communication and hence pragmatics in terms of problem solving. Cf. also S.C. Levinson, *Pragmatics* (Cambridge: CUP, 1983); D. Sperber and D. Wilson, *Relevance: Communication and Cognition* (Oxford: Blackwell, 1986).

12. J.L. Austin, *How to Do Things with Words* (Oxford: OUP, 1978), p. 1.

13. N.R. Norrick, *How Proverbs Mean. Semantic Studies in English Proverbs* (Berlin; Mouton, 1985), p. 27. See also 'Nondirect speech acts and double binds', *Poetics* 10 (1981), pp. 33-47. The writings of A. Krikmann also focus on the understanding of proverb performance through pragmatics, see his *On Denotative Indefiniteness of Proverbs. Remarks on Proverb Semantics 1* (Tallinn: Academy of Sciences of the Estonian SSR, 1974), and *Some Additional Aspects of Semantic Indefiniteness of Proverbs. Remarks on Proverb Semantics 2* (Tallinn: Academy of Sciences of the Estonian SSR, 1974). He observes: 'Proverbs do not function as mere poetic adornments of speech; neither are they used, normally, to meet man's needs for philosophical phrasemongering. As a rule, they are used for some practical, pragmatical purposes in various circumstances of everyday communication. With the aid of a proverb one can aim to provide an endorsement to his statements and opinions, forecast something, express doubts, reproach ... accuse ... justify or excuse ... mock ... comfort ... jeer ... repent ... warn against ... advise ... It is unthinkable to consider the proverb

apart from such pragmatic functions' (p. 3).

14. The importance of the principle of truthfulness in this context has to do with Grice's maxim of quality. The study of pragmatics can be undertaken with reference to Conversational Principles (see Leech's *Principles of Pragmatics*, p. 7). Grice's Cooperative Principle is the most fundamental of these [see H.P. Grice, 'Logic and Conversation', *Syntax and Semantics, Volume 3, Speech Acts*, ed. P. Cole and J. L. Morgan (New York: Academic Press, 1975), pp, 41-58.] It includes four maxims, which are presented by Leech (p. 8) as follows:

Quantity: Give the right amount of information: i.e.

1. Make your contribution as informative as is required.
2. Do not make your contribution more informative than is required.

Quality: Try to make your contribution one that is true: i.e.

1. Do not say what you believe to be false.
2. Do not say that for which you lack adequate evidence.

Relation: Be relevant.

Manner: Be perspicuous: i.e.

1. Avoid obscurity of expression.
2. Avoid ambiguity.
3. Be brief (avoid unnecessary prolixity).
4. Be orderly.

Leech uses this Cooperative Principle as the fundamental basis for 'good (i.e. effective) communicative behaviour': thus, a speaker trying to achieve certain aims must do so within the constraints imposed by this set of maxims (and others, such as Politeness and Irony). The situation we are considering, a double bind, is a clash of maxims in conversation. We should note that the maxims of communicative behaviour are descriptive in nature; they are not intended to depend on moral or stylistic judgments.

15. Norrick (1981), p. 38.

16. *Ibid*., p. 39.

17. We do not wish to suggest that the rhetoric of the proverb is only to be understood in terms of the nondirect speech act. In our culture, it might be more important to consider the proverb as a form of cliché, so that the use might differ from that suggested in this study.

18. The idea of distancing could also include the situation where speakers wish to draw attention to their elegance in speech or their own 'witty' use of traditional sayings.

19. In terms of Grice's Cooperative Principle 'indirection' would be a deliberate breaking of one of the maxims; in fact, a combination of Quantity and Manner, in which the speaker gives more information than is required, and fails to avoid ambiguity.

20. There is some ambiguity in Matthew's account concerning whether v. 24 is addressed to the disciples or the woman: a decision on that matter one way or the other would not greatly effect our reading of the exchange, although if this saying were heard by the woman, then she would have had explained to her the connection between 'house of Israel' and 'children'. This would increase the ambiguity in Mark's telling of the incident, and the skill of the woman in seeing the implicature of 'children' would be thrown into sharper focus.

21. See C.E.B. Cranfield, *The Gospel according to Saint Mark. An Introduction and Commentary* (Cambridge: CUP, 1974), p. 248.

22. Our appreciation of the significance of this narrative owes much to S.Ringe's essay 'A Gentile Woman's Story', *Feminist Interpretations of the Bible*, ed. L.M. Russell (Oxford: Blackwell, 1985), pp. 65-72.

23. Other examples of a similar use of proverbial sayings in conversation would include: Mt. 9.12; 26.41b, 52b; Mk 2.17, 27; Lk. 5.31.

24. Cf. Kirshenblatt-Gimblett, p. 114: 'Since an important aspect of proverb use is the indirection it affords and the tacit understanding it assumes, the proverb user who provides an explanation in order to disambiguate the proverb would be doing so as a last resort'. Jesus' intention is not clear in Luke's account, but the effect is certainly a loss of indirection.

25. J. Jeremias, *The Parables of Jesus* (New York: Charles Scribner, 1972), pp. 192, 193. The explicit basis for this interpretation comes in a footnote: 'The passives in Luke 14.11 are thus a circumlocution for the divine name, and the future tenses refer to the Last Judgment' (p. 193 n. 91). This is to base rather a lot on the grammar of the sentence. We see here Jeremias' commitment to read all the parables in the light of what he sees as the dominant eschatological dimension of Jesus' message. The individual parable and saying is hardly allowed to add anything new to our perception of Jesus' message, but merely illustrates the point on which Jeremias was already decided.

26. I.H. Marshall, *The Gospel of Luke. A Commentary on the Greek Text* (Exeter: Paternoster, 1978), pp. 581, 583.

27. This seems to recall John the Baptist's attack on the Pharisees and Sadducees in chapter 3, where he addresses them as 'brood of vipers' (v. 7), and speaks of the need for the 'fruit' of repentance (v. 8). Cf. also 23.33 for the linking of 'brood of vipers' with the scribes and Pharisees.

28. The saying concerning 'two masters' at Mt. 6.24 and Lk. 16.13 also occurs in very different contexts. Matthew includes it in the extended discourse of the Sermon on the Mount, while Luke connects it to the parable of the unrighteous steward and the sayings which follow it, but it is also illuminated by the narrative comment in v. 14. In Luke the saying has the general force of a command to serve God, but also functions as a rebuke against the Pharisees. In Matthew the saying serves as an introduction to the

discourse about anxiety, which is both a command to serve God and a promise that he will provide.

29. R.H. Gundry, *Matthew. A Commentary on his Literary and Theological Art* (Grand Rapids: Eerdmans, 1982), p. 195.

30. J.A. Fitzmyer, *The Gospel according to Luke I–IX* (Garden City: Doubleday, 1981), p. 642.

31. Marshall *op. cit.*, pp. 269, 270.

32. A basic misunderstanding of proverb performance can be seen in P. Minear's handling of the issue of context in his study of Mk 9.33-35 and related sayings, 'Become Last of All', *Commands of Christ* (Nashville: Abingdon, 1972), pp. 83-97. Minear is interested in the origin of the proverb 'If any one wants to be first, he shall be last of all and servant of all'. Thus he asks: 'Is the narrative necessary to make the saying intelligible? Are the setting and the saying independent or interdependent? Is there evidence of an earlier separation of the two? Does the same saying appear in other contexts and forms? If so, which form best explains the origin of the others?' (pp. 85, 86). We have mentioned the problems involved in making historical judgments about particular proverbs, however, Minear goes on to assert: 'There is no necessary connection between the proverb and its setting; the context adds nothing that could not be inferred from the content of the proverb itself. The saying has rich meaning apart from the context; in fact, the setting limits its meaning' (p. 86). It is a defining feature of the proverb that there should be no necessary connection between the proverb and its setting, and the content of a proverb will always be understandable in a minimal way without a specific context. However, proverb performance involves a particular context adding a particular force to the isolated sense of a proverb. The fact that a saying has 'rich meaning apart from its context' shows nothing, other than the fact that the saying may be proverbial! Unless one starts out with the view that Jesus never spoke in proverbial sayings, then Minear's reasoning does not lead very far.

33. H. Anderson, *The Gospel of Mark* (London: Marshall, Morgan & Scott, 1976), p. 136.

34. W.L. Lane, *The Gospel according to Mark* (Grand Rapids: Eerdmans, 1974), p. 166.

35. It would seem quite reasonable to regard the metaphorical use of 'wisdom' as the creative idea of either Jesus, the tradition, or the evangelist, without having to imagine them thinking of the figure of Wisdom in earlier texts. Indeed, speculation about an allusion merely complicates matters, and relies more for its exegesis of this text on other 'Wisdom' texts. Marshall's exegesis of v. 35 appears to reflect this confusion. On the one hand, he wants to claim that: 'In the present passage .... there is little to suggest that wisdom is thought of as a personal being' (p. 303). However, Marshall is also interested in traditions about the figure of Wisdom and their bearing on this text; thus: 'behind the saying (v. 35) lies .... the Jewish tradition concerning

wisdom as a quasi-personal hypostasis in heaven, a divine agent expressing the mind of God, who preaches to men and longs to dwell among them but is rejected' (p. 303). Elsewhere, Marshall is prepared to go even further in drawing upon Wisdom texts to interpret Luke: 'In its Lucan form it (i.e. v. 35) can hardly mean anything other than that the divine wisdom which sent John and Jesus has been vindicated by its children, i.e., by those who have responded to their message' (p. 298). The problematic nature of appeals to allusion based on such slight evidence is quite clear, and we would suggest that the texts (Lk. 7.35 or Mt. 11.19b) are quite explicable without having to posit an allusion.

36. In an earlier note, chapter three n. 31, we warned against making the unwarranted value judgment that oral performance is somehow more important to the proverbial saying genre than literary collection. The value of pragmatic analysis in the study of conversational uses of proverbs should not lead us to consider the use of proverbs in more extended discourse as some kind of (rhetorical) 'failure'. It is merely another use of the proverbial saying which a pragmatic analysis often finds to be more ambiguous or indirect. It is simply more difficult to see the communicative goal of proverb use in these contexts.

Notes to Chapter 6

1. A related problem concerns the relationship between ethics and eschatology in the message of Jesus. The emphasis on eschatology does not necessarily lead to doubts about the authenticity of ethical material, but it does lead to that material being seen as conditioned by the imminent end. The debate about Jesus' ethical teaching therefore tends to revolve around the relevance of that material for ethical thinking today. For an extreme statement of the interim nature of Jesus' ethics see J.T. Sanders, *Ethics in the New Testament* (London: SCM, 1975): 'To put the matter now most sharply, Jesus does not provide a valid ethics for today. His ethical teaching is interwoven with his imminent eschatology to such a degree that every attempt to separate the two and to draw out only the ethical thread invariably and inevitably draws out also strands of the eschatology, so that both yarns only lie in a heap. Better to leave the tapestry intact, to let Jesus, as Albert Schweitzer appealed to us to do, return to his own time' (p. 29). A less extreme and more persuasive position is argued in A.N. Wilder, *Eschatology and Ethics in the Teaching of Jesus* (New York: Harper & Row, 1950).

2. If we reject the idea of finding a firm basis of 'characteristic' material in the Synoptics, largely through a combination of the dissimilarity test and our understanding of the supposed background to the term Kingdom of God in Jewish literature, then arguing for the coherence of certain aspects of the Gospels will not necessarily aid our attempts at reconstruction.

3. See W. Grundmann, 'Weisheit im Horizont des Reiches Gottes: eine

Studie zur Verkündigung Jesu nach der Spruchüberlieferung Q', *Die Kirche des Anfangs: Festschrift für Heinz Schürmann*, ed. R. Schnackenburg, J. Ernst, & J. Wanke (Leipzig: St-Benno Verlag, p. 178; also J. Riches, *Jesus and the Transformation of Judaism* (London: Darton, Longman & Todd, 1980), p. 148 refers to *1 Enoch* 1-5; C.E.Carlston, 'Wisdom and Eschatology in Q', *Logia. Les Paroles de Jésus*, ed. J. Delobel (Leuven: Leuven University Press, 1982) refers to the Wisdom of Solomon, the *Testaments of the Twelve Patriarchs*, *4 Ezra*, Matthew, the Didache and Hermas as: 'documents from the beginning of our era in which eschatology (or apocalyptic) and wisdom are closely associated' (p. 114). Cf. also our earlier comments on the subject.

4. C.E. Carlston, p. 116.

5. R.A. Edwards, *A Theology of Q: Eschatology, Prophecy and Wisdom* (Philadelphia: Fortress, 1976), p. 147

6. R.L. Jeske, *The Wisdom Structure of Jesus' Eschatology* (Doctoral Dissertation, Ruprecht-Karl University, Heidelberg, 1969); also 'Wisdom and the Future in the Teaching of Jesus', *Dialog* 1 (1972), pp. 108-17. References are to the dissertation.

7. See pp. 35f., 'Wisdom and the Divine Secrets', and pp. 46f., 'The Legitimation of the Apocalyptic Visionary'.

8. J.J. Collins, 'The Court-Tales in Daniel and the Development of Apocalyptic', *JBL* 94 (1975), pp. 218-34.

9. Collins notes that in his critique of von Rad's views on the connection between wisdom and apocalyptic [*Die Apokalyptik in ihrem Verhältnis zu Prophetie und Weisheit* (Munich: Chr. Kaiser, 1969)] P. von der Osten-Sacken fails to take account of the phenomenon of mantic wisdom. This issue is taken up by H.-P. Müller, 'Mantische Weisheit und Apokalyptik', *VT Supp* 22 (Leiden: Brill, 1972), pp. 268-93, where he seeks to defend von Rad by defining more precisely the sort of wisdom which lies behind apocalyptic. This article is also a useful introduction to the phenomenon of mantic wisdom.

10. Jeske's examples with specific referents include *4 Ezra* 8.9; 3.36; 4.12, 46.

11. Mk 8.35-37 par; 10.23b, 25 par; 10.15; 10.31; Lk. 14.11; 6.20b-21b, 17.20-21; 12.54-56; Mt. 16.2-3; 5.3-4, 6.

12. By 'common view' we mean a common set of characteristic interests (e.g. eschatology, and the relationship of present and future), even though there may be some disagreement on detail.

13. If New Testament critics are going to continue to try to represent 'the historical Jesus', then some account of his teaching will need to be given, in spite of the problems involved. Given the unsatisfactory nature of discussions of authenticity some have sought to base their work on what they consider the certain events of Jesus' life. Thus, in his *Jesus the Magician* (San Francisco: Harper & Row, 1978) Morton Smith raises the question of what

people, who did not believe in Jesus, had to say about him, and he focuses attention on the issue of why people came to Jesus. He can offer a reasonably certain answer in the fact that people were attracted by his miracles. Smith then goes on to find external support for this picture of Jesus as magician/ miracle worker, and on this basis he is able to go on to offer an account of why Jesus was crucified. However, to claim that this is an account of 'the historical Jesus' is inadequate. He may be right to be sceptical about the status of the sayings tradition, but to exclude that tradition completely from consideration, and still to claim an accurate portrayal of Jesus is to distort in the same way as does an emphasis on the so-called 'characteristic' teaching of Jesus. Smith may have offered a persuasive answer to the question of why people initially flocked to Jesus, but given his thorough-going scepticism about the sayings tradition he should have restricted himself to offering an answer to that limited question and remained silent about the significance of Jesus' life. If our sources are judged to be inadequate, then we should content ourselves with more limited claims.

14. Cf. the full-length studies on the Kingdom in Mark by A.M. Ambrozic, *The Hidden Kingdom. A Redaction-Critical Study of the References to the Kingdom in Mark's Gospel* (Worcester, Mass: Heffernan, 1972); W. Kelber, *The Kingdom in Mark. A New Place and a New Time* (Philadelphia: Fortress, 1974).

15. The discussion and literature on ἤγγικεν in Mk 1.15 is summarized in Ambrozic, pp. 15f.; cf. also B.D. Chilton, *God in Strength* (Freistadt: F. Plöchl, 1979), pp. 56-58 n. 96. Much of the discussion concerns the possible Aramaic background to the verb, and is therefore of limited value for our interests.

16. Cf. Ambrozic, p. 16, quoting R.F. Berkey: 'EGGIZEIN, PHTHANEIN, and Realized Eschatology', *JBL* 82 (1963), pp. 177-87.

17. M. Black ('The Kingdom of God Has Come', *ET* 63 [1951-52], p. 290) comments on the actual meaning of the phrase as it now stands in Mark, 'The parallel at Mk 1, 15 *peplerotai* ... may be taken to support the translation .... "The Kingdom of God *has come*"'.

18. We would therefore disagree with Ambrozic when he claims that on the basis of rabbinic parallels provided by Dalman and Billerbeck: 'the conclusion to be drawn is that "to enter the kingdom" refers to the future eschatological fulfilment of God's reign' (p. 139). Cf. G. Dalman, *The Words of Jesus* (Edinburgh: T&T Clark, 1902), pp. 116-17.

19. See for example C.E.B. Cranfield, *The Gospel According to Saint Mark* (Cambridge: CUP, 1959), pp. 285-89 where he offers seven possible interpretations.

20. Cf. M. Völkel, 'Zur Deutung des Reiches Gottes bei Lukas', *ZNW* 65 (1974), pp. 57-70; S.G. Wilson, 'Lukan Eschatology', *NTS* 15 (1969-70), pp. 330-47. Wilson brings out the diversity of Luke's teaching about the future. He sees Luke as trying to meet practical pastoral needs rather than

developing a coherent scheme. E. Earle Ellis, 'Present and Future Eschatology in Luke', *NTS* 12 (1965), pp. 27-41; R. Maddox, *The Purpose of Luke-Acts* (Göttingen: Vandenhoeck & Ruprecht, 1982) esp. ch. 5 'The Lukan Eschatology', pp. 100-157; I.H. Marshall, *Luke: Historian and Theologian* (Exeter: Paternoster, 1970), especially pp. 128-36. Marshall's treatment of the Kingdom in Luke is dominated by the temporal question of when the Kingdom will appear (p. 129).This is because he wants to show continuity between Jesus' teaching and Luke's. For Marshall, in Jesus' teaching, 'the term kingdom is used mainly of the action of God in intervening in human history to establish his rule' (p. 129). Jesus spoke both of the presence and the future coming of the Kingdom. This judgment is based on the fact that Jesus' use of the Kingdom idea has its background in the apocalyptic expectation of the establishment of God's rule at the End. Marshall's interests are determined by questions external to Luke; we would agree more with Maddox who does not see Luke's interest as being focused on the temporal question, 'Luke's real concern is not *when* the Kingdom of God will come (as is generally assumed) but *who* will qualify to be admitted to it' (p. 106).

21. Luke has seven uses of 'Kingdom' which are of less significance, 4.5, 11.17, 18, 20, 19.12, 15, 21.10.

22. M. Pamment, 'The Kingdom of Heaven according to the First Gospel', *NTS* 27 (1981), pp. 211-32. Pamment argues, amongst other things, that 'the kingdom of heaven' is an imminent but entirely future reality which is other-worldly in the sense that the world as it is experienced now will no longer exist. Thus, when faced with references to the Kingdom in the present, such as 5.3, 10 she speaks of 'futuristic presents' (p. 213) and again at 18.4 ἐστιν is gnomic (p. 224), also 11.11 (p. 227). This serves to reinforce her main point that 'Kingdom of God' as distinct from 'Kingdom of heaven' represents a present Kingdom (there are, however, problematic exceptions to this e.g. 11.11, 12 [see pp. 227, 228], and 19.23, 24). Our disagreement with Pamment is that in elevating the temporal question above all others, she fails to appreciate the richness of Matthew's language about the Kingdom.

23. J.J. Collins, 'Apocalyptic Eschatology as the Transcendence of Death', *Visionaries and their Apocalypses*, ed. P.D. Hanson (London: SPCK, 1983), pp. 61-84. Collins is concerned with what he calls the later type of apocalyptic, namely Daniel and some intertestamental works (Qumran texts, *1 Enoch*, *Jubilees*, and the *Assumption of Moses*).

24. Pamment asserts p. 219: 'Knowledge of the secrets of the kingdom of heaven means firstly the fact that the kingdom of heaven is about to arrive (Mark's singular μυστήριον refers to this), and secondly to the conditions of entry into the kingdom which have already been outlined in the Gospel.' There appears to be no evidence for this assertion.

25. See the summaries of research on the Kingdom by N. Perrin, *The Kingdom of God in the Teaching of Jesus* (London: SCM, 1963), and G.

Lundström, *The Kingdom of God in the Teaching of Jesus. A History of Interpretation from the Last Decades of the Nineteenth Century to the Present Day* (Edinburgh: Oliver & Boyd, 1963). A recent work by G.R. Beasley-Murray, *Jesus and the Kingdom of God* (Exeter: Paternoster, 1986) is structured around the temporal issue of present or future sayings and parables.

26. Cf. Van A. Harvey, *A Handbook of Theological Terms* (London: Allen & Unwin, 1966), 'Transcendence', pp. 207-208.

27. N. Perrin, *Jesus and the Language of the Kingdom* (London: SCM, 1976). Cf. also the work of B.B. Scott, *Jesus, Symbol-Maker for the Kingdom* (Philadelphia: Fortress, 1981); and M. Borg (1984).

28. A.N. Wilder (1950), and 'Scholars, Theologians and Ancient Rhetoric', *JBL* 75 (1955), pp. 1-11; 'Kerygma, Eschatology and Social Ethics', *The Background of the New Testament and its Eschatology*, ed. W.D. Davies and D. Daube (Cambridge: CUP, 1956); 'Eschatological Imagery and Earthly Circumstance', *NTS* 5 (1958), pp. 229-45; 'Social Factors in Early Christian Eschatology', *Early Christian Origins*, ed. A.Wikgren (Chicago: Quadrangle, 1961), pp. 67-76; 'Eschatology and the Speech-Modes of the Gospel', *Zeit und Geschichte*, ed. E. Dinkler (Tübingen: Mohr, 1964); 'The Rhetoric of Ancient and Modern Apocalyptic', *Int* 25 (1971), pp. 436-53.

29. M.J. Borg, *Conflict, Holiness and Politics in the Teachings of Jesus* (New York: Edwin Mellen, 1984), esp. ch. 8, 'Jesus and the Future'.

30. Borg, pp. 209-21.

31. See also G.B. Caird, *The Language and Imagery of the Bible* (London: Duckworth, 1980), pp. 243-71. Caird has a good review of 'the language of eschatology', arguing against the influential views of Weiss and Schweitzer which attribute a pedestrian mentality to the biblical writers.

32. H. Bald, 'Eschatological or Theocentric Ethics? Notes on the Relationship between Eschatology and Ethics in the Teaching of Jesus', *The Kingdom of God*, ed. B.D. Chilton (London: SPCK, 1984), pp. 133-53. Bald's work is a helpful review of the discussion, and he makes some important points along the way, particularly on the need to reconsider what is meant by Jesus' eschatology. However, his conclusion serves to compound the terminological muddle: 'Jesus' theology is eschatological, because he preaches the coming of God "now"; but his eschatology is theocentric, because it is based on a conception of God which includes eschatology. Jesus' ethics are eschatological and non-eschatological at the same time. This can be the case because Jesus now proclaims the will of God, who is more than his eschatological coming' (p. 152).

33. H. Schürmann, 'Das hermeneutische Hauptproblem der Verkündigung Jesu', *Traditionsgeschichtliche Untersuchungen zu den synoptischen Evangelien* (Düsseldorf: Patmos, 1968), pp. 13-35; A. Vögtle, '"Theo-logie" und "Eschatologie" in der Verkündigung Jesu?', *Neues Testament und Kirche*, ed. J. Gnilka (Freiburg: Herder, 1974), pp. 371-98. Apart from a problem with

Schürmann's Christological emphasis, Vögtle rejects the idea of non-eschatological material based on God's present power in creation. Bald accepts some of Vögtle's criticisms, but in the end he himself favours Schürmann's viewpoint: 'The most important observation is that the tension in Jesus' teaching between statements oriented towards the future (temporally) and non-eschatological (e.g. ethical) statements oriented towards the present cannot be reduced and removed in some timeless, existential interpretation by eliminating the time factor. In my opinon, the idea that Jesus' conception of God is to be regarded as the basis of both ethical and (in the final analysis) eschatological teaching is just as important' (p. 143). We would disagree with Schürmann in that he still maintains the idea of the Kingdom as eschatological over against other theological material.

34. H. Windisch, *The Meaning of the Sermon on the Mount* (Philadelphia: Westminster, 1951). Windisch concludes his opening chapter on 'The Sermon on the Mount and Eschatology': 'In the Sermon on the Mount two great currents of the Synoptic proclamation of Jesus are brought together—purified and radicalized wisdom teaching and prophetic-eschatological proclamation of salvation and judgment. They exhibit a twofold relationship. Sometimes they flow along side by side, unmixed, and sometimes they intermingle because they contain common motives. To these, above all, belongs the idea of God, conceived in its purity. This determines Jesus' "wisdom" as well as his prophetic message, and in both intensifies the demand for radical detachment from all that is outside the sphere of the divine' (pp. 39, 40).

35. H. Conzelmann, *An Outline of the Theology of the New Testament* (London: SCM, 1969), pp. 99f. Conzelmann argues: 'Only in a qualified sense can one describe Jesus' idea of God as eschatological. The concept of the kingdom of God is eschatological. But the idea of God is not exhausted in statements about the coming kingdom of God. Alongside it stand statements about God's present rule which do not look for an imminent end of the world' (p. 99).

36. L. Goppelt, *Theology of the New Testament* I (Grand Rapids: Eerdmans, 1981), esp. pp. 67-76.

37. A. Schweitzer, *The Mystery of the Kingdom of God. The Secret of Jesus' Messiahship and Passion* (London: A & C Black, 1914). The introduction by W. Lowrie is dated 1913.

38. Cf. Pamment, writing on Matthew: 'The ethic of the Sermon on the Mount, and that of the rest of the Gospel .... is not determined by the nearness of the end but is an expression of God's eternal will for man, contra Albert Schweitzer and more recently Jack Sanders. The urgency of the demand is determined by the nearness of the end but not the content of the demand' (p. 216).

39. Bald, p. 151.

40. A point stressed by J. Riches in *Jesus and the Transformation of*

Judaism (London: Darton, Longman & Todd, 1980), esp. ch. 5. Also the essay written with A. Millar, 'Conceptual Change in the Synoptic Tradition', *Alternative Approaches to New Testament Study*, ed. A.E. Harvey (London: SPCK, 1985), pp. 37-60.

41. See C.E. Carlston, 'Proverbs, Maxims, and the Historical Jesus', *JBL* 99 (1980), pp. 91f. He notes the absence of admonitions to seek wisdom; teaching devoted to character building (this is surely questionable); conventional wisdom about women; teaching on family relationships; and the sense of balance which characterizes so much of the wisdom tradition.

42. Cf. R.F. Horton's article, 'Christ's Use of the Book of Proverbs', *The Expositor* 3rd series, 7 (1888), pp. 105-23.

43. Cf. E.P. Sanders, 'Jesus and the Sinners', *JSNT* 19 (1983), pp. 5-36, and *Jesus and Judaism* (London: SCM, 1985).

44. Cf. F.G. Watson, 'Why Was Jesus Crucified?', *Theology* 88 (1985), pp. 105-12.

BIBLIOGRAPHY

Abel, E.L., 'The Psychology of Memory and Rumour Transmission and their Bearing on Theories of Oral Transmission in Early Christianity', *JR* 51 (1971), pp. 270-81.

Abrahams, R.D., 'Introductory Remarks to a Rhetorical Theory of Folklore', *JAF* 81 (1968), pp. 143-58.

—'Proverbs and Proverbial Expressions', *Folklore and Folklife*, ed. R.M. Dorson (Chicago: Chicago University Press, 1972), pp. 117-27.

—with B. Babcock-Abrahams, 'A Sociolinguistic Approach to Proverbs', *MJLF* 1 (1975), pp. 60-64.

Adcock, F.E., *Thucydides and his History* (Cambridge: Cambridge University Press, 1963).

Alonso Schökel, L., 'Sapiential and Covenant Themes in Genesis 2–3', *Studies in Ancient Israelite Wisdom*, ed. J.L. Crenshaw (New York: Ktav, 1976), pp. 468-80.

Alter, R., *The Art of Biblical Narrative* (London: Allen & Unwin, 1981).

Ambrozic, A.M., *The Hidden Kingdom. A Redaction-Critical Study of References to the Kingdom in Mark's Gospel* (Worcester, Mass: Heffernan, 1972).

Amsler, S., 'La sagesse de la Femme', *La Sagesse de l'Ancien Testament*, ed. M. Gilbert (Leuven: Leuven University Press, 1979), pp. 112-16.

Anderson, H., *The Gospel of Mark* (London: Marshall, Morgan & Scott, 1976).

Arewa, E. Ojo, with A. Dundes, 'Proverbs and the Ethnography of Speaking Folklore', *Analytic Essays in Folklore*, ed. A. Dundes (The Hague: Mouton, 1975).

Austin, J.L., *How to Do Things with Words* (Oxford: Oxford University Press, 1978).

Bald, H., 'Eschatological or Theocentric Ethics? Notes on the Relationship between Eschatology and Ethics in the Teaching of Jesus', *The Kingdom of God*, ed. B.D. Chilton (London: SPCK, 1984), pp. 133-53.

Barbour, R.S., *Traditio-Historical Criticism of the Gospels* (London: SPCK, 1972).

Barr, J., *Holy Scripture. Canon, Authority, Criticism* (Oxford: Clarendon, 1983).

Barrett, C.K., *The Gospel according to St John* (London: SPCK, 1978).

Beardslee, W., 'The Wisdom Tradition and the Synoptic Gospels', *JAAR* 35 (1967), pp. 231-40.

—*Literary Criticism of the New Testament* (Philadelphia: Fortress, 1970).

—'Uses of the Proverb in the Synoptic Gospels', *Int* 24 (1970), pp. 61-73.

—*A House for Hope: A Study in Process and Biblical Thought* (Philadelphia: Westminster, 1972).

—'Proverbs in the Gospel of Thomas', *Studies in New Testament and Early Christian Literature: Essays for A.P. Wikgren*, ed. D.E. Aune (Novum Testamentum Supplement, 33; Leiden: Brill, 1972), pp. 92-103.
—'Saving One's Life by Losing it', *JAAR* 47 (1977), pp. 57-72.
—'Parable, Proverb and Koan', *Semeia* 12 (1978), pp. 151-77.
—'Plutarch's Use of Proverbial Sayings', *Semeia* 17 (1980), pp. 101-12.
Beasley-Murray, G.R., *Jesus and the Kingdom of God* (Exeter: Paternoster, 1986).
Berger, P., *The Precarious Vision* (Garden City: Doubleday, 1961).
—with T. Luckmann, *The Social Construction of Reality* (Harmondsworth: Penguin, 1966).
Berkey, R.F., 'EGGIZEIN, PHTHANEIN, and Realized Eschatology', *JBL* 82 (1963), pp. 177-87.
Best, T.F., 'The Sociological Study of the New Testament: Promise and Peril of a New Discipline', *SJT* 36 (1983), pp. 181-94.
Betz, H.D., 'The Logion of the Easy Yoke and of Rest (Matt 11.28-30)', *JBL* 86 (1967), pp. 10-24.
Black, M., 'The Kingdom of God has come', *ET* 63 (1951-52), pp. 289-90.
Blass, F., A. Debrunner & R.W. Funk, *A Greek Grammar of the New Testament and other Early Christian Literature* (Chicago: Chicago University Press, 1961).
Bonnard, P., *La Sagesse en personne annoncée et venue: Jésus Christ* (Paris: Les Editions du Cerf, 1966).
Borg, M.J., *Conflict, Holiness and Politics in the Teachings of Jesus* (New York: Edwin Mellen, 1984).
Breech, J., *The Silence of Jesus. The Authentic Voice of the Historical Man* (Philadelphia: Fortress, 1983).
Brown, R.E., *The Gospel according to John I-XII* (Garden City: Doubleday, 1966).
Brueggemann, W., *In Man We Trust: The Neglected Side of Biblical Faith* (Richmond, VA: John Knox, 1972).
Bultmann, R., 'The New Approach to the Synoptic Problem', *Existence and Faith* (London: Collins, 1964), pp. 39-62.
—'Der religionsgeschichtliche Hintergrund des Prologs zum Johannes-Evangelium', *Exegetica: Aufsätze zur Erforschung des Neuen Testaments* (Tübingen: Mohr, 1967), pp. 10-35.
—*The History of the Synoptic Tradition* (Oxford: Blackwell, 1972).
—'General Truths and Christian Proclamation', *JTC* 4 (1967), pp. 153-62.
Burnett, F.W., *The Testament of Jesus Sophia* (Washington: University Press of America, 1979).
Burney, C.F., *The Poetry of our Lord* (Oxford: Clarendon, 1925).
Caird, G.B., *The Language and Imagery of the Bible* (London: Duckworth, 1980).
Calvert, D.G.A., 'An Examination of the Criteria for Distinguishing the Authentic Words of Jesus', *NTS* 18 (1971-72), pp. 209-19.
Camp, C.V., *Wisdom and the Feminine in the Book of Proverbs* (Sheffield: Almond, 1985).
Carlston, C.E., 'A Positive Criterion of Authenticity?', *BR* 7 (1962), pp. 33-44.
—'Proverbs, Maxims, and the Historical Jesus', *JBL* 99 (1980), pp. 87-105.
—'Wisdom and Eschatology in Q', *Logia. Les Paroles de Jésus*, ed. J. Delobel (Leuven: Leuven University Press, 1982).
Carmignac, J., *Le Mirage de l'Eschatologie* (Paris; Letouzey et Ané, 1979).
Charlesworth, J.H., 'The Historical Jesus in Light of Writings Contemporaneous with Him', *Aufstieg und Niedergang der römischen Welt*, ed. W. Haase, II 25.1 (Berlin: de Gruyter, 1982), pp. 451-76.

Chilton, B.D., *God in Strength. Jesus' Announcement of the Kingdom* (Freistadt: F. Plöchl, 1979; repr. Sheffield: JSOT, 1987).
—*The Kingdom of God* (London: SPCK, 1984).
Christ, F., *Jesus Sophia: die Sophia-Christologie bei den Synoptikern* (Zürich: Zwingli, 1970).
Cobb, J.B., 'A Theology of Story: Crossan and Beardslee', *Orientation by Disorientation. Studies in Literary Criticism and Biblical Literary Criticism, presented in honour of William A. Beardslee*, ed. R.A. Spencer (Pittsburgh: Pickwick, 1980), pp. 151-64.
Collingwood, R.G., *The Idea of History* (Oxford: Oxford University Press, 1961).
Collins, J.J., 'The Court-Tales in Daniel and the Development of Apocalyptic', *JBL* 94 (1975), pp. 218-34.
—'Apocalyptic Eschatology as the Transcendence of Death', *Visionaries and their Apocalypses*, ed. P.D. Hanson (London: SPCK, 1983), pp. 37-60.
Conzelmann, H., *An Outline of the Theology of the New Testament* (London: SCM, 1969).
—'The Mother of Wisdom', *The Future of our Religious Past*, ed. J.M. Robinson (London: SCM, 1971), pp. 230-43.
Cranfield, C.E.B., *The Gospel according to Saint Mark. An Introduction and Commentary* (Cambridge: Cambridge University Press, 1974).
Crenshaw, J.L., 'The Influence of the Wise upon Amos', *ZAW* 79 (1967), pp. 42-52.
—'Method in Determining Wisdom Influence upon Historical Literature', *JBL* 88 (1969), pp. 129-42.
—'Review of Whedbee (1971)', *Int* 26 (1972), pp. 74-76.
—ed. *Studies in Ancient Israelite Wisdom* (New York: Ktav, 1976).
Crossan, J.D., *The Dark Interval: Towards a Theology of Story* (Illinois: Argus Communications, 1975).
—*Raid on the Articulate: Comic Eschatology in Jesus and Borges* (New York: Harper & Row, 1976).
—*A Fragile Craft. The Work of Amos Niven Wilder* (Chico: Scholars Press, 1981).
—*In Fragments. The Aphorisms of Jesus* (New York: Harper & Row, 1983).
—*Four Other Gospels. Shadows on the Contours of Canon* (Minneapolis: Winston, 1985).
Dahl, N.A., 'The Problem of the Historical Jesus', *The Crucified Messiah* (Minneapolis: Augsburg, 1974), pp. 48-89.
Dalman, G., *The Words of Jesus Considered in the Light of Post-Biblical Jewish Writings and the Aramaic Language* (Edinburgh: T & T Clark, 1902).
—*Jesus Jeshua* (London: SPCK, 1929).
Davids, P.H., *The Epistle of James: A Commentary on the Greek Text* (Grand Rapids: Eerdmans, 1982).
Davies, G.I., 'Review of O. Camponovo: *Königtum, Königsherrschaft und Reich Gottes in den frühjüdischen Schriften* (Freiburg: Orbis Biblicus and Orientalis, 1984)', *JTS* 37 (1986).
Davies, S.L., *The Gospel of Thomas and Christian Wisdom* (New York: Seabury, 1983).
Davies, W.D., 'A Quest to be Resumed in New Testament Studies', *New Directions in Biblical Thought*, ed. M.E. Marty (New York: Association, 1960).
—*Paul and Rabbinic Judaism* (London: SPCK, 1979).
Dewey, J., *Markan Public Debate* (Chico: Scholars Press, 1980).
Dewey, K.E., '*Paroimiai* in the Gospel of John', *Semeia* 17 (1980), pp. 81-99.
Dodd, C.H., *The Parables of the Kingdom* (London: Nisbet, 1935).

Downing, F.G., *The Church and Jesus* (London: SCM, 1968).
Duling, D., and N. Perrin, *The New Testament: an Introduction* (New York: Harcourt, Brace Jovanovich, 1982).
Dundes, A., with R.A. George, 'Toward a Structural Definition of the Riddle', *JAF* 76 (1963), pp. 111-18.
—*Analytic Essays in Folklore* (The Hague: Mouton, 1975).
—'The Structure of the Proverb', *The Wisdom of Many. Essays on the Proverb*, ed. A. Dundes and W. Mieder (London: Garland, 1981), pp. 43-64.
Dunn, J.D.G., *Christology in the Making: An Inquiry into the Origins of the Doctrine of the Incarnation* (London: SCM, 1980).
Eagleton, T., *Literary Theory. An Introduction* (Oxford: Blackwell, 1983).
Edwards, O.C., 'Sociology as a Tool for Interpreting the New Testament', *ATR* 65 (1983), pp. 431-48.
Edwards, R.A., *A Theology of Q: Eschatology, Prophecy and Wisdom* (Philadelphia: Fortress, 1976).
Ellis, E.E., 'Present and Future Eschatology in Luke', *NTS* 12 (1965), pp. 27-41.
Erhardt, A.A.T., *The Framework of the New Testament* (Manchester: Manchester University Press, 1964).
Evans-Pritchard, E.E., 'Zandu Proverbs: Final Selection and Comments', *Man* 64 (1974), pp. 1-5.
Farmer, W.R., *The Synoptic Problem. A Critical Analysis* (Dillsboro: Western North Carolina Press, 1976).
Fenn, W.W., *The Theological Method of Jesus* (Boston: Beacon, 1938).
Feuillet, A., 'Jesus et la Sagesse divine d'après les évangiles synoptiques', *RB* 62 (1955), pp. 161-96.
Fichtner, J., 'Isaiah among the Wise', *Studies in Ancient Israelite Wisdom*, ed. J.L. Crenshaw (New York: Ktav, 1976), pp. 429-38.
Finley, M.I., *Ancient History, Evidence and Models* (London: Chatto & Windus, 1985).
Fitzmyer, J.A., *The Gospel according to Luke I-IX* (Garden City: Doubleday, 1981).
Fontaine, C.R., *Traditional Sayings in the Old Testament* (Sheffield: Almond, 1982).
Frei, H., *The Eclipse of Biblical Narrative* (New Haven: Yale University Press, 1974).
—*The Identity of Jesus Christ* (Philadelphia: Fortress, 1975).
Fuller, R.H., *The New Testament in Current Study* (London: SCM, 1963).
—'The Double Commandment of Love: A Test Case for the Criteria of Authenticity', *Essays on the Love Commandment*, ed. L. Schottroff, C. Burchard, M.J. Suggs, and R.H. Fuller (Philadelphia: Fortress, 1979).
Gager, J.G., 'Review of R.M. Grant, A.J. Malherbe, and G. Theissen', *RSR* 5 (1979), pp. 174-80.
—'Shall We Marry Our Enemies? Sociology and the New Testament', *Int* 36 (1982), pp. 256-65.
George, R.A., with A. Dundes, 'Toward a Structural Definition of the Riddle', *JAF* 76 (1963), pp. 111-18.
Gese, H., 'Wisdom, Son of Man, and the Origins of Christology: The Consistent Development of Biblical Theology', *HBT* 3 (1981), pp. 23-57.
Glasson, T.F., 'Schweitzer's Influence: Bane or Blessing?', *The Kingdom of God*, ed. B.D. Chilton (London: SPCK, 1984), pp. 107-20.
Goldmann, L., 'The Sociology of Literature: Status and Problems of Method', *The Sociology of Art and Literature: A Reader*, ed. M.C. Albrecht, J.H. Barnett, and M. Griff (London: Duckworth, 1970), pp. 582-609.

Goody, J., *The Domestication of the Savage Mind* (Cambridge: Cambridge University Press, 1977).

Goodwin, P.A., with J.W. Wenzel, 'Proverbs and Practical Reasoning: A Study in Socio-Logic', *The Wisdom of Many*, ed. A. Dundes and W. Mieder (London: Garland, 1984), pp. 140-60.

Goppelt, L., *Theology of the New Testament* I (Grand Rapids: Eerdmans, 1981).

Gordis, R., 'The Social Background of Wisdom Literature', *Poets, Prophets and Sages: Essays in Biblical Interpretation* (Bloomington: Indiana University Press, 1971), pp. 160-97.

Gottwald, N.K., *The Hebrew Bible. A Socio-Literary Introduction* (Philadelphia: Fortress, 1985).

Grant, F.C., 'The Idea of the Kingdom of God in the New Testament', *Studies in the History of Religions IV. La Regalita Sacra. The Sacral Kingship* (Leiden: Brill, 1959).

Grice, J.P., 'Logic and Conversation', *Syntax and Semantics, Volume Three, Speech Acts*, ed. P. Cole and J.L. Morgan (New York: Academic Press, 1975), pp. 41-58.

Grundmann, W., 'Weisheit im Horizont des Reiches Gottes. Eine Studie zur Verkündigung Jesu nach der Spruchüberlieferung Q', *Die Kirche des Anfangs: Festschrift für H. Schürmann*, ed. R. Schnackenburg, J. Ernst & J. Wanke (Leipzig: St-Benno Verlag, 1978), pp. 175-99.

Gundry, R.H., *Matthew. A Commentary on his Literary and Theological Art* (Grand Rapids: Eerdmans, 1982).

Gunkel, H., 'The Religio-Historical Interpretation of the New Testament', *The Monist* 13 (1902/1903).

Güttgemanns, E., *Candid Questions Concerning Gospel Form Criticism* (Pittsburgh: Pickwick Press, 1979).

Halson, R.P., 'The Epistle of James: Christian Wisdom?', *Studia Evangelica IV* (Berlin: Akademie, 1968), pp. 308-14.

Harnack, A., *What is Christianity?* (London: Williams & Norgate, 1901).

Harrington, D.J., 'The Jewishness of Jesus: Facing Some Problems', *CBQ* 49 (1987), pp. 1-13.

Harvey, A.E., *Jesus and the Constraints of History* (London: Duckworth, 1982).

Harvey, V.A., *A Handbook of Theological Terms* (London: Allen & Unwin, 1966).

—'Religious Faith and the Sociology of Knowledge: The Unburdening of Peter Berger', *RSR* 5 (1979), pp. 1-10.

Hengel, M., *Judaism and Hellenism* (London: SCM, 1974).

—'Jesus als Messianischer Lehrer der Weisheit und die Anfänge der Christologie', *Sagesse et Religion: Colloque de Strasbourg, 1976*, ed. E. Jacob (Paris: Presses Universitaires de France, 1979).

—*The Charismatic Leader and his Followers* (Edinburgh: T & T Clark, 1981).

Hermisson, H.J., *Studien zur israelitischen Spruchweisheit* (Neukirchen-Vluyn: Neukirchener Verlag, 1968).

Herskovits, M.J. and F.S., *Dahomean Narrative* (Evanston: Northwestern University Press, 1958).

Hirsch, E.D., *Validity in Interpretation* (New Haven: Yale University Press, 1967).

Holladay, C.R., *Theios Aner in Hellenistic Judaism: A Critique of the Use of this Category in New Testament Christology* (Missoula: Scholars Press, 1977).

Hollenbach, P.W., 'Recent Historical Jesus Studies and the Social Sciences', *SBL Seminar Papers 1983*, pp. 61-78.

Hooker, M., 'Christology and Methodology', *NTS* 17 (1970/71), pp. 480-87.

—'On Using the Wrong Tool', *Theology* 75 (1972), pp. 570-81.
—'Review of E.P. Sanders: *Jesus and Judaism* (London: SCM, 1985)', *Epworth Review* 13 (1986), p. 89.
Horton, R.F., 'Christ's Use of the Book of Proverbs', *The Expositor* 3rd series, 7 (1888), pp. 105-23.
Isenberg, S.R., 'Some Uses and Limitations of Social Scientific Methodology in the Study of Early Christianity', *SBL Seminar Papers 1980*, pp. 29-49.
Iser, W., *The Act of Reading* (London: Routledge & Kegan Paul, 1978).
Jeremias, J., 'The Present Position in the Controversy concerning the Problem of the Historical Jesus', *ET* 69 (1958), pp. 248-51.
—*New Testament Theology* (London: SCM, 1971).
—*The Parables of Jesus* (New York: Charles Scribner, 1972).
Jeske, R.L., *The Wisdom Structure of Jesus' Eschatology* (Doctoral Dissertation, Ruprecht-Karl University, Heidelberg, 1969).
—'Wisdom and the Future in the Teaching of Jesus', *Dialog* 1 (1972), pp. 108-17.
Johnson, B., 'The Critical Difference: Balzac's "Sarrasine" and Barthes's "S/Z"', *Untying the Text. A Post-Structuralist Reader*, ed. R. Young (London: Routledge & Kegan Paul, 1981).
Johnson, M.D., 'Reflections on a Wisdom Approach to Matthew's Christology', *CBQ* 36 (1974), pp. 44-64.
Johnson, R.A., *The Origins of Demythologizing* (Leiden: Brill, 1974).
Jolles, A., *Einfache Formen* (Tübingen: Max Niemeyer, 1930).
Kähler, M., *The So-called Historical Jesus and the Historic, Biblical Christ* (Philadelphia: Fortress, 1964).
Käsemann, E., *Essays on New Testament Themes* (London: SCM, 1964).
Keck, L.E., *A Future for the Historical Jesus* (London: SCM, 1972).
Kelber, W., *The Kingdom in Mark. A New Place and a New Time* (Philadelphia: Fortress, 1974).
—*The Oral and the Written Gospel* (Philadelphia: Fortress, 1983).
—'Review of Crossan (1983)', *JBL* 104 (1985), pp. 716-19.
Kimmerle, M., 'A Method of Collecting and Classifying Folk Sayings', *WF* 6 (1947), pp. 351-66.
Kirk, J.A., 'The Meaning of Wisdom in James: An Examination of a Hypothesis', *NTS* 16 (1969), pp. 24-38.
Kirshenblatt-Gimblett, B., 'Towards a Theory of Proverb Meaning', *The Wisdom of Many*, ed A. Dundes and W. Mieder (London: Garland, 1981), pp. 111-21.
Kloppenborg, J.S., 'Wisdom Christology in Q', *Laval Théologique et Philosophique* 34 (1978), pp. 129-47.
—*The Formation of Q. Trajectories in Ancient Wisdom Collections* (Philadelphia, Fortress, 1987).
Koester, H., with J.M. Robinson *Trajectories through Early Christianity* (Philadelphia: Fortress, 1971).
—*History, Culture, and Religion of the Hellenistic Age* (Philadelphia: Fortress, 1982).
Krikmann, A., *On Denotative Indefiniteness of Proverbs. Remarks on Proverb Semantics 1* (Tallinn: Academy of Sciences of the Estonian SSR, 1974).
—*Some Additional Aspects of Semantic Indefiniteness of Proverbs. Remarks on Proverb Semantics 2* (Tallinn: Academy of Sciences of the Estonian SSR, 1974).
Küchler, M., *Frühjüdische Weisheitstraditionen: zum Fortgang weisheitlichen Denkens im Bereich des frühjüdischen Jahweglaubens* (Göttingen: Vandenhoeck & Ruprecht, 1979).

Kümmel, W.G., *Promise and Fulfilment. The Eschatological Message of Jesus* (London: SCM, 1984).
Kuusi, M., 'Towards an International Type-System of Proverbs', *FFC* 211 (1972), pp. 5-41.
Lane, W.L., *The Gospel according to Mark* (Grand Rapids: Eerdmans, 1974).
Leech, G., *Principles of Pragmatics* (London: Longman, 1983).
Levinson, S.C., *Pragmatics* (Cambridge: Cambridge University Press, 1983).
Lewis, C.S., 'Bluspels and Flalansferes', *The Importance of Language*, ed. M. Black (Englewood Cliffs: Prentice-Hall, 1962), pp. 36-50.
Lindblom, J., 'Wisdom in the Old Testament Prophets', *VT Supp* 3 (1960), pp. 192-204.
Lindfors, B., 'The Palm-Oil with which Achebe's words are Eaten', *Critical Perspectives on Chinua Achebe*, ed. C.L. Innes and B. Lindfors (London: Heinemann, 1979), pp. 47-66.
Lord, A.B., 'The Gospels as Oral Traditional Literature', *The Relationship among the Gospels*, ed. W.O. Walker (San Antonio: Trinity University Press, 1978).
Luckmann, T. with P. Berger, *The Social Construction of Reality* (Harmondsworth: Penguin, 1966)
Lundström, G., *The Kingdom of God in the Teaching of Jesus. A History of Interpretation from the Last Decades of the Nineteenth Century to the Present Day* (Edinburgh: Oliver & Boyd, 1953).
Lyons, J., *Semantics* (Cambridge: Cambridge University Press, 1977).
Mack, B.L., 'Wisdom Myth and Myth-ology: An Essay in Understanding a Theological Tradition', *Int* 24 (1970), pp. 46-60.
Maddox, R., *The Purpose of Luke-Acts* (Göttingen: Vandenhoeck & Ruprecht, 1982).
McKane, W., *Prophets and Wise Men* (London: SCM, 1965).
—*Proverbs: A New Approach* (London: SCM, 1970).
—'Functions of Language and Objectives of Discourse according to Proverbs 10–30', *La Sagesse de l'Ancien Testament*, ed. M. Gilbert (Leuven: Leuven University Press, 1979), pp. 166-85.
McKenzie, J.L., 'Reflections on Wisdom', *JBL* 86 (1967), pp. 1-9.
MacRae, G.W., 'The Jewish Background of the Gnostic Sophia Myth', *NT* 12 (1970), pp. 86-101.
Man, P.de, *Blindness and Insight. Essays in the Rhetoric of Contemporary Criticism* (London: Methuen, 1983).
Manson, T.W., *The Teaching of Jesus* (Cambridge: Cambridge University Press, 1967).
—'The Quest of the Historical Jesus—Continued', *Studies in the Gospels and Epistles*, ed. M. Black (Philadelphia: Westminster, 1962).
Marshall, I.H., *Luke: Historian and Theologian* (Exeter: Paternoster, 1970).
—*The Gospel of Luke. A Commentary on the Greek Text* (Exeter: Paternoster, 1978).
Mealand, D.L., 'The Dissimilarity Test', *SJT* 31 (1978), pp. 41-50.
Messenger, J.C., 'The Role of Proverbs in a Nigerian Judicial System', *The Study of Folklore*, ed. A. Dundes (Englewood Cliffs: Prentice-Hall, 1965), pp. 299-307.
Millar, A., with J. Riches, 'Conceptual Change in the Synoptic Tradition', *Alternative Approaches to the New Testament*, ed. A.E. Harvey (London: SPCK, 1985), pp. 37-60.
Minear, P., *Commands of Christ* (Nashville: Abingdon, 1972).
Moi T., *Sexual/Textual Politics* (London: Methuen, 1985).

Morgan, D.F., *Wisdom in the Old Testament Traditions* (Oxford: Blackwell, 1981).

Müller, H-P. 'Mantische Weisheit und Apokalyptik', *VT Supp* 22 (Leiden: Brill, 1972), pp. 268-93.

Murphy, R.E., 'A Consideration of the Classification Wisdom Psalms', *VT Supp* 9 (1962), pp. 156-67.

—'Wisdom and Yahwism', *No Famine in the Land: Studies in honour of J.L. McKenzie*, ed. J.W. Flanagan and A.N. Robinson (Missoula: Scholars Press, 1975), pp. 117-26.

—'Wisdom—Theses and Hypotheses', *Israelite Wisdom: Theological and Literary Essays in Honour of Samuel Terrien*, ed. J.G. Gammie, W.A. Brueggemann, W.L. Humphreys & J.M. Ward (Missoula: Scholars Press, 1978), pp. 35-42.

Nauck, W., 'Salt as a Metaphor in Instructions for Discipleship', *Studia Theologica* 6 (1952), pp. 165-78.

Nicol, I.G., 'Schweitzer's Jesus: A Psychology of the Heroic Will', *ET* 86 (1974), pp. 52-55.

Nineham, D., 'Schweitzer Revisited', *Explorations in Theology 1* (London: SCM, 1977), pp. 112-33.

Norrick, N.R., 'Nondirect Speech Acts and Double Binds', *Poetics* 10 (1981), pp. 33-47.

—*How Proverbs Mean. Semantic Studies in English Proverbs* (Berlin: Mouton, 1985).

Oden, R.A., 'Hermeneutics and Historiography: Germany and America', *SBL Seminar Papers 1980*, pp. 135-57.

Okogbule Nwanodi, 'Ibo Proverbs', *Nigerian Magazine* 80 (1964).

Olsen, S.H., *The Structure of Literary Understanding* (Cambridge: Cambridge University Press, 1978).

Orton, D.E., *The Understanding Scribe. Matthew and the Apocalyptic Ideal* (Sheffield: JSOT, 1989).

Pamment, M., 'The Kingdom of Heaven according to the First Gospel', *NTS* 27 (1981), pp. 211-32.

Perkins, P., *Hearing the Parables of Jesus* (New York: Paulist, 1981).

Permyakov, G.L., *From Proverb to Folk-tale* (Moscow: Nauka, 1979).

Perrin, N., *Rediscovering the Teaching of Jesus* (London: SCM, 1967).

—'Wisdom and Apocalyptic in the Message of Jesus', *SBL Seminar Papers 1972*, pp. 543-70.

—*Jesus and the Language of the Kingdom* (London: SCM, 1976).

—*The New Testament: an Introduction* (New York: Harcourt, Brace Jovanovich, 1982), edited after Perrin's death by D. Duling.

—*The Kingdom of God in the Teaching of Jesus* (London: SCM, 1984).

Rad, G. von, 'The Joseph Narrative and Ancient Wisdom', *The Problem of the Hexateuch and Other Essays* (London: Oliver E. Boyd, 1965).

—*Old Testament Theology* I (London: SCM, 1975).

Riches, J., *Jesus and the Transformation of Judaism* (London: Darton, Longman and Todd, 1980).

—with A. Millar, 'Conceptual Change in the Synoptic Tradition', *Alternative Approaches to New Testament Study*, ed. A.E. Harvey (London: SPCK, 1985), pp. 37-60.

Richter, P.J., 'Recent Sociological Approaches to the Study of the New Testament', *Religion* 14 (1984), pp. 77-90.

Ringe, S.H., 'A Gentile Woman's Story', *Feminist Interpretations of the Bible*, ed. L.M. Russell (Oxford: Blackwell, 1985), pp. 65-72.

Ringgren, H., *Word and Wisdom: Studies in the Hypostatization of Divine Qualities and Functions in the Ancient Near East* (Lund: Ohlssons, 1947).
Robinson, J.A.T., *The Priority of John* (London: SCM, 1985).
Robinson, J.M., 'The Formal Structure of Jesus' Message', *Current Issues in New Testament Interpretation*, ed. W. Klassen and G. Snyder (London: SCM, 1962), pp. 91-110.
—with H. Koester, *Trajectories through Early Christianity* (Philadelphia: Fortress, 1971).
—'Jesus as Sophos and Sophia: Wisdom Tradition and the Gospels', *Aspects of Wisdom in Judaism and Early Christianity*, ed. R.L. Wilken. (Notre Dame: University of Notre Dame Press, 1975), pp. 1-16.
—*The New Quest of the Historical Jesus and Other Essays* (Philadelphia: Fortress, 1983).
Rogerson, J.W., *Anthropology of the Old Testament* (Oxford: Blackwell, 1978).
Rohrbaugh, R.L., '"Social Location of Thought" as a Heuristic Concept in New Testament Study', *JSNT* 30 (1987), pp. 103-19.
Roon, A. van, 'The Relation between Christ and the Wisdom of God according to St. Paul', *NT* 16 (1974), pp. 207-39.
Rowland, C., *The Open Heaven* (London: SPCK, 1982).
—*Christian Origins. An Account of the Setting and Character of the Most Important Messianic Sect* (London: SPCK, 1985).
Sanders, E.P., *The Tendencies of the Synoptic Tradition* (Cambridge: Cambridge University Press, 1969).
—*Paul and Palestinian Judaism* (London: SCM, 1977).
—'Jesus and the Sinners', *JSNT* 19 (1983), pp. 5-36.
—*Jesus and Judaism* (London: SCM, 1985).
Sanders, J.T., *Ethics in the New Testament* (London: SCM, 1975).
Schnackenburg, R., *God's Rule and Kingdom* (Freiburg: Herder, 1963).
Schulz, S., *Die Spruchquelle der Evangelisten* (Zurich: Theologischer Verlag, 1972).
Schürmann, H., 'Das hermeneutische Hauptproblem der Verkündigung Jesu', *Traditionsgeschichtliche Untersuchungen zu den synoptischen Evangelien* (Düsseldorf: Patmos, 1968), pp. 13-35.
Schüssler-Fiorenza, E., 'Wisdom Mythology and the Christological Hymns of the New Testament', *Aspects of Wisdom in Judaism and Early Christianity*, ed. R.L. Wilken (Notre Dame: University of Notre Dame Press, 1975), pp. 17-42.
Schweitzer, A., *The Mystery of the Kingdom of God. The Secret of Jesus' Messiahship and Passion* (London: A & C Black, 1914).
—*The Quest of the Historical Jesus* (London: SCM, 1981).
Scott, B.B., *Jesus, Symbol-Maker for the Kingdom* (Philadelphia: Fortress, 1981).
Scroggs, R., 'The Sociological Interpretation of the New Testament: The Present State of Research', *NTS* 26 (1980), pp. 164-79.
Seitel, P., 'Proverbs. A Social Use of Metaphor', *The Wisdom of Many*, ed. A. Dundes and W. Mieder (London: Garland, 1981), pp. 122-39.
Shepherd, M.H., 'The Epistle of James and the Gospel of Matthew', *JBL* 75 (1956), pp. 40-51.
Sheppard, G.T., *Wisdom as a Hermeneutical Construct: A Study in the Sapientializing of the Old Testament* (Berlin: de Gruyter, 1980).
—'Review of J.G. Williams: *Those Who Ponder Proverbs* (Sheffield: Almond, 1981)', *JBL* 102 (1983), pp. 319-20.
Skinner, Q., 'The Limits of Historical Explanation', *Philosophy* 41 (1966), pp. 199-212.

—'Meaning and Understanding in the History of Ideas', *History and Theory* 8 (1969), pp. 3-53.

Smith, D., 'Our Lord's Use of Common Proverbs', *The Expositor* 6 (1902), pp. 441-54.

Smith, J.Z., 'The Social Description of Early Christianity', *RSR* 1 (1975), pp. 19-25.

—'Wisdom and Apocalyptic', *Visionaries and their Apocalypses*, ed. P.D. Hanson (London: SPCK, 1983).

Smith, M., *Jesus the Magician* (San Francisco: Harper & Row, 1978).

Sperber, D. with D. Wilson, *Relevance: Communication and Cognition* (Oxford: Blackwell, 1986).

Spicq, C., 'Le Siracide et la structure littéraire du Prologue de saint Jean', *Memorial Lagrange* (Paris: Gabalda, 1940) pp. 183-95.

Stadter, P.A. (ed.), *The Speeches in Thucydides* (Chapel Hill: North Carolina University Press, 1973).

Stanton, G.N., *Jesus of Nazareth in New Testament Preaching* (Cambridge: Cambridge University Press, 1974).

—'Matthew 11.28-30, Comfortable Words?', *ET* 94 (1982).

Stegemann, W., 'Vagabond Radicalism in Early Christianity?: A Historical and Theological Discussion of a Thesis Proposed by Gerd Theissen', *God of the Lowly: Socio-Historical Interpretations of the Bible*, ed. W. Schottroff & W. Stegemann (Maryknoll: Orbis, 1984), pp. 148-68.

Stephenson, R.H., 'On the Widespread Use of an Inappropriate and Restrictive Model of the Literary Aphorism', *Modern Language Review* 75 (1980), pp. 1-17.

Stone, M.E., 'Coherence and Inconsistency in the Apocalypses: The Case of "the End" in 4 Ezra', *JBL* 102 (1983), pp. 229-43.

Suggs, M.J., *Wisdom, Christology and Law in Matthew's Gospel* (Cambridge, Mass.: Harvard University Press, 1970).

Talmon, S., 'Wisdom in the Book of Esther', *VT* 13 (1963), pp. 419-55.

Tannehill, R.C., *The Sword of his Mouth* (Philadelphia: Fortress, 1975).

Taylor, A., *The Proverb and an Index to the Proverb* (Pennsylvania: Rosenkilde & Baggers, 1962).

Terrien, S., 'Amos and Wisdom', *Israel's Prophetic Heritage*, ed. B.W. Anderson and W. Harrelson (London: SCM, 1962), pp. 108-15.

Theissen, G., 'Itinerant Radicalism: The Tradition of Jesus' Sayings from the Perspective of the Sociology of Literature', *RR* 2 (1975), pp. 84-93.

—*Sociology of Early Palestinian Christianity* (Philadelphia: Fortress, 1978).

Thiselton, A.C., *The Two Horizons. New Testament Hermeneutics and Philosophical Description with special reference to Heidegger, Bultmann, Gadamer, and Wittgenstein* (Exeter: Paternoster Press, 1980).

Thompson, J.M., *The Form and Function of Proverbs in Ancient Israel* (The Hague: Mouton, 1974).

Thompson, W.G., 'Review of Suggs (1970)', *CBQ* 33 (1971), pp. 145-46.

Tiede, D.L., *The Charismatic Figure as Miracle Worker* (Missoula: Scholars Press, 1972).

Turner, N., *Grammar of New Testament Greek. Volume III. Syntax* (Edinburgh: T & T Clark, 1963).

Vögtle, A., '"Theo-logie" und "Eschato-logie" in der Verkündigung Jesu?', *Neues Testament und Kirche*, ed. J. Gnilka (Freiburg: Herder, 1974), pp. 371-98.

Völkel, M., 'Zur Deutung des Reiches Gottes bei Lukas', *ZNW* 65 (1974), pp. 57-70.

Walbank, F.W., *Speeches in Greek Historians* (Oxford: Blackwell, 1965).
Walker, W.O., 'The Quest of the Historical Jesus: A Discussion of Methodology', *ATR* 51 (1969), pp. 38-56.
Watson, F.G., 'Why Was Jesus Crucified?', *Theology* 88 (1985), pp. 105-12.
Weinfeld, M., 'The Origin of Humanism in Deuteronomy', *JBL* 80 (1961), pp. 241-47.
Weiss, J., *Jesus' Proclamation of the Kingdom of God* (Philadelphia: Fortress, 1971, translation of *Die Predigt Jesu vom Reiche Gottes* [Göttingen: Vandenhoeck & Ruprecht, 1892]). Also the revised and significantly enlarged German edition of 1900.
Wenzel, J.W., with P.A. Goodwin, 'Proverbs and Practical Reasoning: A Study in Socio-Logic', *The Wisdom of Many*, ed. A. Dundes and W. Mieder (London: Garland, 1981) pp. 140-60.
Whedbee, J.W., *Isaiah and Wisdom* (Nashville: Abingdon, 1971).
Whybray, R.N., *Wisdom in Proverbs* (London: SCM, 1965).
—*The Succession Narrative* (London: SCM, 1968).
—*The Intellectual Tradition in the Old Testament* (Berlin: de Gruyter, 1974).
Wilckens, U., 'σοφια—Wisdom', *TDNT*, VII, ed. G. Friedrich (Grand Rapids: Eerdmans, 1971), pp. 465-526.
Wilder, A.N., *Eschatology and Ethics in the Teaching of Jesus* (New York: Harper & Brothers, 1950).
—'Scholars, Theologians and Ancient Rhetoric', *JBL* 75 (1955), pp. 1-11.
—'Kerygma, Eschatology and Social Ethics', *The Background of the New Testament and its Eschatology*, ed. W.D. Davies and D. Daube (Cambridge: Cambridge University Press, 1956).
—'Eschatological Imagery and Earthly Circumstance', *NTS* 5 (1958), pp. 229-45.
—'Social Factors in Early Christian Eschatology', *Early Christian Origins*, ed. A. Wikgren (Chicago: Quadrangle, 1961), pp. 67-76.
—'Eschatology and the Speech-Modes of the Gospel', *Zeit und Geschichte*, ed. E. Dinkler (Tübingen: Mohr [Siebeck], 1964), pp. 19-30.
—'The Rhetoric of Ancient and Modern Apocalyptic', *Int* 25 (1971), pp. 436-53.
—*Early Christian Rhetoric: the Language of the Gospel* (Cambridge, MA: Harvard University Press, 1971).
—*Theopoetic: Theology and the Religious Imagination* (Philadelphia: Fortress, 1976).
Williams, J.G., 'The Power of Form: A Study of Biblical Proverbs', *Semeia* 17 (1980), pp. 35-58.
—*Those who Ponder Proverbs: Aphoristic Thinking and Biblical Literature* (Sheffield: Almond, 1981).
Wilson, D., with D. Sperber, *Relevance: Communication and Cognition* (Oxford: Blackwell, 1986).
Wilson, S.G., 'Lukan Eschatology', *NTS* 15 (1969-70), pp. 330-47.
Windisch, H., *The Meaning of the Sermon on the Mount* (Philadelphia: Westminster, 1951).
Wright, N.T., 'Constraints and the Jesus of History', *SJT* 39 (1986), pp. 189-210.
Zeller, D., *Die weisheitlichen Mahnsprüche bei den Synoptikern* (Würzburg: Echter Verlag, 1977).
—'Weisheitliche Überlieferung in der Predigt Jesu', *Religiöse Grunderfahrungen. Quellen und Gestalten*, ed. W. Strolz (Freiburg: Herder, 1978).

INDEXES

INDEX OF BIBLICAL AND EXTRA-BIBLICAL REFERENCES

OLD TESTAMENT

APOCRYPHA

NEW TESTAMENT

PSEUDEPIGRAPHA

INDEX OF AUTHORS

JOURNAL FOR THE STUDY OF THE NEW TESTAMENT
Supplement Series

1 THE BARREN TEMPLE AND THE WITHERED TREE
William R. Telford

2 STUDIA BIBLICA 1978
II. Papers on the Gospels
E.A. Livingstone (ed.)

3 STUDIA BIBLICA 1978
III. Papers on Paul and Other New Testament Authors
E.A. Livingstone (ed.)

4 FOLLOWING JESUS
Discipleship in Mark's Gospel
Ernest Best

5 THE PEOPLE OF GOD
Markus Barth

6 PERSECUTION AND MARTYRDOM IN THE THEOLOGY OF PAUL
John S. Pobee

7 SYNOPTIC STUDIES
The Ampleforth Conferences 1982 and 1983
C.M. Tuckett (ed.)

8 JESUS ON THE MOUNTAIN
A Study in Matthean Theology
Terence L. Donaldson

9 THE HYMNS OF LUKE'S INFANCY NARRATIVES
Their Origin, Meaning and Significance
Stephen Farris

10 CHRIST THE END OF THE LAW
Romans 10.4 in Pauline Perspective
Robert Badenas

11 THE LETTERS TO THE SEVEN CHURCHES OF ASIA IN THEIR LOCAL SETTING
Colin J. Hemer

12 PROCLAMATION FROM PROPHECY AND PATTERN
Lucan Old Testament Christology
Darrell L. Bock

13 JESUS AND THE LAWS OF PURITY
Tradition History and Legal History in Mark 7
Roger P. Booth

14 THE PASSION ACCORDING TO LUKE
The Special Material of Luke 22
Marion L. Soards

15 HOSTILITY TO WEALTH IN THE SYNOPTIC GOSPELS
T.E. Schmidt

16 MATTHEW'S COMMUNITY
The Evidence of his Special Sayings Material
S.H. Brooks

17 THE PARADOX OF THE CROSS IN
THE THOUGHT OF ST PAUL
A.T. Hanson

18 HIDDEN WISDOM AND THE EASY YOKE
Wisdom, Torah and Discipleship in Matthew 11.25-30
C. Deutsch

19 JESUS AND GOD IN PAUL'S ESCHATOLOGY
L.J. Kreitzer

20 LUKE: A NEW PARADIGM
M.D. Goulder

21 THE DEPARTURE OF JESUS IN LUKE-ACTS
The Ascension Narratives in Context
M.C. Parsons

22 THE DEFEAT OF DEATH
Apocalyptic Eschatology in 1 Corinthians 15 and Romans 5
M.C. De Boer

23 PAUL THE LETTER-WRITER
AND THE SECOND LETTER TO TIMOTHY
M. Prior

24 APOCALYPTIC AND THE NEW TESTAMENT:
Essays in Honor of J. Louis Martyn
J. Marcus & M.L. Soards

25 THE UNDERSTANDING SCRIBE
Matthew and the Apocalyptic Ideal
D.E. Orton

26 WATCHWORDS:
Mark 13 in Markan Eschatology
T. Geddert

27 THE DISCIPLES ACCORDING TO MARK:
Markan Redaction in Current Debate
C.C. Black

28 THE NOBLE DEATH:
Greco-Roman Martyrology and Paul's Concept of Salvation
D. Seeley

29 ABRAHAM IN GALATIANS:
Epistolary and Rhetorical Contexts
G.W. Hansen

30 EARLY CHRISTIAN RHETORIC AND 2 THESSALONIANS
F.W. Hughes

31 THE STRUCTURE OF MATTHEW'S GOSPEL:
A Study in Literary Design
D.R. Bauer

32 PETER AND THE BELOVED DISCIPLE:
Figures for a Community in Crisis
K.B. Quast

33 MARK'S AUDIENCE:
The Literary and Social Setting of Mark 4.11-12
M.A. Beavis

34 THE GOAL OF OUR INSTRUCTION:
The Structure of Theology and Ethics in the Pastoral Epistles
P.H. Towner

35 THE PROVERBS OF JESUS:
Issues of History and Rhetoric
A.P. Winton

36 THE STORY OF CHRIST IN THE ETHICS OF PAUL:
An Analysis of the Function of the Hymnic Material in the Pauline Corpus
S.E. Fowl

37 PAUL AND JESUS:
Collected Essays
A.J.M. Wedderburn

38 MATTHEW'S MISSIONARY DISCOURSE:
A Literary Critical Analysis
D.J. Weaver

39 FAITH AND OBEDIENCE IN ROMANS:
A Study in Romans 1–4
G.N. Davies

40 IDENTIFYING PAUL'S OPPONENTS:
The Question of Method in 2 Corinthians
J.L. Sumney

41 HUMAN AGENTS OF COSMIC POWER IN HELLENISTIC JUDAISM AND THE SYNOPTIC TRADITION
M.E. Mills

42 MATTHEW'S INCLUSIVE STORY:
A Study in the Narrative Rhetoric of the First Gospel
D.B. Howell

43 JESUS, PAUL AND TORAH:
Collected Essays
H. Räisänen

44 THE NEW COVENANT IN HEBREWS
S. Lehne